Spartanburg Methodist
Library

33131

D1370964

The
INTERNATIONAL
ALMANAC
of
ELECTORAL HISTORY

THOMAS T. MACKIE & RICHARD ROSE

University of Strathclyde

THE FREE PRESS
A Division of Macmillan Publishing Co., Inc.
New York

Copyright © 1974 by Tom Mackie and Richard Rose

All rights reserved. No part of this book may be reproduced or transmitted in any form or by any means, electronic or mechanical, including photocopying, recording, or by any information storage and retrieval system, without permission in writing from the Publisher.

The Free Press
A Division of Macmillan Publishing Co., Inc.
866 Third Avenue, New York, N.Y. 10022

Collier–Macmillan Canada Ltd.

Library of Congress Catalog Card Number: 74–11577

Printed in the United States of America

printing number
1 2 3 4 5 6 7 8 9 10

329
M21 i

33121

*Spartanburg Methodist College
Library*

THOMAS T. MACKIE received degrees from the London School of Economics and the University of Strathclyde, Glasgow. He is a Lecturer in Politics at the University of Strathclyde, Glasgow.

RICHARD ROSE is a Professor of Politics at the University of Strathclyde, Glasgow. He is the author of many articles and books, including *Electoral Behavior: A Comparative Handbook* (The Free Press).

CONTENTS

ACKNOWLEDGMENTS

Even by the standards of a mutually helpful community of scholars, the authors are much indebted to a wide variety of individuals for providing information and comments necessary and useful in the compilation of this volume.

First of all we wish to acknowledge the prompt and courteous replies to requests for information from national statistical offices, embassies and Commonwealth High Commissions of many lands. Working through masses of official materials from many countries makes one particularly appreciative of the level of accuracy, consistency and clarity of official government reports.

Three libraries have made particularly valuable contributions to the acquisiton of information. The Andersonian Library of the University of Strathclyde promptly responded to many requests for materials. The British Museum, London, and the British Library of Political and Economic Science of the London School of Economics time and again provided materials from the distant past of distant lands. Cumulatively, the characteristic British practice of studying the history and politics of single countries provided a corpus of material well suited for broader analysis.

We would like to thank Professor Basil Chubb, Trinity College, Dublin; F.W.S. Craig of Chichester, Sussex; Professor Hans Daalder and Jan Verhoef of the University of Leiden; Professor Erich Grüner, University of Bern; and Richard M. Scammon of the Elections Research Center, Washington, D.C. for providing unpublished materials from their researches in national electoral history. Students of elections and party systems in many countries made helpful comments and suggestions about difficulties in the interpretation of material. We would particularly like to mention two colleagues at Strathclyde, Keith Hill and Chris Hull, and Alastair Thomas, Leicester Polytechnic. Derek W. Urwin, formerly our colleague at Strathclyde and now of the University of Bergen, gave much guidance; his compendium, *Elections in Western Nations, 1945–1968* (University of Strathclyde Occasional Paper 4 & 5, 1969) is in every sense the precursor of this volume.

The computer processing of the tables of election results was made possible by the work of Michael A. Marsh, now of Trinity College, Dublin, who wrote the necessary computer programmes. All percentages were calculated on an IBM 370–155 computer operated by the Edinburgh Regional Computing Centre. Mrs. R. West typed esoteric materials with speed, accuracy and goodwill. Fred and Phyllis Craig made proofing and publishing the volume move twice as fact as the norm for publishing, and maintained a very high level of accuracy. A grant from the British Social Science Research Council speeded research on which this book is based.

This volume is one of a series of studies in electoral behaviour conducted under the aegis of the Committee on Political Sociology of the International Political Science Association and International Sociological Association. It is complemented by a systematic study of the relationship of social structure and electoral choice, edited by Richard Rose, *Electoral Behavior: a Comparative Handbook* (New York: Free Press, 1973).

Thomas T. Mackie

Richard Rose

Glasgow, Scotland

9th August 1973

INTRODUCTION

Anyone who has ever tried to ascertain seemingly simple facts will know that the task is neither easy nor is it always obvious. This is as true of a public event, such as a general election, as it is of the private negotiations of politicians. When the facts concern elections distant in time or place, difficulties are increased fourfold. Problems increase additionally if one wishes to make comparisons between results in a series of elections within a country: one must then ascertain whether results reported for groups using different names in consecutive elections signify a change in the party system, or only a change in the label that a party employs.

The purpose of this book is to provide a complete and accurate compilation of election results in Western nations since the beginning of competitive national elections. By doing this, we hope to save other students of politics many hours searching for esoteric information, drawing erroneous conclusions from ambiguous information or, even worse, repeating the mistakes enshrined in popular but sometimes inaccurate secondary sources. We hope the data stimulate greater awareness of the variety of electoral systems and electoral outcomes found in the Western world today. In addition, we hope to stimulate a greater interest in the evolution of electoral and party systems within each country represented here. Generalizations about parties and elections often err because they are unwittingly restricted to a single country at a single time in its modern history. A first analysis of the patterns implicit in the tables herein is contained in Richard Rose and Derek W. Urwin, "Persistence and Change in Western Party Systems", *Political Studies* 18:287-319 (1970).

In establishing terms of reference for this volume, the needs of users, including the authors, have been foremost. A reference volume must be detailed yet clear. Information must be reliable, yet sometimes no uncontroverted source of facts exists. The span of nations and elections covered should be broad, but 'muddled', 'stolen' or 'manufactured' results should not be reported as if they were equal in meaning to those from free elections. The selection of materials for inclusion thus requires a number of editorial decisions.

The countries included in this volume are industrial societies conducting competitive elections regularly since the end of the Second World War. The study is confined to industrial nations because of the many differences—social, economic and political—between such countries and those holding elections in Latin America, or in former colonies of the British or French Empires. We would welcome compilations about such countries prepared by those expert in their distinctive party and electoral systems. Information is also excluded from East European and other countries which once held competitive elections but no longer do so in ways recognizable to Western scholars. These terms of reference result in a universe of 23 countries.

Because the electoral histories of Western nations differ greatly from each other, there can be no intellectual justification for reporting results for different countries from the same arbitrarily chosen starting date. The starting point chosen for each country is the first election in which the great majority of seats for the national parliament were contested and most candidates fought under common cross-local labels. The practice of contesting elections developed gradually in most western nations. In America it has not been completed yet, for at each Congressional election dozens of seats in the House of Representatives remain uncontested. It is a pre-condition of aggregating constituency results that candidates in different constituencies adopt a common party label. Without party labels, one can only enumerate the votes of individual candidates. Without parties, general elections are neither general nor nationwide. Of the 23 countries included here, 12 first held national elections in the 19th century. The United States has had the longest unbroken history of national elections.

The elections reported here have been held under a wide variety of franchise laws. To have stipulated as a condition of inclusion here that the franchise be 'democratic' would have involved considerable (and anachronistic) problems of definition. Is an election democratic when a majority of a nation's adult population can vote, or only when the whole of its population can vote? Is a franchise democratic when the vote is granted to all males, or only when women have the right to vote equally with men? Does the grant of plural votes to some as well as a single vote to everyone invalidate a country's claim to a democratic franchise? What registration requirements are consistent with a democratic franchise? The answers to such questions are by no means easy, nor are they a matter of general agreement. Moreover, it is a simple matter to show that the answer to any of these questions can be a matter of degree. The introductory comments for each chapter describe the evolution of the national franchise laws, thus allowing each reader to decide whether or when a country's elections meet his own definition of democracy. The tables describe to what extent election outcomes change as the franchise is extended. The Republic of South Africa is the only country reported here in which the majority of the adult population is still excluded from the vote.

The organization of information in each chapter follows a standard pattern. The evolution of the electoral system and franchise laws are first described, and exact dates given for each election. A list of political parties includes the name of each party in English and in its national language. This is important, inasmuch as authors writing in English are by no means consistent in the translations employed, nor will an English-language name help when using documents published in a country's own language. For instance, the use of the names Left and Liberals by different authors in describing Danish parties may inadvertently conceal that they both refer to the same historical party, the Venstre. The customary description of the Swiss Radical Party, while true to the party's French title has somewhat different connotations from the German title Freisinnig-demokratische Partei (Free-thinking Democrats).

Election results are reported in sets of four standard tables, giving the total number and percentage of votes for each party, and the number and percentage of seats that each party wins. Votes are reported for every party that has at least once secured more than one per cent of the vote in a national election. This condition includes many small parties, while avoiding 'one man' parties and esoteric electoral groupings. Parties with less votes are reported when this aids in comparison cross-nationally (e.g., Communists), or when the separatist character of a party may lead it to regard its 'nation' as smaller than that of the electorate (e.g., Welsh Nationalists). In nearly every country, the chief (or only) national election concerns the choice of representatives for the nation's parliament. Where a country has a bi-cameral legislature, contests for the more important chamber are cited. In the United States, the primacy of the Presidential election justifies an exception. In countries where elections are fought in single-member constituencies, unopposed returns and the number and percentage of seats contested by each party are reported, if available. Wherever possible, official publications are the source of vote totals.

Because the initial impetus to compile the data came from frustrations with the inconsistencies, omissions and uncertainties of existing sources, a special effort has been made to present data in as clear a form as possible. The production of percentage figures from a computerized file of the raw data has provided a number of useful checks for internal consistency, and missing information. Nonetheless, it would be arrogant to claim that this volume is free from all errors. The editors would welcome corrections to incorporate in subsequent editions carrying forward this record of competitive elections in Western nations.

CONVENTIONS AND SIGNS

1. Percentages: Valid Votes, Invalid Votes and Total Votes are expressed as percentages of the Electorate. The Total Vote is the sum of the Valid and Invalid Vote. Share Invalid is the proportion invalid of the Total Vote. Party Votes are expressed as a percentage of the Valid Vote. Percentages are rounded to one decimal place. Because of rounding percentage totals do not always sum to exactly 100 percent.

2. Did not contest election: —

3. Data not available: n.a.

4. A bracket groups two or more parties for which only aggregated votes or seats are given. This is usually because of a formal electoral alliance at the national level. Occasionally sources provide only grouped data for parties which did not form an electoral alliance.

5. Arrows are used when a party splits into two groups and is later reunited.

6. The number to the left of each party refers to the entry in the first table of each chapter, giving in full the name of the party in English and the appropriate national language.

Chapter 1

AUSTRALIA

The Commonwealth of Australia was established as a federation of six British colonies in 1901. The colonies already enjoyed a large measure of self government. Their assemblies were elected on a very broad franchise. Manhood suffrage and the secret ballot were the norm, although some colonies still retained plural voting. In some states women already had the vote. With the founding of the Australian Labor Party in 1890, organized political parties began to develop. (Aitken and Kahan, 1973)

The Australian Parliament consists of a Senate and a House of Representatives. In the Commonwealth's first election in 1901 the franchise was granted to all those qualified to vote in the larger of the state assemblies, with the proviso that plural voting rights were not admitted. Election was by plurality in single-member constituencies. In 1902 universal adult suffrage with a minimum age of 21 was introduced. The alternative vote system was introduced in 1918 and compulsory voting in 1924. In 1922 the Northern Territory was given representation in the House of Representatives. Similar provision was made for the Australian Capital Territory, Canberra, in 1948. In both cases, members were only allowed to vote on measures concerning their own territories. The Australian Capital Territory Representative has had full voting rights since 1967 and the Northern Territory member since 1968.

The Country Party has usually contested elections in alliance with the principal anti-Labor party.

Sources:

Aitken, D. and Kahan, M., "Australia" in R. Rose (ed.) *Electoral Behavior: a Comparative Handbook* (New York: Free Press, 1973).

Hughes, C.A. and Graham, B.D., *A Handbook of Australian Government and Politics* (Canberra: Australian University Press, 1968).

Table 1.1
POLITICAL PARTIES IN AUSTRALIA SINCE 1901

	Party Names	Elections contested	Number contested
1	Australian Labor Party—ALP	1901ff	28
2	Free Trade	1901-1903	2
3	Protectionists	1901-1906	3
4	Anti-Socialists[1]	1906	1
5	Western Australia Party[2]	1906	1
6	Liberal Party 1[3]	1910-1914	3
7	Nationalist Party[4]	1917-1929	6
8	Country Party[5]	1919ff	21
9	Liberal Union[6]	1922	1
10	Liberal Party II[7]	1922	1
11	Country Progressive Party[8]	1928-1929	2
12	United Australia Party—UAP[9]	1931-1943	5
13	Communist Party	1931-1937; 1943ff	15
14	New South Wales Labor Party[10]	1931-1934	2
15	Social Credit Party	1934-1937	2
16	Non-Communist Labor[11]	1940	1
17	State Labor Party[11]	1940-1943	2
18	Queensland Country Party	1943	1
19	Liberal Democrats	1943	1
20	Country-National Party[12]	1943	1
21	One Parliament for Australia Party	1943	1
22	Services Party of Australia	1946	1
23	Lang Labor Party[13]	1946-1949	2
24	Australian Liberal Party[14]	1946ff	11
25	Democratic Labor Party—DLP[15]	1955ff	7
26	Australia Party	1969ff	2

[1] Former Free Traders.

[2] A local alliance of Liberals and Free Traders.

[3] A merger of the Protectionists and Free Traders in 1906.

[4] A merger of the Liberal Party and part of the Labor Party in 1917.

[5] The Country Party was formally established in January 1920. Figures for the 1919 election refer to candidates sponsored by the farmers and graziers organizations (Hughes and Graham, 1968 : 320 and 325).

[6] A dissident faction of Nationalists in Victoria.

[7] A dissident group of South Australian Nationalists.

[8] Country Party dissidents in Victoria.

[9] A merger of the Nationalist Party and former members of the Labor Party in 1931. The Emergency Committee, an electoral alliance formed in the same year by the Country Party and the UAP in South Australia, is included. The Liberal and Country League, (LCL) the successor to the Emergency Committee, is also included with the UAP.

[10] A faction of the Labor Party which ran candidates against federal Labor in New South Wales in 1931 and 1934. Recognized as the official New South Wales branch of the federal Labor Party in 1936. (Hughes and Graham, 1968 : 345 and 451).

[11] Labor Party factions in New South Wales.

[12] An electoral alliance of the UAP and elements of the Country Party in Queensland.

[13] A splinter group of the federal Labor Party in New South Wales formed in 1943. (Hughes and Graham, 1968 : 454).

[14] A merger of anti-Labor groups including the UAP and the LCL.

[15] In 1955 the Anti-Communist Labor Party. Since 1958 includes the Queensland Labor Party.

Table 1.2
DATES OF ELECTIONS
TO THE HOUSE OF REPRESENTATIVES 1901–1972

1.	30 March 1901	15.	23 October 1937
2.	16 December 1903	16.	21 September 1940
3.	12 December 1906	17.	21 August 1943
4.	13 April 1910	18.	28 September 1946
5.	31 May 1913	19.	10 December 1949
6.	5 September 1914	20.	28 April 1951
7.	5 May 1917	21.	29 May 1954
8.	13 December 1919	22.	10 December 1955
9.	16 December 1922	23.	22 November 1958
10.	14 November 1925	24.	9 December 1961
11.	17 November 1928	25.	30 November 1963
12.	12 August 1929	26.	26 November 1966
13.	19 December 1931	27.	25 October 1969
14.	15 September 1934	28.	2 December 1972

Sources: Hughes and Graham (1968) and Keesings Contemporary Archives.

Table 1.3 AUSTRALIA Total Votes 1901–1917

	1901[1]	1903	1906	1910	1913	1914	1917
Electorate	987,754	1,893,586	2,109,562	2,258,482	2,760,216	2,811,515	2,835,327
Valid Votes	505,972	720,938	951,688	1,322,582	1,900,369	1,686,763	1,883,434
Invalid Votes	8,468	18,463	36,865	27,044	55,354	40,143	51,044
Total Votes	514,440	739,401	988,553	1,349,626	1,955,723	1,726,906	1,934,478

PARTY VOTES

	1901[1]	1903	1906	1910	1913	1914	1917
1 Australian Labor Party	79,736	223,163	348,711	660,864	921,099	858,451	827,541
2 Free Trade	151,960	247,774	–	–	–	–	–
3 Protectionists	185,943	214,091	202,499[2]	–	–	–	–
4 Anti-Socialists	–	–	363,257	–	–	–	–
5 Western Australia Party	–	–	22,154	–	–	–	–
6 Liberal Party l	–	–	–	596,350	930,076	796,397	–
7 Nationalist Party	–	–	–	–	–	–	1,021,138
Others	8,384	35,910	15,067	65,368	49,194	31,915	34,755

[1] Party votes in 1901 exclude constituencies in South Australia and Tasmania.
[2] Includes Independent Protectionists with 46,074 votes.

Source: Hughes and Graham, 1968.

Table 1.4   AUSTRALIA   Percentage of Votes 1901–1917

	1901	1903	1906	1910	1913	1914	1917
Valid Votes	51.2	38.1	45.1	58.6	68.8	60.0	66.4
Invalid Votes	0.9	1.0	1.7	1.2	2.0	1.4	1.8
Total Votes	52.1	39.0	46.9	59.8	70.9	61.4	68.2
Share Invalid	1.6	2.5	3.7	2.0	2.8	2.3	2.6
PARTY VOTES							
1 Australian Labor Party	18.7	31.0	36.6	50.0	48.5	50.9	43.9
2 Free Trade	35.7	34.4	–	–	–	–	–
3 Protectionists	43.6	29.7	21.3	–	–	–	–
4 Anti-Socialists	–	–	38.2	–	–	–	–
5 Western Australia Party	–	–	2.3	–	–	–	–
6 Liberal Party I	–	–	–	45.1	48.9	47.2	–
7 Nationalist Party	–	–	–	–	–	–	54.2
Others	2.0	5.0	1.6	4.9	2.6	1.9	1.8

7

Table 1.5 AUSTRALIA Number of Seats Won in the House of Representatives 1901–1917

	1901	1903	1906	1910	1913	1914	1917
1 Australian Labor Party	14	23	26	43	37	42	22
2 Free Trade	28	25	–	–	–	–	–
3 Protectionists	31	26	20[2]	–	–	–	–
4 Anti-Socialists	–	–	27	–	–	–	–
5 Western Australia Party	–	–	2	–	–	–	–
6 Liberal Party I	–	–	–	31	38	32	–
7 Nationalist Party	–	–	–	–	–	–	53
Others	2[1]	1[1]	0	1	0	1	0
Total Seats	**75**	**75**	**75**	**75**	**75**	**75**	**75**
Unopposed Returns	6	17	7	4	3	13	10

[1] Revenue Tariff.
[2] Including four Independent Protectionists.

Source: Hughes and Graham, 1968.

Table 1.6   AUSTRALIA   Percentage of Seats Won in the House of Representatives 1901–1917

	1901	1903	1906	1910	1913	1914	1917
1 Australian Labor Party	18.7	30.7	34.7	57.3	49.3	56.0	29.3
2 Free Trade	37.3	33.3	–	–	–	–	–
3 Protectionists	41.3	34.7	26.6	–	–	–	–
4 Anti-Socialists	–	–	36.0	–	–	–	–
5 Western Australia Party	–	–	2.7	–	–	–	–
6 Liberal Party I	–	–	–	41.3	50.7	42.7	–
7 Nationalist Party	–	–	–	–	–	–	70.7
Others	2.7	1.3	0.0	1.3	0.0	1.3	0.0

Table 1.7   AUSTRALIA   Number of Candidates 1901—1917

		1901	1903	1906	1910	1913	1914	1917
1	Australian Labor Party	27	39	57	67	69	60	62
2	Free Trade	59	47	–	–	–	–	–
3	Protectionists	86	50	33	–	–	–	–
4	Anti-Socialists	–	–	59	–	–	–	–
5	Western Australia Party	–	–	5	–	–	–	–
6	Liberal Party I	–	–	–	70	72	62	–
7	Nationalist Party	–	–	–	–	–	–	65
	Others	9	10	7	20	13	5	7
	Total Seats	181	146	161	157	154	127	134

Source: Hughes and Graham, 1968.

Table 1.8   AUSTRALIA   Percentage of Seats Contested 1901–1917

	1901	1903	1906	1910	1913	1914	1917
1 Australian Labor Party	34.7	50.7	76.0	89.3	92.0	80.0	82.7
2 Free Trade	68.0	56.0	–	–	–	–	–
3 Protectionists	76.0	53.3	42.7	–	–	–	–
4 Anti-Socialists	–	–	74.7	–	–	–	–
5 Western Australia Party	–	–	6.7	–	–	–	–
6 Liberal Party I	–	–	–	93.3	94.7	82.7	–
7 Nationalist Party	–	–	–	–	–	–	86.7

11

Table 1.9   AUSTRALIA   Total Votes 1919–1943[1]

	1919	1922	1925	1928	1929	1931	1934	1937	1940	1943
Electorate	2,849,862	2,980,424	3,302,016	3,444,766	3,539,120	3,649,954	3,902,677	4,080,038	4,329,346	4,4f ˆ37
Valid Votes	1,909,231	1,572,514	2,916,638	2,595,085	2,879,250	3,172,034	3,551,385	3,603,341	3,876,986	4,1z2,491
Invalid Votes	68,612	74,349	70,562	133,730	78,297	114,440	126,338	95,928	102,023	122,878
Total Votes	1,977,843	1,646,863	2,987,200	2,728,815	2,957,547	3,286,474	3,677,723	3,699,269	3,979,009	4,245,369

PARTY VOTES

	1919	1922	1925	1928	1929	1931	1934	1937	1940	1943
1 Australian Labor Party	811,244	665,145	1,313,627	1,158,505	1,406,327	859,513	952,251	1,555,737	1,556,941	2,058,578
14 New South Wales Labor	–	–	–	–	–	335,309	510,480	–	–	–
16 Non-Communist Labor	–	–	–	–	–	–	–	–	202,721	–
17 State Labor Party	–	–	–	–	–	–	–	–	101,191	29,752
8 Country Party	176,884	197,513	313,363	271,686	295,640	388,544	447,968	560,279	531,397	287,000
7 Nationalist Party	860,519	553,920	1,238,397	1,014,522	975,979	–	–	–	–	–
12 United Australia Party	–	–	–	–	–	1,319,371	1,313,561	1,214,526	1,171,788	807,415
10 Liberal Party II	–	73,939	–	–	–	–	–	–	–	–
11 Country Progressive Party	–	–	–	41,713	27,942	–	–	–	–	–
20 Country-National Party	–	–	–	–	–	–	–	–	–	166,419
19 Liberal Democrats	–	–	–	–	–	–	–	–	–	42,149
18 Queensland Country Party	–	–	–	–	–	–	–	–	–	61,196
13 Communist Party	–	–	–	–	–	8,511	47,449	17,153	–	81,816
15 Social Credit Party	–	–	–	–	–	–	166,589	79,432	–	–
21 One Parliament for Australia	–	–	–	–	–	–	–	–	–	–
Others	60,584[2]	81,977	51,251	108,659	173,362[3]	260,786	113,037	176,214[4]	312,948	501,054

[1] All figures for party votes refer to the number of first preference votes polled. All figures exclude the Northern Territory.
Source: Hughes and Graham, 1968.

Table 1.10   AUSTRALIA

Percentage of Votes 1919–1943

	1919	1922	1925	1928	1929	1931	1934	1937	1940	1943
Valid Votes	67.0	52.8	88.3	75.3	81.4	86.9	91.0	88.3	89.6	92.3
Invalid Votes	2.4	2.5	2.1	3.9	2.2	3.1	3.2	2.4	2.4	2.8
Total Votes	69.4	55.3	90.5	79.2	83.6	90.0	94.2	90.7	91.9	95.0
Share Invalid	3.5	4.5	2.4	4.9	2.6	3.5	3.4	2.6	2.6	2.9
PARTY VOTES										
1 Australian Labor Party	42.5	42.3	45.0	44.6	48.8	27.1	26.8	43.2	40.2	49.9
14 New South Wales Labor	–	–	–	–	–	10.6	14.4	–	–	–
16 Non-Communist Labor	–	–	–	–	–	–	–	–	5.2	–
17 State Labor Party	–	–	–	–	–	–	–	–	2.6	0.7
8 Country Party	9.3	12.6	10.7	10.5	10.3	12.2	12.6	15.5	13.7	7.0
7 Nationalist Party	45.1	35.2	42.5	39.1	33.9	–	–	–	–	–
12 United Australia Party	–	–	–	–	–	41.6	37.0	33.7	30.2	19.6
10 Liberal Party II	–	4.7	–	–	–	–	–	–	–	–
11 Country Progressive Party	–	–	–	1.6	1.0	–	–	–	–	–
20 Country-National Party	–	–	–	–	–	–	–	–	–	4.0
19 Liberal Democrats	–	–	–	–	–	–	–	–	–	1.0
18 Queensland Country Party	–	–	–	–	–	–	–	–	–	1.5
13 Communist Party	–	–	–	–	–	0.3	1.3	0.5	–	2.0
15 Social Credit Party	–	–	–	–	–	–	4.7	2.2	–	–
21 One Parliament for Australia	–	–	–	–	–	–	–	–	–	2.1
Others	3.2	5.2	1.8	4.2	6.0	8.2	3.2	4.9	8.1	12.2

13

Table 1.11   AUSTRALIA   Number of Seats Won in the House of Representatives 1919–1943

		1919	1922	1925	1928	1929	1931	1934	1937	1940	1943
1	Australian Labor Party	26	29	23	31	46	14	18	29	32	49
14	New South Wales Labor	–	–	–	–	–	4	9	–	–	–
16	Non-Communist Labor	–	–	–	–	–	–	–	–	4	–
17	State Labor Party	–	–	–	–	–	–	–	–	0	0
8	Country Party	11	14	14	13	10	16	14	16	14	7
7	Nationalist Party	37	26	37	29	14	–	–	–	–	–
12	United Australia Party	–	–	–	–	–	40	33	28	23	13
10	Liberal Party II	–	5	–	–	–	–	–	–	–	–
11	Country Progressive Party	–	–	–	1	1	–	–	–	–	–
20	Country-National Party	–	–	–	–	–	–	–	–	–	3
19	Liberal Democrats	–	–	–	–	–	–	–	–	–	0
18	Queensland Country Party	–	–	–	–	–	–	–	–	–	1
13	Communist Party	–	–	–	–	–	0	0	0	–	0
15	Social Credit Party	–	–	–	–	–	–	0	0	–	–
21	One Parliament for Australia	–	–	–	–	–	–	–	–	–	–
	Others	1[1]	1	1	1	4	4[2]	1[3]	1[3]	1	1
	Total Seats	**75**	**75**	**75**	**75**	**75**	**75**	**74**	**74**	**74**	**74**
	Unopposed Returns	2	5	1	12	9	4	1	4	1	1

[1] Independent Nationalist.
[2] Including 3 Independent UAP.
[3] Independent UAP.

14

Table 1.12   AUSTRALIA

Percentage of Seats Won in the House of Representatives 1919–1943

		1919	1922	1925	1928	1929	1931	1934	1937	1940	1943
1	Australian Labor Party	34.7	38.7	30.7	41.3	61.3	18.7	24.3	39.2	43.2	66.2
14	New South Wales Labor	–	–	–	–	–	5.3	12.2	–	–	–
16	Non-Communist Labor	–	–	–	–	–	–	–	–	5.4	–
17	State Labor Party	–	–	–	–	–	–	–	–	0.0	0.0
8	Country Party	14.7	18.7	18.7	17.3	13.3	21.3	18.9	21.6	18.9	9.5
7	Nationalist Party	49.3	34.7	49.3	38.7	18.7	–	–	–	–	–
12	United Australia Party	–	–	–	–	–	53.3	44.6	37.8	31.1	17.6
10	Liberal Party II	–	6.7	–	–	–	–	–	–	–	–
11	Country Progressive Party	–	–	–	1.3	1.3	–	–	–	–	–
20	Country-National Party	–	–	–	–	–	–	–	–	–	4.1
19	Liberal Democrats	–	–	–	–	–	–	–	–	–	0.0
18	Queensland Country Party	–	–	–	–	–	–	–	–	–	1.4
13	Communist Party	–	–	–	–	–	0.0	0.0	0.0	–	0.0
15	Social Credit Party	–	–	–	–	–	–	0.0	0.0	–	–
21	One Parliament for Australia	–	–	–	–	–	–	–	–	–	0.0
	Others	1.3	1.3	1.3	1.3	5.3	1.3	1.4	1.4	1.4	1.4
	Unopposed Returns	2.7	6.7	1.3	16.0	12.0	5.3	1.4	5.4	1.4	1.4

Table 1.13 AUSTRALIA   Number of Candidates 1919–1943

		1919	1922	1925	1928	1929	1931	1934	1937	1940	1943
1	Australian Labor Party	69	61	75	55	59	61	66	71	73	72
14	New South Wales Labor	–	–	–	–	–	28	28	–	–	–
16	Non-Communist Labor	–	–	–	–	–	–	–	–	18	–
17	State Labor Party	–	–	–	–	–	–	–	–	19	6
8	Country Party	19	32	18	14	18	27	29	25	28	17
7	Nationalist Party	71	68	65	55	57	–	–	–	–	–
12	United Australia Party	–	–	–	–	–	60	60	49	64	47
10	Liberal Party II	–	11	–	–	–	–	–	–	–	–
11	Country Progressive Party	–	–	–	2	1	–	–	–	–	–
20	Country-National Party	–	–	–	–	–	–	–	–	–	7
19	Liberal Democrats	–	–	–	–	–	–	–	–	–	9
18	Queensland Country Party	–	–	–	–	–	–	–	–	–	5
13	Communist Party	–	–	–	–	–	10	21	2	–	17
15	Social Credit Party	–	–	–	–	–	–	36	16	–	–
21	One Parliament for Australia	–	–	–	–	–	–	–	–	–	23
	Others	22	22	6	12	16	40	20	23	65	136
	Total Seats	**191**	**194**	**164**	**138**	**151**	**226**	**260**	**186**	**267**	**338**

16

Table 1.14   AUSTRALIA   Percentage of Seats Contested 1919–1943

		1919	1922	1925	1928	1929	1931	1934	1937	1940	1943
1	Australian Labor Party	92.0	81.3	97.3	72.0	77.3	81.3	83.8	90.5	98.6	95.9
14	New South Wales Labor	–	–	–	–	–	37.3	37.8	–	–	–
16	Non-Communist Labor	–	–	–	–	–	–	–	–	24.3	–
17	State Labor Party	–	–	–	–	–	–	–	–	25.7	6.8
8	Country Party	25.3	36.0	22.7	18.7	20.0	26.7	28.4	29.7	28.4	20.3
7	Nationalist Party	88.0	82.7	82.7	69.3	72.0	–	–	–	–	–
12	United Australia Party	–	–	–	–	–	73.3	78.4	64.9	60.8	58.1
10	Liberal Party II	–	13.3	–	–	–	–	–	–	–	–
11	Country Progressive Party	–	–	–	2.7	1.3	–	–	–	–	–
20	Country-National Party	–	–	–	–	–	–	–	–	–	9.5
19	Liberal Democrats	–	–	–	–	–	–	–	–	–	12.2
18	Queensland Country Party	–	–	–	–	–	–	–	–	–	6.8
13	Communist Party	–	–	–	–	–	13.3	28.4	2.7	–	23.0
15	Social Credit Party	–	–	–	–	–	–	47.3	21.6	–	–
21	One Parliament for Australia	–	–	–	–	–	–	–	–	–	31.1

Table 1.15   AUSTRALIA   Total Votes 1946–1972[1]

	1946	1949	1951	1954	1955	1958	1961	1963	1966	1969	1972
Electorate	4,739,853	4,913,654	4,867,713	4,829,546	4,779,974	5,412,865	5,692,364	5,875,595	6,193,881	6,606,233	7,073,930
Valid Votes	4,344,744	4,620,780	4,582,744	4,576,438	4,395,535	5,018,012	5,281,509	5,507,445	5,709,749	6,114,118	6,601,050
Invalid Votes	109,197	93,580	88,671	62,506	130,239	148,088	139,011	101,961	182,578	159,493	146,194
Total Votes	4,453,941	4,714,360	4,671,415	4,638,944	4,525,774	5,166,100	5,420,520	5,609,406	5,892,327	6,273,611	6,747,244
PARTY VOTES											
1 Australian Labor Party	2,159,953	2,124,214	2,183,958	2,292,881	1,987,792	2,154,023	2,534,680	2,507,168	2,282,834	2,870,792	3,273,549
23 Lang Labor Party	69,138	32,870	–	–	–	–	–	–	–	–	–
8 Country Party	493,736	500,349	444,798	392,044	319,103	465,320	446,475	489,498	561,926	523,232	622,826
24 Australian Liberal Party	1,402,820	1,816,304	1,857,086	1,758,897	1,774,827	1,863,563	1,771,001	2,045,571	2,291,964	2,125,987	2,115,085
13 Communist Party	64,811	40,941	45,759	56,675	51,001	26,337	22,902	32,053	23,056	4,920	8,105
22 Services Party of Australia	54,000	–	–	–	–	–	–	–	–	–	–
25 Democratic Labor Party[2]	–	–	–	–	227,083	469,723	459,489	407,416	417,411	367,977	346,415
26 Australia Party	–	–	–	–	–	–	–	–	–	53,646	159,916
Others	100,286	106,102	51,143	75,941	35,730	39,046	46,962	25,739	132,558	167,564	75,154

[1] All figures for party votes refer to the number of first preference votes polled. Figures include the Northern Territory and the Australian Capital Territory.
[2] In 1955 the Anti-Communist Labor Party.

Sources: Hughes and Graham, 1968; and figures provided by the Chief Electoral Officer, Canberra.

18

Table 1.16   AUSTRALIA   Percentage of Votes 1946–1972

	1946	1949	1951	1954	1955	1958	1961	1963	1966	1969	1972
Valid Votes	91.7	94.0	94.1	94.8	92.0	92.7	92.8	93.7	92.2	92.6	93.3
Invalid Votes	2.3	1.9	1.8	1.3	2.7	2.7	2.4	1.7	2.9	2.4	2.1
Total Votes	94.0	95.9	96.0	96.1	94.7	95.4	95.2	95.5	95.1	95.0	95.4
Share Invalid	2.5	2.0	1.9	1.3	2.9	2.9	2.6	1.8	3.1	2.5	2.2
PARTY VOTES											
1 Australian Labor Party	49.7	46.0	47.7	50.1	45.2	42.9	48.0	45.5	40.0	47.0	49.6
23 Lang Labor Party	1.6	0.7	–	–	–	–	–	–	–	–	–
8 Country Party	11.4	10.8	9.7	8.6	7.3	9.3	8.5	8.9	9.8	8.6	9.4
24 Australian Liberal Party	32.3	39.3	40.5	38.4	40.4	37.1	33.5	37.1	40.1	34.8	32.0
13 Communist Party	1.5	0.9	1.0	1.2	1.2	0.5	0.4	0.6	0.4	0.1	0.1
22 Services Party of Australia	1.2	–	–	–	–	–	–	–	–	–	–
25 Democratic Labor Party	–	–	–	–	5.2	9.4	8.7	7.4	7.3	6.0	5.2
26 Australia Party	–	–	–	–	–	–	–	–	–	0.9	2.4
Others	2.3	2.3	1.1	1.7	0.8	0.8	0.9	0.5	2.3	2.7	1.1

19

Table 1.17

Table 1.17   AUSTRALIA   Number of Seats Won in the House of Representatives 1946—1972

		1946	1949	1951	1954	1955	1958	1961	1963	1966	1969	1972
1	Australian Labor Party	43	49	55	59	48	47	62	52	41	59	67
23	Lang Labor Party	1	0	–	–	–	–	–	–	–	–	–
8	Country Party	11	19	16	17	18	19	17	20	21	20	20
24	Australian Liberal Party	18	55	52	47	57	58	45	52	61	46	38
13	Communist Party	0	0	0	0	0	0	0	0	0	0	0
22	Services Party of Australia	0	–	–	–	–	–	–	–	–	–	–
25	Democratic Labor Party[1]	–	–	–	–	0	0	0	0	0	0	0
26	Australia Party	–	–	–	–	–	–	–	–	–	0	0
	Others	1	0	0	0	0	0	0	0	1	0	0
	Total Seats	74	123	123	123	123	124	124	124	124	125	125

[1] In 1955 the Anti-Communist Labor Party.

Sources: Hughes and Graham, 1968; and figures provided by the Chief Electoral Officer, Canberra.

Table 1.18   AUSTRALIA   Percentage of Seats Won in the House of Representatives 1946–1972

		1946	1949	1951	1954	1955	1958	1961	1963	1966	1969	1972
1	Australian Labor Party	58.1	39.0	44.7	48.0	39.0	37.9	50.0	41.9	33.1	47.2	53.6
23	Lang Labor Party	1.4	0.0	–	–	–	–	–	–	–	–	–
8	Country Party	14.9	15.4	13.0	13.8	14.6	15.3	13.7	16.1	16.9	16.0	16.0
24	Australian Liberal Party	24.3	44.7	42.3	38.2	46.3	46.8	36.3	41.9	49.2	36.8	30.4
13	Communist Party	0.0	0.0	0.0	0.0	0.0	0.0	0.0	0.0	0.0	0.0	0.0
22	Services Party of Australia	0.0	–	–	–	–	–	–	–	–	–	–
25	Democratic Labor Party	–	–	–	–	0.0	0.0	0.0	0.0	0.0	0.0	0.0
26	Australia Party	–	–	–	–	–	–	–	–	–	0.0	0.0
	Others	1.4	0.0	0.0	0.0	0.0	0.0	0.0	0.0	0.8	0.0	0.0

Table 1.19   AUSTRALIA   Number of Candidates 1946–1972

		1946	1949	1951	1954	1955	1958	1961	1963	1966	1969	1972
1	Australian Labor Party	73	122	121	115	112	123	124	123	124	124	125
23	Lang Labor Party	11	10	–	–	–	–	–	–	–	–	–
8	Country Party	24	35	23	20	21	24	25	24	27	26	36
24	Australian Liberal Party	61	103	98	96	99	103	104	99	104	107	107
13	Communist Party	14	35	27	42	27	19	21	21	16	7	16
22	Services Party of Australia	24	–	–	–	–	–	–	–	–	–	–
25	Democratic Labor Party[1]	–	–	–	–	39	113	113	101	113	113	121
26	Australia Party	–	–	–	–	–	–	–	–	–	37	60
	Others	22	51	19	16	46	30	27	32	66	90	70
	Total	**229**	**356**	**288**	**289**	**344**	**412**	**414**	**400**	**450**	**499**	**535**

[1] In 1955 the Anti-Communist Labor Party.

Sources: Hughes and Graham, 1968; and figures provided by the Chief Electoral Officer, Canberra.

Table 1.20 AUSTRALIA Percentage of Seats Contested 1946–1972

		1946	1949	1951	1954	1955	1958	1961	1963	1966	1969	1972
1	Australian Labor Party	98.6	99.2	98.4	93.5	91.1	99.2	100.0	99.2	100.0	99.2	100.0
23	Lang Labor Party	14.9	8.1	–		–	–	–	–	–	–	–
8	Country Party	32.4	28.5	18.7	16.3	17.1	19.4	20.2	19.4	21.8	20.8	28.8
24	Australian Liberal Party	82.4	83.7	79.7	78.0	80.5	83.1	83.9	79.8	83.9	85.6	85.6
13	Communist Party	18.9	28.5	22.0	34.1	22.0	15.3	16.9	16.9	12.9	5.6	12.8
22	Services Party of Australia	32.4	–	–	–	–	–	–	–	–	–	–
25	Democratic Labor Party	–	–	–	–	31.7	91.1	91.1	81.5	91.1	90.4	96.8
26	Australia Party	–	–	–	–	–	–	–	–	–	29.6	48.0

23

Chapter 2

AUSTRIA

Until 1918 the territory that was to become the Republic of Austria consisted of a number of predominantly German-speaking provinces in one-part of the multi-national Austro-Hungarian Empire. The Austrian House of Assembly consisted of four estates or curia, representing large landowners, cities, chambers of commerce and trade, and the rural communes. In 1897 a fifth curia was added in which all men over 24 could vote; this comprised 72 of the 425 seats. Voting figures for the elections of 1897 and 1900/01 are available in *Österreichische Statistik* 49 (1) 1897 and *Ibid.*, 59 (3) 1901. The calculation of aggregate voting statistics for these elections is inhibited by the curia system, and by the fact that in most of the fifth curia constituencies elections were indirect.

In 1907 the estates system was abolished and replaced by universal male suffrage. Direct and secret elections in single-member constituencies using the two-ballot majority system were introduced. (A detailed description of the complex pattern of Austrian election laws may be found in Stiefbold and Metzler-Andelberg, 1969: 15–30). The extension of the franchise was followed by the growth of political parties based on the different linguistic groups which made up the Empire. Czech, Polish, Ruthene, Slovene, Croat, Italian and Rumanian parties emerged. Among the German-speaking population the Social Democrats and the Christian Social Party, both founded in 1889, made rapid advances. By 1907 they dominated the provinces of Upper and Lower Austria, Carinthia, Salzburg, Styria, Tyrol and Vorarlberg, which were later to form the core of the Austrian republic, as the 1907 and 1911 election results show:

	14 May 1907			13 June 1911		
	Votes	%	seats	Votes	%	seats
Electorate	1,488,350			1,546,987		
Christian Social Party	658,198	52.3	94	555,986	45.5	70
Social Democrats	264,431	21.0	28	310,663	25.4	33
German Agrarians	16,656	1.3	0	9,214	0.8	1
German Conservatives	15,260	1.2	1	12,308	1.0	1
German National Party	8,481	0.7	2	26,779	2.2	5
German Peoples Party	83,073	6.6	15	55,182	4.5	14
German Progressive Party	20,211	1.6	2	–	–	–
Italian Parties	57,704	4.6	10	47,719	3.9	9
Slovene Parties	57,020	4.5	8	53,063	4.3	8
German Farmers League	–	–	–	15,301	1.2	0

(Continued)

	14 May 1907			13 June 1911		
	Votes	%	seats	Votes	%	seats
German Freedom Party	–	–	–	62,789	5.1	15
Upper Austrian Farmers League	–	–	–	22,009	1.8	0
Others	77,108	6.1	2	53,214	4.4	6
Total	1,258,142		162	1,224,927		162

Source: *Österreichische Statistik* 7 (1) 1912: 8-10.

In 1918 various national groups which formed the Habsburg Empire successfully claimed their independence. The predominantly German-speaking provinces established an independent democratic republic. In 1934 the Social Democratic Party was suppressed and Austria became a one-party corporate state. Four years later it was absorbed by Nazi Germany. After the defeat of Germany in 1945, Austria was re-established as a separate state under four-power Allied military occupation; this continued until the signature of the Austrian State Treaty in 1955 established the Second Austrian Republic.

In 1919 proportional representation using the d'Hondt system replaced the majority system used in the Empire. Women were given the vote and the voting age reduced to 20. In 1920 a second-stage seat distribution at national level which employed the d'Hondt system was introduced. In 1923 the Hagenbach-Bischoff system replaced the d'Hondt at the constituency level. The second-stage distribution continued to be calculated according to the d'Hondt method, but in four constituency groupings (Wahlkreisverbande) rather than for the country as a whole. In order to participate in the second stage, a party had to win at least one constituency seat.

The Second Austrian Republic retained its predecessor's electoral system. In 1968 the voting age was reduced to 19. In 1970 the number of Wahlkreisverbände was reduced to two and the method of computing the constituency quotient was altered. It is now calculated by dividing the total vote by the number of seats rather than the number of seats plus one. Provincial laws have prescribed compulsory voting in federal elections in the Tyrol and Vorarlberg since 1919 and in Styria since 1949.

Sources:

Kaiserlich-Königliche Statistische Zentral-Commission 'Ergebnisse der Reichstratswahlen im Jahre 1897'. *Österreichische Statistik,* 49 (1) 1897. Election results for December 1900–January 1901, 1907 and 1911 are published in the same series.

Österreichischen Statistischen Zentralamt, *Statistisches Handbuch für die Republik Österreich,* 1971 :/ 442-443.

Stiefbold, R.A.A., Leupold-Löwenthal, G. Ress, W. Lichem and D. Marvik (eds.) *Wahlen und Parteien in Österreich: Österreichisches Wahlhandbuch,* Band III Teil C. *"Wahlstatistik",* Vienna: Institute for Advanced Studies and Scientific Research, 1966.

Stiefbold, R. and R. Metzler-Andelberg, "Austria", in S. Rokkan and J. Meyriat (eds.) *International Guide to Electoral Statistics* (Paris: Mouton, 1969: 15-46).

Table 2.1
POLITICAL PARTIES IN AUSTRIA SINCE 1919

Party Names	Elections contested	Number contested
1 Social Democrats (Sozialdemokratische Partei—SDP); since 1945 the Socialist Party of Austria (Sozialistische Partei Österreichs—SPÖ)	1919ff	14
2 Christian Social Party (Christlich-soziale Partei—CSP); since 1945 the Austrian Peoples Party (Österreichische Volkspartei—ÖVP)	1919ff	14
3 German Nationalists[1]	1919ff	5
4 Czechs[2]	1919-1923	3
5 Communist Party (Kommunistische Partei Österreichs—KPÖ)[3]	1920ff	13
6 Carinthian Unity List (Kärntner Einheitsliste)[4]	1923	1
7 Fatherland Front (Heimatblock)	1930	1
8 National Socialist German Workers Party (Hitler Movement) (Nationalsozialistischer Deutsche Arbeiterpartei: Hitlerbewegung)	1930	1
9 League of Independents (Wahlpartei der Unabhängigen)—WdU; since 1956 the Freedom Party—(Freiheitliche Partei Österreichs—FPÖ)	1949ff	8
10 Democratic Progressive Party (Demokratische Fortschrittliche Partei—DFP)[5]	1966	1

[1] In 1919 several nationalist parties whose elected deputies formed the Grossdeutsche Partei; in 1920 the Greater German Peoples Party (Grossdeutsche Volkspartei—GdVP), the Austrian Farmers Party (Österreichisches Bauernpartei), the Carinthian Farmers League (Kärntner Bauernbund) and the National Socialist Party (Nationalsozialistische Partei). In 1923 the Grossdeutsche Volkspartei, the Austrian Land League (Landbund fur Osterreich—LbÖ) and the Burgenland Farmers League (Burgenlandische Bauernbund). In 1927 the Grossdeutsche Volkspartei formed an alliance with the Christlich soziale Partei whilst the Landbund ran independently. In 1930 the Grossdeutsche Volkspartei and the Landbund formed an electoral alliance (the Nationalwirtschaftsblock und Landbund—NWbLb).

[2] Representatives of the Czech-speaking minority in Lower Austria and Vienna.

[3] In 1949 the Left Block (Linksblock); in 1953 the Austrian Peoples Opposition (Wahlgemeinschaft Österreichisches Volksopposition); from 1956 to 1966 Communists and Left Socialists (Kommunisten und Links-sozialisten).

[4] An electoral alliance in Carinthia between the Christlichsoziale Partei, the Grossdeutsche Volkspartei and the Kärntner Bauernbund).

[5] Formed by ex-members of the Socialist Party led by Franz Olah, the former Minister of the Interior.

Table 2.2
DATES OF ELECTIONS TO THE NATIONALRAT 1919–1971[1]

1.	16 February 1919	8.	22 February 1953
2.	17 October 1920	9.	13 May 1956
3.	21 October 1923	10.	10 May 1959
4.	24 April 1927	11.	18 November 1962
5.	9 November 1930	12.	6 March 1966
6.	25 October 1945	13.	1 March 1970
7.	9 October 1949	14.	10 October 1971

[1] In 1919 the Nationalversammlung.

Sources: Stiefbold and Metzler-Andelberg, 1969 : 31-35.

Table 2.3   AUSTRIA   Total Votes 1919–1930

	1919	1920[1]	1923	1927	1930
Electorate	3,554,242	3,752,212	3,849,484	4,119,626	4,121,282
Valid Votes	2,973,454	2,980,328	3,312,606	3,636,712	3,688,068
Invalid Votes	24,843	n.a.	38,249	36,927	29,098
Total Votes	2,998,297	n.a.	3,350,855	3,673,639	3,717,166
PARTY VOTES					
1 Social Democrats	1,211,814	1,072,709	1,311,870	1,539,088	1,517,146
5 Communist Party	–	27,386	22,164	16,181	20,951
2 Christian Social Party	1,068,382	1,245,531	1,459,047	1,753,346[2]	1,314,956
3 German Nationalists	545,938	514,127	358,958	229,977[3]	471,944[4]
4 Czechs	67,514	39,002	7,580	–	–
6 Carinthian Unity List	–	–	95,465	–	–
7 Fatherland Front	–	–	–	–	227,401
8 National Socialists	–	–	–	–	111,627
Others	79,806	81,573	57,522	98,120	24,043

[1] Includes elections held in Carinthia on 19 June 1921 and Burgenland on 18 June 1922.
[2] An electoral alliance, the Unity List (Einheitsliste) of the Christian Social Party and the Greater German Peoples Party.
[3] Landbund Party only.
[4] Includes 43,689 votes cast for Independent Landbund Lists in Upper Austria and Salzburg.

Source: Stiefbold *et al.* 1966 25ff.

Table 2.4　　AUSTRIA　　Percentage of Votes 1919—1930

	1919	1920	1923	1927	1930
Valid Votes	83.7	79.4	86.1	88.3	89.5
Invalid Votes	0.7	n.a.	1.0	0.9	0.7
Total Votes	84.4	n.a.	87.0	89.2	90.2
Share Invalid	0.8	n.a.	1.1	1.0	0.8
PARTY VOTES					
1 Social Democrats	40.8	36.0	39.6	42.3	41.1
5 Communist Party	–	0.9	0.7	0.4	0.6
2 Christian Social Party	35.9	41.8	44.0	48.2	35.7
3 German Nationalists	18.4	17.3	10.8	6.3	12.8
4 Czechs	2.3	1.3	0.2	–	–
6 Carinthian Unity List	–	–	2.9	–	–
7 Fatherland Block	–	–	–	–	6.2
8 National Socialists	–	–	–	–	3.0
Others	2.7	2.7	1.7	2.7	0.7

31

Table 2.5 AUSTRIA   Number of Seats Won in the Nationalrat 1919–1930

	1919	1920	1923	1927	1930
1 Social Democrats	69	69	68	71	72
5 Communist Party	–	0	0	0	0
2 Christian Social Party	63	85	80	73	66
3 German Nationalists	24	28	11	21^2	19
4 Czechs	1	0	0	–	–
6 Carinthian Unity List	–	–	6^1	–	–
7 Fatherland Front	–	–	–	–	8
8 National Socialists	–	–	0	0	0
Others	2	1	0	0	0
Total Seats	159	183	165	165	165

[1] Two Christian Socials and four German Nationalists.
[2] Includes 12 Greater German Peoples Party candidates elected as part of the Unity List with the Christian Social Party.

Source: Stiefbold et al., 1966 : 25ff.

Table 2.6   AUSTRIA   Percentage of Seats Won in the Nationalrat 1919–1930

		1919	1920	1923	1927	1930
1	Social Democrats	43.4	37.7	41.2	43.0	43.6
5	Communist Party	–	0.0	0.0	0.0	0.0
2	Christian Social Party	39.6	46.4	48.5	44.2	40.0
3	German Nationalists	15.1	15.3	6.7	12.7	11.5
4	Czechs	0.6	0.0	0.0	–	–
6	Carinthian Unity List	–	–	3.6	–	–
7	Fatherland Front	–	–	–	–	4.8
8	National Socialists	–	–	–	–	0.0
	Others	1.3	0.5	0.0	0.0	0.0

Table 2.7   AUSTRIA   Total Votes 1945—1972

	1945	1949	1953	1956	1959	1962	1966	1970	1971
Electorate	3,449,605	4,391,815	4,586,870	4,614,464	4,696,603	4,805,351	4,886,818	5,045,841	4,984,448
Valid Votes	3,217,354	4,193,733	4,318,688	4,351,908	4,362,856	4,456,131	4,531,885	4,588,961	4,556,990
Invalid Votes	35,975	56,883	76,831	75,803	61,802	49,876	52,085	41,890	50,626
Total Votes	3,253,329	4,250,616	4,395,519	4,427,711	4,424,658	4,506,007	4,583,970	4,630,851	4,607,616

PARTY VOTES

	1945	1949	1953	1956	1959	1962	1966	1970	1971
1 Socialist Party	1,434,898	1,623,524	1,818,517	1,873,295	1,953,935	1,960,685	1,928,985	2,221,981	2,280,168
5 Communist Party	174,257	213,066	228,159	192,438	142,578	135,520	18,636	44,750	61,762
2 Peoples Party	1,602,227	1,846,581	1,781,777	1,999,986	1,928,043	2,024,501	2,191,109	2,051,012	1,964,713
9 League of Independents/ Freedom Party	–	489,273	472,866	283,749	336,110	313,895	242,570	253,425	248,473
10 Democratic Progressive Party	–	–	–	–	–	–	148,528	–	–
Others	5,972	21,289	17,369	2,440	2,190	21,530	2,057	17,793	1,874

Source: *Statistiches Handbuch*, 1972 : 442.

34

Table 2.8   AUSTRIA   Percentage of Votes 1945—1972

	1945	1949	1953	1956	1959	1962	1966	1970	1971
Valid Votes	93.3	95.5	94.2	94.3	92.9	92.7	92.7	90.9	91.4
Invalid Votes	1.0	1.3	1.7	1.6	1.3	1.0	1.1	0.8	1.0
Total Votes	94.3	96.8	95.8	96.0	94.2	93.8	93.8	91.8	92.4
Share Invalid	1.1	1.3	1.7	1.7	1.4	1.1	1.1	0.9	1.1
PARTY VOTES									
1 Socialist Party	44.6	38.7	42.1	43.0	44.8	44.0	42.6	48.4	50.0
5 Communist Party	5.4	5.1	5.3	4.4	3.3	3.0	0.4	1.0	1.4
2 Peoples Party	49.8	44.0	41.3	46.0	44.2	45.4	48.3	44.7	43.1
9 League of Independents/ Freedom Party	–	11.7	10.9	6.5	7.7	7.0	5.4	5.5	5.5
10 Democratic Progressive Party	–	–	–	–	–	–	3.3	–	–
Others	0.2	0.5	0.4	0.1	0.1	0.5	0.0	0.4	0.0

Table 2.9   AUSTRIA   Number of Seats Won in the Nationalrat 1945—1972

	1945	1949	1953	1956	1959	1962	1966	1970	1971
1 Socialist Party	76	67	73	74	78	74	74	81	93
5 Communist Party	4	5	4	3	0	0	0	0	0
2 Peoples Party	85	77	74	82	79	85	85	79	80
9 League of Independents/ Freedom Party	–	16	14	6	8	6	6	5	10
10 Democratic Progressive Party	–	–	–	–	–	–	0	–	–
Others	0	0	0	0	0	0	0	0	0
Total Seats	165	165	165	165	165	165	165	165	183

Source: *Statistiches Handbuch*, 1972 : 442.

Table 2.10   AUSTRIA   Percentage of Seats Won in the Nationalrat 1945—1972

	1945	1949	1953	1956	1959	1962	1966	1970	1971
1 Socialist Party	46.1	40.6	44.2	44.8	47.3	44.8	44.8	49.1	50.8
5 Communist Party	2.4	3.0	2.4	1.8	0.0	0.0	0.0	0.0	0.0
2 Peoples Party	51.5	46.7	44.8	49.7	47.9	51.5	51.5	47.9	43.7
9 League of Independents/ Freedom Party	–	9.7	8.5	3.6	4.8	3.6	3.6	3.0	5.5
10 Democratic Progressive Party	–	–	–	–	–	–	0.0	–	–
Others	0.0	0.0	0.0	0.0	0.0	0.0	0.0	0.0	0.0

Chapter 3

BELGIUM

Belgium became an independent state in 1830. The 1831 Constitution set up a two-chamber parliament consisting of a Chamber of Representatives (In Dutch, Kamer der Volksvertegenwoordigers; in French, Chambre des Représentants) and a Senate (Senaat/Sénat). Distinct Catholic and Liberal parties appeared in the 1830's but full details are not available of the political composition of the parliament or of national elections before 1847. (For a discussion of the parliamentary arena, see Lebas, 1960). The Liberals formed a national party organization in 1846, but the Catholics did not follow suit until the 1860's (Lorwin, 1966:155).

During the period of the *régime censitaire,* from 1830 to 1893, the suffrage for voters to the Chamber of Representatives was confined to men over 25 who paid a minimum direct tax. Until 1848, when a uniform rate of 20 florins was introduced, the tax qualification varied between rural and urban areas and between provinces. The secret ballot was introduced in 1877. Universal male suffrage, modified by plural voting, was introduced in 1893. Voting was made compulsory. All married men over 35 who occupied a house whose taxable value was at least five francs received an extra vote, as did all owners of property worth more than 2,000 francs and recipients of rents and dividends of more than 1,000 francs. Electors with a higher education diploma were entitled to two extra votes. No one could have more than three votes. In 1893, of a total of 1,370,000 voters, approximately 850,000 had only one vote, 290,000 had two votes and 220,000 three votes; thus plural voters were fewer in number than those with only one vote, but in aggregate they cast more ballots. (Gilissen, 1958: 125). Until 1899 a majority system was used in predominantly multi-member constituencies. If insufficient candidates received a majority of votes on the first round, a run-off election was held in which the number of candidates was restricted to twice the number of seats to be filled.

In 1899 the d'Hondt system of Proportional Representation replaced the majority system. Seats were allocated at the constituency level. The 1919 electoral law provided for a second allocation of seats at the provincial level in order to achieve greater proportionality. In each constituency an electoral divisor was calculated by dividing the number of votes cast by the number of seats. The number of seats awarded to each party was decided by dividing its total vote by the electoral divisor. If any seats remained unallocated each party's constituency votes were transferred to a provincial pool, where a second allocation was made using the d'Hondt method. At the same time plural voting was abolished and the voting age reduced to 21. Mothers and widows of soldiers who had died in the war were enfranchised, but women were not given the vote on the same basis as men until 1948.

Until 1919 partial elections were the norm. Nationwide elections were held only when the parliament was dissolved. Only eight such elections were held from 1847 to 1914. Partial elections always took place in two alternate groups of provinces. The first group consisted of Antwerp, Brabant, West Flanders, Luxembourg and Namur; the second of East Flanders, Hainaut, Liège and Limburg. The overall distribution of seats in the chamber after each partial and general election is presented in Table 3.7-8 and 3.13-14.

Sources:

Annuaire Statistique de la Belgique 1967 (Brussels: Institut National de Statistique, 1967.

Ibid, 1970

Gilissen, J., *Le régime répresentatif en Belgique depuis 1790.* (Brussels: Renaissance du Livre, 1958).

Hill, K., "Belgium: political change in a segmented society." in R. Rose (ed.) *Electoral Behavior: a Comparative Handbook* (New York: Free Press, 1973).

Lebas, C., *L'union des catholiques et des libéraux de 1839 a 1847* (Louvain: Editions Nauwelaerts, 1960).

Lorwin, V., "Belgium: religion, class and language in national politics." in R.A. Dahl (ed.) *Political Oppositions in Western Democracies* (New Haven: Yale University Press, 1966).

Ministère de l'Intérieur, *Elections Législatives-Chambre des Représentants: Résultats Officiels des Elections du 23 Mai 1965 et du 31 Mars 1968* (Brussels: Institut National de Statistique, n.d.)

Ibid., *Résultats des Elections du 7 Novembre 1971* (1972).

Moine, W. *Résultats des élections belges entre 1847 et 1914* (Brussels: Institut Belge de Science Politique, 1970).

de Smet, R.E. Evalenko, R. and Fraeys, W., *Atlas des élections belges 1919– 1954* (Brussels: Université Libre de Bruxelles, Institut de Sociologie Solvay, 1958).

Ibid. *Supplement comportant les résultats des élections législatives du ler juin 1958* (1961).

Ibid., *Deuxième supplement comportant les résults des eléctions législatives du 26 mars 1961* (1962).

Zombek–Fuks, F. and Fraeys, W., "Belgique." in S. Rokkan and J. Meyriat (eds.) *International Guide to Electoral Statistics* (Paris: Mouton, 1969) pp.47–57.

Table 3.1
POLITICAL PARTIES IN BELGIUM SINCE 1847

	Party Names	Elections contested	Number contested
1	Catholic Party (Katholieke Partij/Parti Catholique) Since 1945 the Christian Social Party (Christelijke Volkspartij—CVP/Parti Social Chrétien—PSC)[1]	1847ff	53
2	Liberal Party (Liberale Partij/Parti Libéral) Renamed the Party of Liberty and Progress (Partij voor Vrijheid en Vooruitgang—PVV/ Parti de la Liberté et du Progrès—PLP) in 1961	1847ff	53
3	Belgian Workers Party (Belgische Werklieden- partij—BWP/Parti Ouvrier Belge—POB). Renamed the Belgian Socialist Party (Belgische Socialistische Partij—BSP/Parti Socialiste Belge— PSB) in 1945	1890ff	29
4	Daensists (Christene Volkspartij)[2]	1894-1914	11
5	Liberal-Workers/Socialist Party Cartels	1894-1898; 1906-1912; 1946; 1950-1958	11
6	Dissident Catholic Lists[4]	1919-1936; 1945-1954; 1961-1965	12
7	Ex-Servicemen (Combattants)	1919-1922	2
8	Flemish Nationalists. Until 1932 the Front Party (Frontpartij). In 1936 and 1939 the Flemish National League (Vlaams Nationaal Verbond— VNV). In 1949 the Flemish Concentration (Vlaamse Concentratie). Since 1954 the Flemish Christian Peoples Union (Christelijke Vlaamse Volksunie)	1919-1939; 1949; 1954ff	14
9	Middle Class Party (Classes Moyennes)	1919-1928	4
10	Communist Party (Belgische Communistische Partij—BCP/Parti Communiste Belge—PCB).	1921ff	15
11	Rexists (Rex)	1936-1939	2
12	Democratic Union (Union Démocratique Belge— UDB)	1946	1
13	Francophone Démocratic Front (Front Democratique des Francophones—FDF)	1965ff	3
14	Walloon Démocratic Front (Front Démocratique Wallon)	1965	1
15	Walloon Front (Front Wallon)	1965	1
16	Walloon Workers Party (Parti Wallon des Travailleurs)	1965-1968	2
17	Walloon Rally (Rassemblement Wallon)	1968ff	2

[1] Before the First World War Catholic Party organization was very weak. In 1921 a Catholic Union (Union Catholique Belge) was established. In 1937 the party was reformed as the Catholic Block (Bloc Catholique Belge), a federation of separate Flemish and French-speaking parties: the Katholieke Vlaamsche Volkspartij—KVV and the Parti Catholique Social—PCS.

[2] Founded by the Abbé Daens in 1894.

[3] Provincial level electoral alliances between the Liberal Party and the Workers Party and later the Socialist Party. For an estimate of the total votes cast for these parties including their share of the alliance votes see Hill, 1973, Table 6A.

[4] Various Catholic Lists presented independently of the Catholic and Christian Social parties as identified in de Smet, 1958ff.

Table 3.2
DATES OF ELECTIONS
TO THE KAMER DER VOLKSVERTEGENWOORDIGERS/
CHAMBRE DES REPRESENTANTS 1847–1971

1.	8 June 1847 (B)		28.	5 July 1896 (A)
2.	13 June 1848 (G)		29.	22 May 1898 (B)
3.	11 June 1850 (A)		30.	27 May 1900 (G)
4.	8 June 1852 (B)		31.	25 May 1902 (A)
5.	13 June 1854 (A)		32.	29 May 1904 (B)
6.	10 June 1856 (B)		33.	27 May 1906 (A)
7.	10 December 1857 (G)		34.	24 May 1908 (B)
8.	14 June 1859 (A)		35.	22 May 1910 (A)
9.	11 June 1861 (B)		36.	2 June 1912 (G)
10.	9 June 1863 (A)		37.	24 May 1914 (B)
11.	11 August 1864 (G)		38.	16 November 1919
12.	12 June 1866 (B)		39.	20 November 1921
13.	9 June 1868 (A)		40.	5 May 1925
14.	14 June 1870 (B)		41.	26 May 1929
15.	2 August 1870 (G)		42.	27 November 1932
16.	11 June 1872 (A)		43.	24 May 1936
17.	9 June 1874 (B)		44.	2 April 1939
18.	13 June 1876 (A)		45.	17 February 1946
19.	11 June 1878 (B)		46.	29 June 1949
20.	8 June 1880 (A)		47.	4 June 1950
21.	13 June 1882 (B)		48.	11 April 1954
22.	10 June 1884 (A)		49.	1 June 1958
23.	8 June 1886 (B)		50.	26 March 1961
24.	12 June 1888 (A)		51.	23 May 1965
25.	10 June 1890 (B)		52.	31 March 1969
26.	14 June 1892 (G)		53.	7 November 1971
27.	14 October 1894 (G)			

(G) indicates a general election during the period 1847 to 1914; (A) a partial election held in the provinces of Antwerp, Brabant, Luxembourg, Namur and West Flanders; (B) a partial election held in East Flanders, Hainaut, Liège and Limburg.
Since 1914 all elections have been general elections.
Election dates from 1847 to 1898 refer to the first ballot.

Sources: Moine (1970) and Zombek-Fuks and Fraeys (1969).

Table 3.3 BELGIUM   Total Votes 1847–1892[1]

	1847	1848*	1850	1852	1854	1856	1857*	1859	1861	1863	1864*	1866	1868
Electorate	22,572	**79,076**	40,435	42,053	45,884	45,573	**90,543**	49,672	47,555	52,519	**103,717**	51,465	55,297
Valid Votes[2]	17,541	**44,311**	27,954	29,092	28,008	27,640	**71,783**	27,778	27,778	39,109	**79,566**	36,025	30,721
Total Votes	18,906	**52,955**[3]	30,150	31,727	32,037	31,261	**76,219**	37,972[4]	30,538	40,565	**83,949**	38,933	34,079
PARTY VOTES													
1 Catholic Party	8,298	**13,122**	11,618	12,404	11,921	15,168	**32,503**	12,726	11,799	21,310	**39,750**	15,060	16,918
2 Liberal Party	9,142	**30,806**	15,320	16,688	16,087	12,472	**39,280**	15,052	15,979	17,799	**39,576**	20,965	13,619
Others	101	**383**	1,016	–	–	–	–	–	–	–	**240**	–	184

	1870 (June)	1870* (Aug.)	1872	1874	1876	1878	1880	1882	1884	1886	1888	1890	1892*
Electorate	51,435	**107,099**	54,933	52,074	63,278	57,640	62,936	55,517	69,276	57,692	73,276	59,452	**136,707**
Valid Votes	30,871	**72,873**	30,470	33,395	42,740	36,051	42,301	41,689	54,790	36,944	53,517	38,210	**104,728**
Total Votes	33,373	**79,083**	36,179[5]	36,082	45,184	38,748	45,787	46,676	58,156	42,263	58,791[6]	43,873	**114,717**
PARTY VOTES													
1 Catholic Party	13,698	**39,705**	20,949	15,864	22,952	17,085	20,700	19,681	33,428	17,979	31,273	17,253	**56,199**
2 Liberal Party	17,173	**32,448**	9,455	17,531	19,788	18,966	21,283	22,001	21,294	18,965	19,967	20,829	**47,518**
3 Workers Party	–	–	–	–	–	–	–	–	–	–	–	98	167
Others	–	**720**	66	–	–	–	318	7	68	–	2,277	30	844

[1] General election results are shown in bold type.   [2] Until 1900 each elector was entitled to as many votes as there were seats in his constituency. Party votes have been estimated by dividing the number of valid votes cast by the number of seats in the constituency.   [3] Excluding the Oudenaarde constituency for which party votes are not available.   [4] Excluding the Ieper constituency for which party votes are not available.   [5] Excluding the Nivelles constituency for which party votes are not available.   [6] Excluding the Marche constituency for which party votes are not available.

Table 3.4 BELGIUM   Percentage of Votes 1847–1892

	1847	1848*	1850	1852	1854	1856	1857*	1859	1861	1863	1864*	1866	1868
Total Votes	83.7	67.0	74.5	74.4	69.8	71.7	84.2	76.2	64.2	77.2	81.9	75.6	61.6
PARTY VOTES													
1 Catholic Party	47.3	29.6	41.6	42.6	42.6	54.9	45.3	45.8	42.5	54.5	50.0	41.8	55.1
2 Liberal Party	52.1	69.5	54.8	57.4	57.4	45.1	54.7	54.2	57.5	45.5	49.7	58.2	44.3
Others	0.6	0.9	3.6	–	–	–	–	–	–	–	0.3	–	0.6

	1870 (June)	1870* (Aug.)	1872	1874	1876	1878	1880	1882	1884	1886	1888	1890	1892*
Total Votes	64.8	73.8	65.8	69.3	71.4	67.2	72.7	84.1	83.9	73.3	80.2	73.8	83.9
PARTY VOTES													
1 Catholic Party	44.4	54.5	68.8	47.5	53.7	47.4	48.9	47.2	61.0	48.7	58.4	45.2	53.6
2 Liberal Party	55.6	44.5	31.0	52.5	46.3	52.6	50.3	52.8	38.9	51.3	37.3	54.5	45.4
3 Workers Party	–	–	–	–	–	–	–	–	–	–	–	0.3	0.2
Others	–	1.0	0.2	–	–	–	0.8	0.0	0.1	–	4.3	0.1	0.8

Source: Moine, 1970 : 128-129.

Table 3.5 BELGIUM Number of Seats Won in the Chambre des Représentants 1847–1892[1]

	1847	1848*	1850	1852	1854	1856	1857*	1859	1861	1863	1864*	1866	1868
1 Catholic Party	21	26	22	23	26	33	38	27	22	34	53	18	33
2 Liberal Party	33	82	32	31	28	21	70	31	36	24	63	43	30
Total Seats	54	108[2]	54	54	54	54	108	58[3]	58	58	116	61	63

	1870 (June)	1870* (Aug.)	1872	1874	1876	1878	1880	1882	1884	1886	1888	1890	1892*
1 Catholic Party	30	73	43	26	42	18	40	20	67	32	66	29	92
2 Liberal Party	31	51	20	35	21	48	26	49	2	37	3	40	60
3 Workers Party	–	–	–	–	–	–	–	–	–	–	–	–	0
Total Seats	61	124	63	61	63	66	66	69	69	69	69	69	152

[1] In Dutch Kamer der Volksvertegenwoordigers.
[2] Including one unopposed return.
[3] Including 12 unopposed returns.

Table 3.6   BELGIUM   Percentage of Seats Won in the Chambre des Représentants 1847–1892

	1847	1848*	1850	1852	1854	1856	1857*	1859	1861	1863	1864*	1866	1868
1 Catholic Party	38.9	24.1	40.7	42.6	48.1	61.1	35.2	46.6	37.9	58.6	45.7	29.5	49.2
2 Liberal Party	61.1	75.9	59.3	57.4	51.9	38.9	64.8	53.4	62.1	41.4	54.3	70.5	47.6

	1870 (June)	1870* (Aug.)	1872	1874	1876	1878	1880	1882	1884	1886	1888	1890	1892*
1 Catholic Party	49.2	58.9	68.3	42.6	66.7	27.3	60.6	30.0	97.1	46.4	95.7	42.0	60.5
2 Liberal Party	50.8	41.1	31.7	57.4	33.3	72.7	39.4	70.0	2.9	53.6	4.3	58.0	39.5

Table 3.7   BELGIUM   Distribution of Seats in the Chambre des Représentants 1847–1892[1]

	1847	1848*	1850	1852	1854	1856	1857*	1859	1861	1863	1864*	1866	1868
1 Catholics	53	25	39	51	54	63	38	47	50	57	52	52	50
2 Liberals	55	83	69	57	54	45	70	69	66	59	64	70	72
Total	108	108	108	108	108	108	108	116	116	116	116	122	122

	1870 (June)	1870* (Aug.)	1872	1874	1876	1878	1880	1882	1884	1886	1888	1890	1892*
1 Catholics	61	72	71	68	67	60	58	59	86	98	98	94	92
2 Liberals	61	52	53	56	57	72	74	79	52	40	40	44	60
Total	122	124	124	124	124	132	132	138	138	138	138	138	152

[1] This table presents the number of seats held by each party in the Chamber after both general and partial elections.

Source: J. Gillissen, 1958 : 188-189.

Table 3.8 BELGIUM   Percentage Distribution of Seats in the Chambre des Représentants 1847–1892

	1847	1848*	1850	1852	1854	1856	1857*	1859	1861	1863	1864*	1866	1868
1 Catholics	49.1	23.1	36.1	47.2	50.0	58.3	35.2	40.5	43.1	49.1	44.8	42.6	41.0
2 Liberals	50.9	76.9	63.9	52.8	50.0	41.7	64.8	39.5	56.9	50.1	55.2	57.4	59.0

	1870 (June)	1870* (Aug.)	1872	1874	1876	1878	1880	1882	1884	1886	1888	1890	1892*
1 Catholics	50.0	59.0	57.3	54.8	54.0	45.5	43.9	42.8	62.3	71.0	71.0	68.1	60.5
2 Liberals	50.0	41.0	42.7	45.2	46.0	55.5	56.1	57.2	37.7	29.0	29.0	31.9	39.5

Table 3.9   BELGIUM   Total Votes 1894–1914

	1894*	1896	1898	1900*	1902	1904	1906	1908	1910	1912*	1914
Electorate[1]	2,111,127[2]	1,076,151	1,093,103	2,269,414	1,164,185	1,216,735	1,259,242	1,304,864	1,365,116	2,814,181	1,436,962
Valid Votes	1,802,980[3]	884,009	902,944	2,051,014	1,064,926	1,107,940	1,172,828	1,200,906	1,274,496	2,621,771	1,334,581
Invalid Votes	—	—	—	83,717	38,642	35,463	28,950	38,725	32,258	62,327	—
Total Votes	1,733,568[3]	928,734[4]	989,112	2,134,331	1,103,568	1,143,403	1,201,778	1,239,631	1,306,754	2,684,098	—
PARTY VOTES											
1 Catholic Party	921,607	492,547	373,375	994,245	596,382	486,643	636,446	517,679	676,846	1,337,315	570,806
2 Liberal Party	503,929	166,794	170,839	498,799	266,891	283,411	197,021	236,503	232,663	303,895	326,922
3 Workers Party	237,920	74,762	190,492	461,095	159,370	287,847	72,224	271,870	85,326	243,338	404,701
5 Liberal–Workers Party Cartels	94,129	129,227	123,256	—	—	—	234,677	135,546	243,063	679,734	—
4 Daensists	21,849	12,195	22,978	61,131	26,435	20,761	10,602	15,396	13,960	48,716[5]	22,219
Others	23,546	8,484	22,004	35,744	15,848	29,278	21,858	23,912	22,638	8,773	9,933

[1] Period of plural voting: the total number of votes to which electors were entitled rather than the number of electors.
[2] Of which Brussels 236,283.
[3] Excludes the Brussels constituency for which figures are not available.
[4] Excluding the Tielt constituency for which figures are not available.
[5] Including votes cast for a Liberal-Socialist-Daensist alliance in Brugge.

Source: Moine, 1970 : 128-129.

Table 3.10   BELGIUM   Percentage of Votes 1894—1914

	1894*	1896	1898	1900*	1902	1904	1906	1908	1910	1912*	1914
Valid Votes	–	–	–	90.4	91.5	91.1	93.1	92.0	93.4	93.2	92.9
Invalid Votes	n.a.	n.a.	n.a.	3.6	2.9	2.9	2.3	3.0	2.3	2.2	n.a.
Total Votes	n.a.	91.8	95.4	94.0	94.8	94.0	95.4	95.0	95.7	95.4	n.a.
PARTY VOTES											
1 Catholic Party	51.1	55.7	41.4	48.5	56.0	43.9	54.3	43.1	53.1	51.1	42.8
2 Liberal Party	28.0	18.9	18.9	24.3	25.1	25.6	16.8	19.7	18.3	11.6	24.5
3 Workers Party	13.2	8.5	21.0	22.5	15.0	26.0	6.2	22.6	6.7	9.3	30.3
5 Liberal—Workers Party Cartels	5.2	14.6	13.7	–	–	–	20.0	11.3	19.1	25.9	–
4 Daensists	1.2	1.4	2.5	3.0	2.5	1.9	0.9	1.3	1.1	1.9	1.7
Others	1.3	1.0	2.4	1.7	1.5	2.6	1.9	2.0	1.8	0.3	0.8

Table 3.11   BELGIUM   Number of Seats Won in the Chambre des Représentants 1894—1914

	1894*	1896	1898	1900*	1902	1904	1906	1908	1910	1912*	1914
1 Catholic Party	103	72	37	86	54	38	50	37	49	101	41
2 Liberal Party	20	4	9	33	20	22	23	21	24	44	20
3 Workers Party	28	1	27	32	10	19	12	22	12	39	26
4 Daensists	1	0	0	1	1	1	0	1	0	2	1
Others	0	0	2[3]	0	0	1[4]	0	0	0	0	0
Total Seats	152[1]	77[2]	75	152	85	81	85	81	85	186	88

[1] Including one unopposed return.
[2] Including four unopposed returns
[3] Independent Catholics.
[4] Independent Catholic.

Source: Moine : 128-129.

Table 3.12   BELGIUM   Percentage of Seats Won in the Chambre des Représentants 1894—1914

	1894*	1896	1898	1900*	1902	1904	1906	1908	1910	1912*	1914
1 Catholic Party	67.8	93.5	49.3	56.7	63.5	46.9	58.8	45.7	57.6	54.3	46.6
2 Liberal Party	13.2	5.2	12.0	21.7	23.5	27.2	27.1	25.9	28.2	23.7	22.7
3 Workers Party	18.4	1.3	36.0	21.1	11.8	23.5	14.1	27.2	14.1	21.0	29.5
4 Daensists	0.7	0.0	0.0	0.7	1.2	1.2	0.0	1.2	0.0	1.1	0.0
Others	0.0	0.0	2.7	0.0	0.0	1.2	0.0	0.0	0.0	0.0	0.0

Table 3.13   BELGIUM   Distribution of Seats in the Chambre des Représentants 1894—1914[1]

	1894*	1896	1898	1900*	1902	1904	1906	1908	1910	1912*	1914
1 Catholics	104	111	112	86	96	93	89	87	86	101	99
2 Liberals	20	13	13	34	34	42	46	43	44	44	45
3 Workers Party	28	28	27	31	34	29	30	35	35	39	40
4 Daensists	0	0	0	1	2	2	1	1	1	2	2
Total Seats	152	152	152	152	166	166	166	166	166	186	186

[1] This table presents the number of seats held by each party in the Chambre after both general and partial elections.

Source: Gilissen, 1958 : 190.

54

Table 3.14　BELGIUM　Percentage Distribution of Seats in the Chambre des Représentants 1894—1914

	1894*	1896	1898	1900*	1902	1904	1906	1908	1910	1912*	1914
1 Catholics	68.4	73.0	73.7	56.6	57.8	56.0	53.6	52.4	51.8	54.3	53.2
2 Liberals	13.2	8.9	8.9	22.4	20.5	25.3	27.7	25.9	26.5	23.7	24.2
3 Workers Party	18.4	18.4	17.8	20.4	20.5	17.5	18.1	21.1	21.1	21.0	21.5
4 Daensists	0.0	0.0	0.0	0.7	1.2	1.2	0.7	0.7	0.7	1.1	1.1

Table 3.15   BELGIUM   Total Votes 1919–1939

	1919	1921	1925	1929	1932	1936	1939
Electorate	2,102,710	2,226,797	2,346,096	2,497,446	2,555,743	2,652,707	2,667,341
Valid Votes	1,760,745	1,931,967	2,079,624	2,230,065	2,335,192	2,362,454	2,338,437
Invalid Votes	100,145	97,326	98,572	116,664	74,361	148,812	150,442
Total Votes	1,860,890	2,029,293	2,178,196	2,346,729	2,409,553	2,511,266	2,488,879
PARTY VOTES							
1 Catholic Party	645,462	715,041	751,058	788,914	899,887	653,717	764,843
6 Dissident Catholic Lists	37,245	82,509[2]	52,400[2]	69,988[2,3]	4,664	26,460[4]	–
2 Liberal Party	310,853	343,929	304,467	369,114	333,567	292,972	401,991
3 Workers Party	645,075	672,445	820,116	803,347	866,817	758,485	705,969
7 Ex-Servicemen	19,075	20,633	–	–	–	–	–
8 Flemish Nationalists	45,863	58,790	80,407	140,616	138,456	168,355	193,528
9 Middle Class Party	18,267	9,754	9,999	3,569	–	–	–
10 Communist Party	–	939	34,149	42,237	65,694	143,223	125,428
11 Rexists	–	–	–	–	–	271,491	103,821
Others	40,301[1]	27,802	27,324	12,584	26,107	47,751	42,857[5]

[1] Includes Renovation Nationale, 12,246 votes.

[2] Includes several Christian Workers (Kristelijke Arbeiders) lists in West Flanders with 17,763 votes in 1921, 27,516 votes in 1925 and 52,642 votes in 1929.

[3] Includes Liste De Lille with 19,205 votes.

[4] Includes Démocrates Chrétiens with 22,224 votes.

[5] Includes Frenssen (Technocrates) with 10,843 votes and Combattants with 10,630 votes.

Sources: de Smet et al., 1958 : 10-11, Annuaire statistique, 1967 : 584.

Table 3.16 BELGIUM   Percentage of Votes 1919–1939

	1919	1921	1925	1929	1932	1936	1939
Valid Votes	83.7	86.8	88.6	89.3	91.4	89.1	87.7
Invalid Votes	4.8	4.4	4.2	4.7	2.9	5.6	5.6
Total Votes	88.5	91.1	92.8	94.0	94.3	94.7	93.3
Share Invalid	5.4	4.8	4.5	5.0	3.1	5.9	6.0
PARTY VOTES							
1 Catholic Party	36.6	37.0	36.1	35.4	38.5	27.7	32.7
6 Dissident Catholic Lists	2.1	4.3	2.5	3.1	0.2	1.1	–
2 Liberal Party	17.6	17.8	14.6	16.6	14.3	12.4	17.2
3 Workers Party	36.6	34.8	39.4	36.0	37.1	32.1	30.2
7 Ex-Servicemen	1.1	1.1	–	–	–	–	–
8 Flemish Nationalists	2.6	3.0	3.9	6.3	5.9	7.1	8.3
9 Middle Class Party	1.0	0.5	0.5	0.2	–	–	–
10 Communist Party	–	0.0	1.6	1.9	2.8	6.1	5.4
11 Rexists	–	–	–	–	–	11.5	4.4
Others	2.3	1.4	1.3	0.6	1.1	2.0	1.8

Table 3.17 BELGIUM Number of Seats won in the Chambre des Représentants 1919–1939

	1919	1921	1925	1929	1932	1936	1939
1 Catholic Party	73	76	75	71	79	61	73
6 Dissident Catholic Lists	0	4[2]	3[3]	6[4]	0	2[5]	–
2 Liberal Party	34	33	23	28	24	23	33
3 Workers Party	70	68	78	70	73	70	64
7 Ex-Servicemen	2	1	–	–	–	–	–
8 Flemish Nationalists	5	4	6	11	8	16	17
9 Middle Class Party	1	0	2	0	–	–	–
10 Communist Party	–	0	2	1	3	9	9
11 Rexists	–	–	–	–	–	21	4
Others	1[1]	0	0	0	0	0	2[6]
Total Seats	186	186	187	187	187	202	202

[1] Renovation Nationale
[2] Includes two Kristelijke Arbeiders.
[3] Kristelijke Arbeiders.
[4] Kristelijke Arbeiders 5, Liste De Lille one.
[5] Démocrates Chrétiens.
[6] Frenssen and Combattants.

Source: de Smet et al., 1958 : 14-15

Table 3.18   BELGIUM   Percentage of Seats won in the Chambre des Représentants 1919—1939

	1919	1921	1925	1929	1932	1936	1939
1 Catholic Party	39.2	40.9	40.1	38.0	42.2	30.2	36.1
6 Dissident Catholic Lists	0.0	2.2	1.6	3.2	0.0	1.0	–
2 Liberal Party	18.3	17.7	12.3	15.0	12.8	11.4	16.3
3 Workers Party	37.6	36.6	41.7	37.4	39.0	34.7	31.7
7 Ex-Servicemen	1.1	0.5	–	–	–	–	–
8 Flemish Nationalists	2.7	2.2	3.2	5.9	4.3	7.9	8.4
9 Middle Class Party	0.5	0.0	0.0	0.0	–	–	–
10 Communist Party	–	0.0	1.1	0.5	1.6	4.5	4.5
11 Rexists	–	–	–	–	–	10.4	2.0
Others	0.5	0.0	0.0	0.0	0.0	0.0	1.0

59

Table 3.19 BELGIUM Total Votes 1946–1971

	1946	1949	1950	1954	1958	1961	1965	1968	1971
Electorate	2,724,796	5,635,452	5,635,452	5,863,092	5,954,858	6,036,165	6,091,534	6,170,167	6,271,240
Valid Votes	2,365,638	5,030,886	4,942,807	5,160,486	5,302,353	5,265,025	5,181,935	5,177,952	5,281,633
Invalid Votes	95,158	289,377	276,469	302,644	272,774	308,836	396,941	376,700	459,637
Total Votes	2,460,796	5,320,263	5,219,276	5,463,130	5,575,127	5,573,861	5,578,876	5,554,652	5,741,270

PARTY VOTES

	1946	1949	1950	1954	1958	1961	1965	1968	1971
1 Christian Social Party	1,006,293	2,190,898	2,356,608	2,123,408	2,465,549	2,182,652	1,785,211	1,643,785[3]	1,587,195
6 Dissident Catholic Lists	348	4,327	332	44,796[1]	—	42,081[2]	14,007	—	—
2 Liberal Party	211,143	767,180	556,102	626,983	585,999	649,376	1,120,081	1,080,894	865,657
3 Socialist Party	746,738	1,496,539	1,705,781	1,927,015	1,897,646	1,933,424	1,465,503	1,449,172[5]	1,438,626[7]
5 Liberal-Socialist Cartels	37,844	—	87,252	109,982	111,284	—	—	—	—
8 Flemish Nationalists	—	103,896	—	113,632	104,823	182,407	333,409	506,697	586,917
10 Communist Party	300,099	376,765	234,541	184,108	100,145	162,238	236,702	170,625	161,517
12 Democratic Union	51,095	—	—	—	—	—	—	—	—
13 Francophone Democratic Front	—	—	—	—	—	—	68,966	130,258	235,316
14 Walloon Democratic Front	—	—	—	—	—	—	5,709	—	—
15 Walloon Front	—	—	—	—	—	—	24,245	—	—
16 Walloon Workers Party	—	—	—	—	—	—	23,582	3,474	—
17 Walloon Rally	—	—	—	—	—	—	—	175,186	357,929[8]
Others	12,078	91,281	2,191	30,562	36,907	112,857[3]	104,520	17,861	48,476

[1] Rassemblement Social Chrétien de la Liberté. [2] Rassemblement National. [3] Includes Liste L'Allemand and allied lists with 36,276 votes. [4] Includes 236,283 votes for the Cartel Vanden Boeynants in Brussels. [5] Includes 46,065 votes for Rode Leeuwen, a separate Flemish Socialist list in Brussels. [6] Includes 23,765 votes for Walloon Rally – FDF cartels in the Nivelles constituency. [7] Includes 43,555 votes for Rode Leeuwen. [8] Includes 50,710 votes for Walloon Rally – FDF cartels in the Leuven and Nivelles constituencies.

Table 3.20   BELGIUM   Percentage of Votes 1946—1971

	1946	1949	1950	1954	1958	1961	1965	1968	1971
Valid Votes	86.8	89.3	87.7	88.0	89.0	87.2	85.1	83.9	84.2
Invalid Votes	3.5	5.1	4.9	5.2	4.6	5.1	6.5	6.1	7.3
Total Votes	90.3	94.4	92.6	93.2	93.6	92.3	91.6	90.0	91.5
Share Invalid	3.9	5.4	5.3	5.5	4.9	5.5	7.1	6.8	8.0
PARTY VOTES									
1 Christian Social Party	42.5	43.5	47.7	41.1	46.5	41.5	34.4	31.8	30.1
6 Dissident Catholic Lists	0.0	0.1	0.0	0.9	–	0.8	0.3	–	–
2 Liberal Party	8.9	15.2	11.3	12.1	11.1	12.3	21.6	20.9	16.4
3 Socialist Party	31.6	29.7	34.5	37.3	35.8	36.7	28.2	28.0	27.2
5 Liberal-Socialist Cartels	1.6	–	1.8	2.1	2.1	–	–	–	–
8 Flemish Nationalists	–	2.1	–	2.1	2.0	3.5	6.4	9.8	11.1
10 Communist Party	12.7	7.5	4.7	3.6	1.9	3.1	4.6	3.3	3.1
12 Democratic Union	2.2	–	–	–	–	–	–	–	–
13 Francophone Democratic Front	–	–	–	–	–	–	1.3	2.5	4.5
14 Walloon Democratic Front	–	–	–	–	–	–	0.1	–	–
15 Walloon Front	–	–	–	–	–	–	0.5	–	–
16 Walloon Workers Party	–	–	–	–	–	–	0.5	0.0	–
17 Walloon Rally	–	–	–	–	–	–	–	3.4	6.8
Others	0.5	1.8	0.0	0.6	0.7	2.1	2.1	0.3	0.9

Sources: Annuaire Statistique, 1967 : 584; de Smet et al., 1958 : 10-11; Ibid, 1961 : 12; Ibid., 1962 : 3; Ministère de l'Intérieur, n.d., 324-325; Ibid, 1972 : 193.

Table 3.21   BELGIUM   Number of Seats won in the Chambre des Représentants 1946—1971

	1946	1949	1950	1954	1958	1961	1965	1968	1971
1 Christian Social Party	92	105	108	95	104	96	77	69	67
6 Dissident Catholic Lists	0	0	0	1[1]	–	1[2]	0	–	–
2 Liberal Party	17	29	20	25	21	20	48	47	34
3 Socialist Party	69	66	77	86	84	84	64	59	61
8 Flemish Nationalists	–	0	–	1	1	5	12	20	21
10 Communist Party	23	12	7	4	2	5	6	5	5
12 Democratic Union	1	–	–	–	–	–	–	–	–
13 Francophone Democratic Front	–	–	–	–	–	–	3	5	10
14 Walloon Democratic Front	–	–	–	–	–	–	0	–	–
15 Walloon Front	–	–	–	–	–	–	1	–	–
16 Walloon Workers Party	–	–	–	–	–	–	1	0	–
17 Walloon Rally	–	–	–	–	–	1[3]	–	7	14
Others	0	0	0	0	0		0	0	0
Total Seats	202	212	212	212	212	212	212	212	212

[1] Rassemblement Social Chrétien de la Liberté.
[2] Rassemblement National.
[3] Liste l'Allemand.

Sources: *Annuaire Statistique*, 1967 : 592-593; Ministère de l'Intérieur, 1972 : 193.

Table 3.22   BELGIUM   Percentage of Seats won in the Chambre des Représentants 1946—1971

	1946	1949	1950	1954	1958	1961	1965	1968	1971
1 Christian Social Party	45.5	49.5	50.9	44.8	49.1	45.3	36.6	32.5	31.6
6 Dissident Catholic Lists	0.0	0.0	0.0	0.5	–	0.5	0.0	–	–
2 Liberal Party	8.4	13.7	9.4	11.8	9.9	9.4	22.6	22.2	16.0
3 Socialist Party	34.2	31.1	36.3	40.6	39.6	39.6	30.2	27.8	28.8
8 Flemish Nationalists	–	0.0	–	0.5	0.5	2.4	5.7	9.4	9.9
10 Communist Party	11.4	5.7	3.3	1.9	0.9	2.4	2.8	2.4	2.4
12 Democratic Union	0.5	–	–	–	–	–	–	–	–
13 Francophone Democratic Front	–	–	–	–	–	–	1.4	2.4	4.7
14 Walloon Democratic Front	–	–	–	–	–	–	0.0	–	–
15 Walloon Front	–	–	–	–	–	–	0.5	–	–
16 Walloon Workers Party	–	–	–	–	–	–	0.5	0.0	–
17 Walloon Rally	–	–	–	–	–	–	–	3.3	6.6
Others	0.0	0.0	0.0	0.0	0.0	0.5	0.0	0.0	0.0

Chapter 4
CANADA

The Dominion of Canada was established in 1867 as a federation of most of the British colonies in North America. (Newfoundland did not join until 1949.) Two parties soon developed out of pre-federation political groupings. Although they were far from cohesive organizations in the early years of the Confederation, the Liberal and Conservative parties immediately established themselves as, and have remained, the two dominant Canadian political parties.

The Canadian parliament consists of a directly elected House of Commons and a nominated Senate. Suffrage laws were the exclusive concern of the provinces until 1917, except for the period from 1885 to 1898. The franchise therefore varied somewhat; in all cases it was confined to adult males who met property or income requirements. In 1888 Manitoba introduced adult male suffrage with only very minor restrictions; lower franchise requirements were gradually adopted elsewhere. Women were given the vote in Manitoba, Saskatchewan and Alberta in 1916 and in British Columbia and Ontario in 1917. In the same year, federal legislation enfranchised close female relatives of servicemen, and women serving in the armed forces. In 1920 universal adult suffrage was established for federal elections. In 1970 the voting age was reduced to 18. A plurality system in predominantly single-member constituencies has always been used. The secret ballot was introduced in 1874.

Sources:

Beck, J.M., *Pendulum of Power: Canada's Federal Elections* (Scarborough, Ontario: Prentice-Hall, 1968).

Qualter, T.H., *The Election Process in Canada* (Toronto: McGraw-Hill, 1970).

Twenty-eighth General Election, 1968. Report of the Chief Electoral Officer (Ottawa: the Queen's Printer, 1969).

Table 4.1
POLITICAL PARTIES IN CANADA SINCE 1867

	Party Names	Elections contested	Number contested
1	Government[1]	1867	1
2	Opposition[2]	1867	1
3	Conservative Party; in 1942 renamed the Progressive Conservative Party	1872ff	28
4	Liberal Party	1872ff	28
5	Patrons of Industry	1891-1896	2
6	McCarthyites	1896	1
7	Labor Party	1900-1949	13
8	Communist Party	1921; 1925-1940 1962-1968	9
9	National Progressive Party	1921-1930	4
10	Cooperative Commonwealth Federation—CCF; in 1961 renamed the New Democratic Party—NDP	1935ff	12
11	Reconstruction Party	1935	1
12	Social Credit	1935ff	12
13	Bloc Populaire	1945	1
14	Union des Electeurs	1949	1
15	Ralliement des Créditistes de Quebec[3]	1965-1968	2

[1] An alliance of different groups supporting Confederation.

[2] An alliance of anti-Confederation groups.

[3] Originally the Quebec branch of the Social Credit Party, it became a separate party in 1963. In 1971 the two parties were reunited as the Social Credit Party.

Table 4.2
DATES OF ELECTIONS
TO THE HOUSE OF COMMONS 1867–1972

1.	7 August – 20 September 1867	15.	29 October 1925
2.	20 July – 12 October 1872	16.	14 September 1926
3.	22 January 1874	17.	28 July 1930
4.	17 September 1878	18.	14 October 1935
5.	20 June 1882	19.	26 March 1940
6.	22 February 1887	20.	11 June 1945
7.	5 March 1891	21.	27 June 1949
8.	23 June 1896	22.	10 August 1953
9.	7 November 1900	23.	10 June 1957
10.	3 November 1904	24.	31 March 1958
11.	26 October 1908	25.	8 April 1963
12.	21 September 1911	26.	18 November 1965
13.	7 December 1917	27.	25 June 1968
14.	6 December 1921	28.	30 October 1972

Sources: For the 1867, 1872, 1874 and 1972 elections the Chief Electoral Officer, Ottawa; for all other elections Beck, 1968.

Table 4.3 CANADA Total Votes 1867–1900

	1867	1872	1874	1878	1882	1887	1891	1896	1900
Valid Votes	268,217	318,342	322,619	533,941	515,504	722,722	778,522	899,046	950,763
PARTY VOTES									
1 Government	134,269	–	–	–	–	–	–	–	–
2 Opposition	131,364	–	–	–	–	–	–	–	–
3 Conservatives	–	159,006	146,465	280,224	261,293	362,632	397,731	414,838	450,790
4 Liberals	–	156,365	173,477	247,043	241,400	352,184	366,817	405,185	487,193
5 Patrons of Industry	–	–	–	–	–	–	2,198	36,655	–
6 McCarthyites	–	–	–	–	–	–	–	17,532	–
7 Labor Party	–	–	–	–	–	–	–	–	2.924
Others	2,584	2,971	2,677	6,674	12,811	7,906	11,776	24,836	9,856

Source: Beck, 1968.

Table 4.4   CANADA   Percentage of Votes 1867–1900

PARTY VOTES	1867	1872	1874	1878	1882	1887	1891	1896	1900
1 Government	50.1	–	–	–	–	–	–	–	–
2 Opposition	49.0	–	–	–	–	–	–	–	–
3 Conservatives	–	49.9	45.4	52.5	50.7	50.2	51.1	46.1	47.4
4 Liberals	–	49.1	53.8	46.3	46.8	48.7	47.1	45.1	51.2
5 Patrons of Industry	–	–	–	–	–	–	0.3	4.1	–
6 McCarthyites	–	–	–	–	–	–	–	2.0	–
7 Labor Party	–	–	–	–	–	–	–	–	0.3
Others	1.0	0.9	0.8	1.2	2.5	1.1	1.5	2.8	1.0

69

Table 4.5 CANADA — Number of Seats Won in the House of Commons 1867–1900

	1867	1872	1874	1878	1882	1887	1891	1896	1900
1 Government	108	–	–	–	–	–	–	–	–
2 Opposition	72	–	–	–	–	–	–	–	–
3 Conservatives	–	104	67	142	139	126	121	88	80
4 Liberals	–	96	138	64	71	89	94	118	133
5 Patrons of Industry	–	–	–	–	–	–	0	2	–
6 McCarthyites	–	–	–	–	–	–	–	4	–
7 Labor Party	–	–	–	–	–	0	0	1	0
Others	0	0	1	0	1	0	0	1	0
Total Seats	181[1]	200	206	206	211	215	215	213	213
Unopposed Returns	46	52	55	11	25	10	8	3	5

[1] No candidate returned in Kamouraska (Quebec) because of riots.

Source: Beck, 1968.

Table 4.6   CANADA   Percentage of Seats Won in the House of Commons 1867–1900

	1867	1872	1874	1878	1882	1887	1891	1896	1900
1 Government	60.0	–	–	–	–	–	–	–	–
2 Opposition	40.0	–	–	–	–	–	–	–	–
3 Conservatives	–	52.0	32.5	68.9	65.9	58.6	56.3	41.3	37.6
4 Liberals	–	48.0	67.0	31.1	33.6	41.4	43.7	55.4	62.4
5 Patrons of Industry	–	–	–	–	–	–	0.0	0.9	–
6 McCarthyites	–	–	–	–	–	–	–	1.9	–
7 Labor Party	–	–	–	–	–	–	–	–	0.0
Others	0.0	0.0	0.5	0.0	0.5	0.0	0.0	0.5	0.0
Unopposed Returns	25.0	26.0	26.7	5.3	11.8	4.7	3.7	1.4	2.3

71

Table 4.7   CANADA   Number of Candidates 1867–1900

	1867	1872	1874	1878	1882	1887	1891	1896	1900
1 Government	161	–	–	–	–	–	–	–	–
2 Opposition	149	–	–	–	–	–	–	–	–
3 Conservatives	–	174	163	202	209	212	212	207	207
4 Liberals	–	167	181	194	178	207	203	192	212
5 Patrons of Industry	–	–	–	–	–	–	2	30	–
6 McCarthyites	–	–	–	–	–	–	–	11	–
7 Labor Party	–	–	–	–	–	–	–	–	3
Others	21	23	19	23	24	20	20	29	15
Total	331	364	363	419	411	439	437	469	437

Source: Beck, 1968.

72

Table 4.8   CANADA   Percentage of Seats Contested 1867–1900

	1867	1872	1874	1878	1882	1887	1891	1896	1900
1 Government	89.0	–	–	–	–	–	–	–	–
2 Opposition	82.3	–	–	–	–	–	–	–	–
3 Conservatives	–	87.0	79.1	98.1	99.1	98.6	98.6	97.2	97.2
4 Liberals	–	83.5	87.9	94.2	84.4	96.3	94.4	90.1	99.5
5 Patrons of Industry	–	–	–	–	–	–	0.9	14.1	–
6 McCarthyites	–	–	–	–	–	–	–	5.2	–
7 Labor Party	–	–	–	–	–	–	–	–	1.4

Table 4.9 CANADA Total Votes 1904—1940

	1904	1908	1911	1917	1921	1925	1926	1930	1935	1940
Electorate	n.a.	n.a.	1,820,742	2,093,799	4,435,310	4,608,636	4,665,381	5,153,971	5,918,207	6,588,888
Valid Votes	1,030,788	1,174,709	1,307,528	1,885,329	3,123,903	3,152,525	3,256,508	3,898,527	4,406,854	4,620,260
Invalid Votes	n.a.	n.a.	7,425	7,412	15,403	15,885	16,554	24,100	45,821	52,271
Total Votes	n.a.	n.a.	1,314,953	1,892,741	3,139,306	3,168,410	3,273,062	3,922,627	4,452,675	4,672,531
PARTY VOTES										
3 Conservatives	478,729	550,351	666,074	1,074,701	945,681	1,465,331	1,474,283	1,903,815	1,305,565	1,416,230
4 Liberals	536,370	592,596	623,554	751,493	1,272,660	1,256,824	1,500,302	1,761,352	1,975,841	2,381,443
7 Labor Party	2,159	1,320	1,742	34,558	71,321	55,330	48,352	29,315	15,206	6,270
8 Communist Party	–	–	–	–	810	–	–	7,034	31,221	14,616
9 National Progressive Party	–	–	–	–	714,620	282,152	171,516	109,745	–	–
10 C.C.F.	–	–	–	–	–	–	–	–	387,056	393,230
11 Reconstruction Party	–	–	–	–	–	–	–	–	384,095	–
12 Social Credit	–	–	–	–	–	–	–	–	180,301	123,033
Others	13,530	30,442	16,158	24,577	118,811	92,888	62,055	87,266	127,569	285,438

Sources: Beck, 1968; and figures provided by the Chief Electoral Officer, Ottawa.

74

Table 4.10   CANADA   Percentage of Votes 1904–1940

	1904	1908	1911	1917	1921	1925	1926	1930	1935	1940
Valid Votes	n.a.	n.a.	71.8	90.0	70.4	68.4	69.8	75.6	74.5	70.1
Invalid Votes	n.a.	n.a.	0.4	0.4	0.3	0.3	0.4	0.5	0.8	0.8
Total Votes	n.a.	n.a.	72.2	90.4	70.8	68.7	70.2	76.1	75.2	70.9
Share Invalid	n.a.	n.a.	0.6	0.4	0.5	0.5	0.5	0.6	1.0	1,1
PARTY VOTES										
3 Conservatives	46.4	46.8	50.9	57.0	30.3	46.5	45.3	48.8	29.6	30.7
4 Liberals	52.0	50.4	47.7	39.9	40.7	39.9	46.1	45.2	44.8	51.5
7 Labor Party	0.2	0.1	0.1	1.8	2.3	1.8	1.5	0.8	0.3	0.1
8 Communist Party	–	–	–	–	0.0	–	–	0.2	0.7	0.3
9 National Progressive Party	–	–	–	–	22.9	9.0	5.3	2.8	–	–
10 C.C.F.	–	–	–	–	–	–	–	–	8.8	8.5
11 Reconstruction Party	–	–	–	–	–	–	–	–	8.7	–
12 Social Credit	–	–	–	–	–	–	–	–	4.1	2.7
Others	1.3	2.6	1.2	1.3	3.8	2.9	1.9	2.2	2.9	6.2

Table 4.11   CANADA   Number of Seats Won in the House of Commons 1904—1940

	1904	1908	1911	1917	1921	1925	1926	1930	1935	1940
3 Conservatives	75	85	134	153	50	116	91	137	40	40
4 Liberals	138	135	87	82	116	99	128	91	173	181
7 Labor Party	0	0	0	0	2	2	3	2	0	0
8 Communist Party	–	–	–	–	0	–	–	0	0	0
9 National Progressive Party	–	–	–	–	64	24	20	12	–	–
10 C.C.F.	–	–	–	–	–	–	–	–	7	8
11 Reconstruction Party	–	–	–	–	–	–	–	–	1	–
12 Social Credit	–	–	–	–	–	–	–	–	17	10
Others	1	1	0	0	3	4	3	3	7	6
Total Seats	214	221	221	235	235	245	245	245	245	245
Unopposed Returns	5	3	4	32	0	0	1	1	0	0

Source: Beck, 1968.

Table 4.12   CANADA   Percentage of Seats Won in the House of Commons 1904–1940

	1904	1908	1911	1917	1921	1925	1926	1930	1935	1940
3 Conservatives	35.0	38.5	60.6	65.1	21.3	47.3	37.1	55.9	16.3	16.3
4 Liberals	64.5	61.1	39.4	34.9	49.4	40.4	52.2	37.1	70.6	73.9
7 Labor Party	0.0	0.0	0.0	0.0	0.9	0.8	1.2	0.8	0.0	0.0
8 Communist Party	–	–	–	–	0.0	–	–	0.0	0.0	0.0
9 National Progressive Party	–	–	–	–	27.2	9.8	8.2	4.9	–	–
10 C.C.F.	–	–	–	–	–	–	–	–	2.9	3.3
11 Reconstruction Party	–	–	–	–	–	–	–	–	0.4	–
12 Social Credit	–	–	–	–	–	–	–	–	6.9	4.1
Others	0.5	0.5	0.0	0.0	1.3	1.6	1.2	1.2	2.9	2.4
Unopposed Returns	2.3	1.4	1.8	13.6	0.0	0.0	0.4	0.4	0.0	0.0

Table 4.13   CANADA   Number of Candidates 1904–1940

	1904	1908	1911	1917	1921	1925	1926	1930	1935	1940
3 Conservatives	208	215	218	210	208	234	233	234	232	213
4 Liberals	214	218	220	220	202	215	220	232	242	244
7 Labor Party	2	1	5	22	24	20	17	9	6	2
8 Communist Party	–	–	–	–	1	–	–	9	13	10
9 National Progressive Party	–	–	–	–	148	72	37	22	–	–
10 C.C.F.	–	–	–	–	–	–	–	–	118	96
11 Reconstruction Party	–	–	–	–	–	–	–	–	174	–
12 Social Credit	–	–	–	–	–	–	–	–	45	29
Others	20	28	18	25	52	38	23	40	62	74
Total	444	462	461	477	635	599	530	540	892	668

Source: Beck, 1968.

78

Table 4.14   CANADA   Percentage of Seats Contested 1904—1940

	1904	1908	1911	1917	1921	1925	1926	1930	1935	1940
3 Conservatives	97.2	97.3	98.6	89.4	88.5	95.5	95.1	95.5	94.7	86.9
4 Liberals	100.0	98.6	99.5	93.6	86.0	87.8	89.8	94.7	98.8	99.6
7 Labor Party	0.9	0.5	2.3	9.4	10.2	8.2	6.9	3.7	2.4	0.8
8 Communist Party	–	–	–	–	0.4	–	–	3.7	5.3	4.1
9 National Progressive Party	–	–	–	–	63.0	29.4	15.1	9.0	–	–
10 C.C.F.	–	–	–	–	–	–	–	–	48.2	39.2
11 Reconstruction Party	–	–	–	–	–	–	–	–	71.0	–
12 Social Credit	–	–	–	–	–	–	–	–	18.4	11.8

Table 4.15 CANADA Total Votes 1945–1972

	1945	1949	1953	1957	1958	1962	1963	1965	1968	1972
Electorate	6,952,445	7,893,629	8,401,691	8,902,125	9,131,200	9,700,325	9,910,757	10,274,904	10,860,888	12,909,179
Valid Votes	5,246,130	5,848,971	5,641,272	6,605,980	7,287,297	7,690,134	7,894,076	7,713,316	8,125,996	9,667,760
Invalid Votes	59,063	54,601	60,691	74,710	69,842	82,522	64,560	83,412	91,920	298,388
Total Votes	5,305,193	5,903,572	5,701,963	6,680,690	7,357,139	7,772,656	7,958,636	7,796,728	8,217,916	9,966,148
PARTY VOTES										
3 Conservatives	1,435,747	1,736,226	1,749,579	2,572,926	3,908,633	2,865,582	2,591,614	2,499,913	2,554,880	3,383,277
4 Liberals	2,146,330	2,897,662	2,751,307	2,702,573	2,447,909	2,861,834	3,293,790	3,099,519	3,696,945	3,718,654
8 Communist Party	–	–	–	–	–	6,360	4,324	4,285	4,465	–
10 C.C.F./N.D.P.	816,259	782,410	636,310	707,659	692,398	1,036,853	1,037,857	1,381,658	1,378,260	1,714,208
12 Social Credit	214,998	135,217	305,551	436,663	188,356	896,574	940,703	282,454	62,956	737,421
15 Ralliement des Créditistes	–	–	–	–	–	–	–	359,438	361,045	–
13 Bloc Populaire	186,822	–	–	–	–	–	–	–	–	–
14 Union des Electeurs	–	85,198	–	–	–	–	–	–	–	–
Others	445,874[1]	212,258[2]	198,525	186,159	50,001	22,931	25,788	86,049	67,445	114,200

[1] Includes 423 votes cast for the Labor Party.
[2] Includes 415 votes cast for the Labor Party.

Sources: Beck, 1968; and figures provided by the Chief Electoral Officer, Ottawa.

Table 4.16   CANADA   Percentage of Votes 1945–1972

	1945	1949	1953	1957	1958	1962	1963	1965	1968	1972
Valid Votes	75.5	74.1	67.1	74.2	79.8	79.3	79.7	75.1	74.8	74.9
Invalid Votes	0.8	0.7	0.7	0.8	0.8	0.9	0.7	0.8	0.8	2.3
Total Votes	76.3	74.8	67.9	75.0	80.6	80.1	80.3	75.9	75.7	77.2
Share Invalid	1.1	0.9	1.1	1.1	0.9	1.1	0.8	1.1	1.1	3.0
PARTY VOTES										
3 Conservatives	27.4	29.7	31.0	38.9	53.6	37.3	32.8	32.4	31.4	35.0
4 Liberals	40.9	49.5	48.8	40.9	33.6	37.2	41.7	40.2	45.5	38.5
8 Communist Party	–	–	–	–	–	0.1	0.1	0.1	0.1	–
10 C.C.F./N.D.P.	15.6	13.4	11.3	10.7	9.5	13.5	13.1	17.9	17.0	17.7
12 Social Credit	4.1	2.3	5.4	6.6	2.6	11.7	11.9	3.7	0.8	7.6
15 Ralliement des Créditistes	–	–	–	–	–	–	–	4.7	4.4	–
13 Bloc Populaire	3.6	–	–	–	–	–	–	–	–	–
14 Union des Electeurs	–	1.5	–	–	–	–	–	–	–	–
Others	8.5	3.6	3.5	2.8	0.7	0.3	0.3	1.1	0.8	1.2

Table 4.17 CANADA Number of Seats Won in the House of Commons 1945—1972

	1945	1949	1953	1957	1958	1962	1963	1965	1968	1972
3 Conservatives	67	41	51	112	208	116	95	97	72	107
4 Liberals	125	193	171	105	49	100	129	131	155	109
8 Communist Party	–	–	–	–	–	0	0	0	0	–
10 C.C.F./N.D.P.	28	13	23	25	8	19	17	21	22	31
12 Social Credit	13	10	15	19	0	30	24	5	0	15
15 Ralliement des Créditistes	–	–	–	–	–	–	–	9	14	–
13 Bloc Populaire	2	–	–	–	–	–	–	–	–	–
14 Union des Electeurs	–	0	–	–	–	–	–	–	–	–
Others	10	5	5	4	0	0	0	2	1	2
Total Seats	**245**	**262**	**265**	**265**	**265**	**265**	**265**	**265**	**264**	**264**
Unopposed Returns	0	0	2	2	1	0	0	0	0	0

Sources: Beck, 1968; and figures provided by the Chief Electoral Officer, Ottawa.

82

Table 4.18   CANADA   Percentage of Seats Won in the House of Commons 1945—1972

	1945	1949	1953	1957	1958	1962	1963	1965	1968	1972
3 Conservatives	27.3	15.6	19.2	42.3	78.5	43.8	35.8	36.6	27.3	40.5
4 Liberals	51.0	73.7	64.5	39.6	18.5	37.7	48.7	49.4	58.7	41.3
8 Communist Party	–	–	–	–	–	0.0	0.0	0.0	0.0	–
10 C.C.F./N.D.P.	11.4	5.0	8.7	9.4	3.0	7.2	6.4	7.9	8.3	11.7
12 Social Credit	5.3	3.8	5.7	7.2	0.0	11.3	9.1	1.9	0.0	5.7
15 Ralliement des Créditistes	–	–	–	–	–	–	–	3.4	5.3	–
13 Bloc Populaire	0.8	–	–	–	–	–	–	–	–	–
14 Union des Electeurs	–	0.0	–	–	–	–	–	–	–	–
Others	4.1	1.9	1.9	1.5	0.0	0.0	0.0	0.8	0.4	0.8
Unopposed Returns	0.0	0.0	0.7	0.7	0.3	0.0	0.0	0.0	0.0	0.0

Table 4.19   CANADA   Number of Candidates 1945—1972

	1945	1949	1953	1957	1958	1962	1963	1965	1968	1972
3 Conservatives	204	250	248	257	265	265	265	265	263	264
4 Liberals	241	260	264	265	265	264	265	265	263	263
8 Communist Party	–	–	–	–	–	8	7	11	14	–
10 C.C.F./N.D.P.	205	180	170	162	169	218	232	255	263	251
12 Social Credit	95	28	72	115	82	230	224	86	31	164
15 Ralliement des Créditistes	–	–	–	–	–	–	–	77	71	–
13 Bloc Populaire	37	–	–	–	–	–	–	–	–	–
14 Union des Electeurs	–	55	–	–	–	–	–	–	–	–
Others	170[1]	75[2]	143	63	50	31	30	52	62	174
Total	952	848	897	862	831	1,016	1,023	1,011	967	1,116

[1] Including one Labor Party candidate.
[2] Including two Labor Party candidates.

Sources: Beck, 1968; and figures provided by the Chief Electoral Officer, Ottawa.

84

Table 4.20   CANADA   Percentage of Seats Contested 1945–1972

	1945	1949	1953	1957	1958	1962	1963	1965	1968	1972
3 Conservatives	83.3	95.4	93.6	97.0	100.0	100.0	100.0	100.0	99.6	100.0
4 Liberals	98.4	99.2	99.6	100.0	100.0	99.6	100.0	100.0	99.6	99.6
8 Communist Party	–	–	–	–	–	3.0	2.6	4.2	5.3	–
10 C.C.F./N.D.P.	83.7	68.7	64.2	61.1	63.8	82.3	87.5	96.2	99.6	95.1
12 Social Credit	38.8	10.7	27.2	43.4	30.9	86.8	84.5	32.5	11.7	62.1
15 Ralliement des Créditistes	–	–	–	–	–	–	–	29.1	26.9	–
13 Bloc Populaire	15.1	–	–	–	–	–	–	–	–	–
14 Union des Electeurs	–	21.0	–	–	–	–	–	–	–	–

Chapter 5

DENMARK

The 1849 Danish Constitution established a two-chamber parliament, the Rigsdag. The two houses, the Landsting and the Folketing, had equal powers but were chosen in different ways. The Folketing was elected on a broad franchise. All men over 30, except for servants and farm workers who did not have their own households and those who had been or were receiving poor relief, were entitled to vote. Elections were held in single-member constituencies. Voting was by show of hands. The candidate who, in the opinion of the election committee, won a plurality of the vote was declared elected. If there was only one candidate, he had to win a majority of the votes cast. If the election committee's decision was challenged, a roll-call vote took place; in the case of a single candidate, the electors simply voted yes or no. If the candidate failed to win a majority a second vote was arranged.

The Landsting was chosen indirectly by the same electorate as the Folketing until 1866. Thereafter, 12 members were appointed by the King, one by the Faroese Lagting and 53 elected indirectly. Half of the electors were chosen by plurality by the Folketing electorate and the remainder by the largest taxpayers. In the rural areas the largest taxpayers were themselves the Landsting electors. The members of the Landsting were chosen by proportional representation, using Andrae's method, a system very similar to the single transferable vote.

Political parties began to appear in Denmark after the constitutional reform of 1849. After 1866 a division developed between the Conservatives (Højre) and the Liberals (Venstre) about the role of the King and the relative powers of the two houses of the Rigsdag. However, both groups were initially poorly organized and unstable. Organized political parties did not begin to develop until the 1880's. The Social Democrats, founded in 1871, won their first parliamentary seat in 1884. The Højre and the Venstre established national organizations in 1883 and 1888 respectively (Miller, 1968, 57–59).

Party votes were not recorded in the official statistics until 1901. A secondary source (Møller, 1950:308) provides estimates of party votes from 1884:

	1884	1887	1890	1893	1895	1898
Electorate	322,000	338,000	358,000	363,000	376,000	399,000
Conservatives	55,000	87,000	92,000	78,000	64,000	58,000
%	38.7	38.3	39.7	34.8	28.8	25.9
Liberals	80,000	132,000	123,000	63,000	90,000	98,000
%	56.3	58.1	53.0	28.1	40.5	43.8
Social Democrats	7,000	8,000	17,000	20,000	25,000	32,000
%	4.9	3.5	7.3	8.9	11.3	14.3
Moderate Left	—	—	—	63,000	43,000	36,000
%	—	—	—	28.1	19.4	16.1
Total[1]	142,000	227,000	232,000	224,000	222,000	224,000

[1] including the Faroe Islands.

The Liberals (Venstre) dominated the Folketing until the conservative wing broke away to form the Moderate Liberals:

	1884	1887	1890	1892	1895	1898
Conservatives	19	27	24	31	25	16
Liberals	81	74	75	30	54	63
Social Democrats	2	1	3	2	8	12
Moderate Liberals	—	—	—	39	27	23
Total[1]	102	102	102	102	114	114

[1] including the Faroe Islands

Source: Møller, 1950: 308

In 1901 open voting was replaced by the secret ballot. Beginning with the 1901 election full details of voting by party are available from the official statistics. A candidate needed to win a plurality of the votes cast in order to be elected.

In 1915 universal adult suffrage was introduced. The voting age was reduced to 29 and proportional representation using the d'Hondt system was introduced in Copenhagen. A number of supplementary seats (tillaegsmandater) were distributed on a proportional basis in order to ensure that overall representation in the Folketing was as proportional as possible. In 1920 proportional representation was extended to the rest of Denmark and from the third election in 1920 the voting age was reduced to 25. In 1915 the Landsting franchise was made equivalent to that for the Folketing, but the age qualification was increased to 35; 18 members were chosen by the previous Landsting, one by the Faroese Lagting and 53 indirectly. The electors for the Landsting were chosen in multi-member constituencies by the d'Hondt method. From the second election in 1920 the number of indirectly elected members was increased to 55 and the number chosen by the Landsting to 19.

In 1938 the Rigsdag approved constitutional changes which would have involved the abolition of the Landsting and its replacement by an upper chamber, partly chosen by the Folketing and partly directly elected by proportional representation. The proposal was approved by referendum but by an insufficient majority to pass into law. In 1940 Denmark was invaded by Nazi Germany. The Folketing continued to meet during the occupation. The Communist Party was outlawed in 1941 but free elections were allowed in 1943.

In 1953 a new Constitution was introduced. The Landsting was abolished. The Saint-Laguë system (with an initial divisor of 1.4) replaced the d'Hondt system for elections to the Folketing. The voting age was reduced to 23. The voting age was further reduced to 21 in 1961 and to 20 in 1971.

The Faroe Islands have been represented in the Rigsdag since 1850. In 1948 the islands were given internal self government and the number of representatives in the Folketing increased to two. Greenland has sent two representatives to the Folketing since 1953. The Faroes and Greenland are excluded from the following tables unless specifically stated otherwise. For further details see Thomas, 1973: 53–57.

Sources:

Danmarks Statistik, *Folketingsvalgene 1901ff* (Copenhagen, 1901ff).

Holm, A., *Rigsdagsvalgene i hundrede aar* (Copenhagen: Fremad, 1949).

Institute of Political Science, Aarhus University "Denmark" in S. Rokkan and J. Meyriat (eds.) *International Guide to Electoral Statistics* (Paris: Mouton, 1969) pp.58–76.

Miller, K.E. "The Danish electoral system." *Parliamentary Affairs* 18:71–81 (1965).

Miller, K.E., *The Government and Politics of Denmark* (Boston: Houghton Mifflin, 1968).

Moller, P., *Politisk haandbog: en samling konkrete oplysninger* (Copenhagen: Hagerup, 1950).

Thomas, A., *Parliamentary Parties in Denmark, 1945–1972* (Glasgow: University of Strathclyde, Occasional Paper No. 13, 1973).

Table 5.1
POLITICAL PARTIES IN DENMARK SINCE 1884

	Party Names	Elections contested	Number contested
1	Conservatives. Until 1915 the Right (Hojre). Since 1915 the Conservative Peoples Party (Konservative Folkeparti)	1884ff	35
2	Liberals (Venstre) Literally, the Left; since 1970 the Left-Liberal Party of Denmark (Venstre-Danmarks Liberale Parti)	1884ff	35
3	Social Democrats (Socialdemokratiet)	1884ff	35
4	Moderate Liberals (Moderate Venstre) Literally Moderate Left	1892-1909	7
5	Radicals (Radikale Venstre)	1906ff	27
6	Industry Party (Erhvervspartiet)[1]	1918-1924	5
7	Schleswig Party (Slesvigske Parti)[2]	Sept. 1920-1939; 1947-1964; 1968ff	16
8	Communist Party (Danmarks Kommunistiske Parti)[3]	1924-1939; 1945ff	17
9	Justice Party (Retsforbundet)[4]	1924ff	18
10	Farmers Party (Bondepartiet)[5]	1935-1943	3
11	National Socialists (National Socialistisk Arbejder Parti)	1935-1943	3
12	Danish Union (Dansk Samling)	1939-1947; 1953; 1964	6
13	National Cooperation (Nationalt Samvirke)	1939	1
14	Independents Party (Uafhaengige)	Sept. 1953-1968	6
15	Socialist Peoples Party (Sosialistisk Folkeparti)[6]	1960ff	5
16	Liberal Centre (Liberalt Centrum)	1966-1968	2
17	Left Socialist Party (Venstresocialisterne)[7]	1968ff	2
18	Christian Peoples Party (Kristeligt Folkeparti)	1971	1

[1] In 1918 the Industry List (Erhvervlisten).

[2] The party representing the German-speaking minority. From 1947 to September, 1953 non-party candidates were nominated to represent this minority. Votes for these candidates are included with the Schleswig Party.

[3] Founded in November 1919 as the Left Socialist Party of Denmark (Danmarks Venstresocialistiske Parti).

[4] In 1924 the Retspartiet. Often known as the Single-Tax Party.

[5] In 1935 the Free Peoples Party (Frie Folkeparti).

[6] Established in 1959 by Aksel Larsen, the former leader of the Communist Party.

[7] Founded in 1967 as the result of a split in the Socialist Peoples Party.

Table 5.2
DATES OF ELECTIONS
TO THE FOLKETING 1884–1971

1.	25 June 1884	19.	2 December 1926
2.	28 January 1887	20.	24 April 1929
3.	21 January 1890	21.	16 November 1932
4.	20 April 1892	22.	22 October 1935
5.	9 April 1895	23.	3 April 1939
6.	5 April 1898	24.	23 March 1943
7.	3 April 1901	25.	30 October 1945
8.	16 June 1903	26.	28 October 1947
9.	29 May 1906	27.	5 September 1950
10.	25 May 1909	28.	21 April 1953
11.	20 May 1910	29.	22 September 1953
12.	20 May 1913	30.	14 May 1957
13.	7 May 1915	31.	15 November 1960
14.	22 April 1918	32.	22 September 1964
15.	26 April 1920	33.	22 November 1966
16.	6 July 1920	34.	23 January 1968
17.	21 September 1920	35.	21 September 1971
18.	11 April 1924		

Sources: Holm, 1949 : 13 and *Folketingsvalget den 21 Sept. 1971,* 1972 : 50-51.

Table 5.3   DENMARK   Total Votes 1901–1913[1]

	1901	1903	1906	1909	1910	1913
Electorate	404,271	416,748	438,341	460,553	470,392	491,422
Valid Votes	198,590	216,202	301,316	320,687	348,856	362,540
Invalid Votes	2,710	3,065	3,482	2,854	2,918	2,877
Total Votes	201,300	219,255	304,798	323,541	351,774	365,417
PARTY VOTES						
1 Conservatives	51,787	47,286	63,335	64,189	64,904	81,404
2 Liberals	78,319	99,644	93,632	96,285	118,902	103,251
4 Moderate Liberals	23,753	17,167	20,487	–	–	–
3 Social Democrats	38,398	46,646	76,612	93,079	98,718	107,365
5 Radicals	–	–	38,151	51,165	64,884	67,903
Others	6,333	5,459	9,099	15,969	1,448	2,617

[1] The 1915 election is excluded. The election was held in order to amend the constitution. Only ten constituencies were contested and in five of these there was only one candidate (*Folketingsvalgene den 15 mai 1915* : 8-9). The Faroe Islands are included.

Sources: *Folketingsvalgene, 1901* ff. and figures provided by Danmarks Statistik.

Table 5.4 DENMARK   Percentage of Votes 1901–1913

	1901	1903	1906	1909	1910	1913
Valid Votes	49.1	51.9	68.7	69.6	74.2	73.7
Invalid Votes	0.7	0.7	0.8	0.7	0.6	0.6
Total Votes	49.8	52.6	69.3	70.3	74.8	74.4
Share Invalid	1.3	1.4	1.1	0.9	0.8	0.8
PARTY VOTES						
1 Conservatives	26.0	21.9	21.0	20.0	18.6	22.5
2 Liberals	39.4	46.1	31.1	30.0	34.1	28.6
4 Moderate Liberals	12.0	7.9	6.8	–	–	–
3 Social Democrats	19.3	21.6	25.4	29.0	28.3	29.6
5 Radicals	–	–	12.7	16.0	18.6	18.7
Others	3.2	2.5	3.0	5.0	0.4	0.7

93

Table 5.5   DENMARK   Seats Won in the Folketing 1901—1913

	1901	1903	1906	1909	1910	1913
1 Conservatives	8	12	12	21	13	7
2 Liberals	76	73	56	48	57	44
4 Moderate Liberals	16	12	9	–	–	–
3 Social Democrats	14	16	24	24	24	32
5 Radicals	–	–	9	15	20	31
Others	0	1	4	6	0	0
Total Seats	114	114	114	114	114	114

Source: Danmarks Statistik.

94

Table 5.6   DENMARK   Percentage of Seats Won in the Folketing 1901—1913

	1901	1903	1906	1909	1910	1913
1 Conservatives	7.0	10.5	10.5	18.4	11.4	6.1
2 Liberals	66.7	64.0	49.1	42.1	50.0	38.6
4 Moderate Liberals	14.0	10.5	7.9	—	—	—
3 Social Democrats	12.3	14.0	21.1	21.1	21.1	28.1
5 Radicals	—	—	7.9	13.1	17.5	27.2
Others	0.0	0.9	3.5	5.3	0.0	0.0

Table 5.7 DENMARK Total Votes 1918–1943

	1918	1920 (April)	1920 (July)	1920 (Sept.)	1924	1926	1929	1932	1935	1939	1943
Electorate	1,218,901	1,274,377	1,276,302	1,576,716	1,637,564	1,742,604	1,786,092	1,902,835	2,044,997	2,159,356	2,280,716
Valid Votes	916,929	1,024,386	953,561	1,211,583	1,282,937	1,337,647	1,420,246	1,547,082	1,646,438	1,699,889	2,010,783
Invalid Votes	3,468	3,082	2,004	2,673	4,147	3,579	2,904	4,039	4,694	9,667	29,800
Total Votes	920,397	1,027,468	955,565	1,214,256	1,287,084	1,341,226	1,423,150	1,551,121	1,651,132	1,709,556	2,040,583
PARTY VOTES											
1 Conservatives	167,743	201,499	180,293	216,733	242,955	275,793	233,935	289,531	293,393	301,625	421,523
2 Liberals	269,646	350,563	344,351	411,661	362,682	378,137	402,121	381,862	292,247	309,355	376,850
3 Social Democrats	262,796	300,345	285,166	389,653	469,949	497,106	593,191	660,839	759,102	729,619	894,632
5 Radicals	189,521	122,160	109,931	147,120	166,476	150,931	151,746	145,221	151,507	161,834	175,179
6 Industry Party	11,934	29,464	25,627	27,403	2,102	–	–	–	–	–	–
7 Schleswig Party	–	–	–	7,505	7,715	10,422	9,787	9,868	12,617	15,016	–
8 Communist Party	–	3,859	2,493	5,160	6,219	5,678	3,656	17,179	27,135	40,893	–
9 Justice Party	–	–	–	–	12,643	17,463	25,810	41,238	41,199	33,783	31,323
10 Farmers Party	–	–	–	–	–	–	–	–	52,793	50,829	24,572
11 National Socialists	–	–	–	–	–	–	–	757	16,257	31,032	43,309
12 Danish Union	–	–	–	–	–	–	–	–	–	8,553	43,367
13 National Cooperation	–	–	–	–	–	–	–	–	–	17,350	–
Others	15,289	16,316	6,690	6,460	12,196	2,117	–	587	188	–	28

Source: *Folketingsvalget den 21 Sept. 1971*, 1972 : 50-55.

96

Table 5.8   DENMARK   Percentage of Votes 1918—1943

	1918	1920 (April)	1920 (July)	1920 (Sept.)	1924	1926	1929	1932	1935	1939	1943
Valid Votes	75.2	80.4	74.7	76.8	78.3	76.8	79.5	81.3	80.5	78.7	88.2
Invalid Votes	0.3	0.2	0.2	0.2	0.3	0.2	0.2	0.2	0.2	0.4	1.3
Total Votes	75.5	80.6	74.9	77.0	78.6	77.0	79.7	81.5	80.7	79.2	89.5
Share Invalid	0.4	0.3	0.2	0.2	0.3	0.3	0.2	0.3	0.3	0.6	1.5
PARTY VOTES											
1 Conservatives	18.3	19.7	18.9	17.9	18.9	20.6	16.5	18.7	17.8	17.7	21.0
2 Liberals	29.4	34.2	36.1	34.0	28.3	28.3	28.3	24.7	17.8	18.2	18.7
3 Social Democrats	28.7	29.3	29.9	32.2	36.6	37.2	41.8	42.7	46.1	42.9	44.5
5 Radicals	20.7	11.9	11.5	12.1	13.0	11.3	10.7	9.4	9.2	9.5	8.7
6 Industry Party	1.3	2.9	2.7	2.3	0.2	–	–	–	–	–	–
7 Schleswig Party	–	–	–	0.6	0.6	0.8	0.7	0.6	0.8	0.9	–
8 Communist Party	–	0.4	0.3	0.4	0.5	0.4	0.3	1.1	1.6	2.4	–
9 Justice Party	–	–	–	–	1.0	1.3	1.8	2.7	2.5	2.0	1.6
10 Farmers Party	–	–	–	–	–	–	–	–	3.2	3.0	1.2
11 National Socialists	–	–	–	–	–	–	–	0.0	1.0	1.8	2.2
12 Danish Union	–	–	–	–	–	–	–	–	–	0.5	2.2
13 National Cooperation	–	–	–	–	–	–	–	–	–	1.0	–
Others	1.7	1.6	0.7	0.5	1.0	0.2	–	0.0	0.0	–	0.0

Table 5.9   DENMARK   Number of Seats Won in the Folketing 1918–1943

	1918	1920 (April)	1920 (July)	1920 (Sept.)	1924	1926	1929	1932	1935	1939	1943
1 Conservatives	22	28	26	27	28	30	24	27	26	26	31
2 Liberals	44	48	51	51	44	46	43	38	28	30	28
3 Social Democrats	39	42	42	48	55	53	61	62	68	64	66
5 Radicals	32	17	16	18	20	16	16	14	14	14	13
6 Industry Party	1	4	4	3	0	–	–	–	–	–	–
7 Schleswig Party	–	0	–	1	1	1	1	1	1	0	–
8 Communist Party	–	0	0	0	0	0	0	2	2	3	1
9 Justice Party	–	–	–	–	0	2	3	4	4	3	2
10 Farmers Party	–	–	–	–	–	–	–	–	5	4	2
11 National Socialists	–	–	–	–	–	–	–	0	0	3	3
12 Danish Union	–	–	–	–	–	–	–	–	–	1	3
13 National Cooperation	–	–	–	–	–	–	–	–	–	0	–
Others	1	0	0	0	0	0	–	0	0	–	0
Total Seats	139	139	139	148	148	148	148	148	148	148	148

Source: *Folketingsvalget den 21 Sept. 1971, 1972* : 50-55.

98

Table 5.10   DENMARK   Percentage of Seats Won in the Folketing 1918–1943

	1918	1920 (April)	1920 (July)	1920 (Sept.)	1924	1926	1929	1932	1935	1939	1943
1 Conservatives	15.8	20.1	18.7	18.2	18.9	20.3	16.2	18.2	17.6	17.6	20.9
2 Liberals	31.7	34.5	36.7	34.5	29.7	31.1	29.1	25.7	18.9	20.3	18.9
3 Social Democrats	28.1	30.2	30.2	32.4	37.2	35.8	41.2	41.9	45.9	43.2	44.6
5 Radicals	23.0	12.2	11.5	12.2	13.5	10.8	10.8	9.5	9.5	9.5	8.8
6 Industry Party	0.7	2.9	2.9	2.0	0.0	–	–	–	–	–	–
7 Schleswig Party	–	–	–	0.7	0.7	0.7	0.7	0.7	0.7	0.0	–
8 Communist Party	–	0.0	0.0	0.0	0.0	0.0	0.0	1.4	1.4	2.0	–
9 Justice Party	–	–	–	–	0.0	1.4	2.0	2.7	2.7	2.0	1.4
10 Farmers Party	–	–	–	–	–	–	–	–	3.4	2.7	1.4
11 National Socialists	–	–	–	–	–	–	–	0.0	0.0	2.0	2.0
12 Danish Union	–	–	–	–	–	–	–	–	–	0.7	2.0
13 National Cooperation	–	–	–	–	–	–	–	–	–	0.0	–
Others	0.7	0.0	0.0	0.0	0.0	0.0	–	0.0	0.0	–	0.0

Table 5.11   DENMARK   Total Votes 1945—1971

	1945	1947	1950	1953 (April)	1953 (Sept.)	1957	1960	1964	1966	1968	1971
Electorate	2,381,983	2,435,306	2,516,118	2,571,311	2,695,554	2,772,159	2,842,336	3,088,269	3,162,352	3,208,646	3,332,044
Valid Votes	2,049,184	2,084,141	2,054,330	2,070,903	2,166,391	2,310,175	2,431,947	2,631,384	2,794,007	2,854,647	2,883,900
Invalid Votes	6,131	4,874	5,614	6,712	5,645	10,922	7,989	9,472	8,297	10,158	20,196
Total Votes	2,055,315	2,089,015	2,059,944	2,077,615	2,172,036	2,321,097	2,439,936	2,640,856	2,802,304	2,864,805	2,904,096
PARTY VOTES											
1 Conservatives	373,688	259,324	365,236	358,509	364,960	383,843	435,764	527,798	522,028	581,051	481,335
2 Liberals	479,158	574,895	438,188	456,896	499,656	578,932	512,041	547,770	539,027	530,167	450,904
3 Social Democrats	671,755	834,089	813,224	836,507	894,913	910,170	1,023,794	1,103,667	1,068,911	974,833	1,074,777
5 Radicals	167,073	144,206	167,969	178,942	169,295	179,822	140,979	139,702	203,858	427,304	413,620
7 Schleswig Party	—	7,464	6,406	8,438	9,721	9,202	9,058	9,274	—	6,831	6,743
8 Communist Party	255,236	141,094	94,523	98,940	93,824	72,315	27,298	32,390	21,553	29,706	39,564
9 Justice Party	38,459	94,570	168,784	116,288	75,449	122,759	52,330	34,258	19,905	21,124	50,231
12 Danish Union	63,760	24,724	—	16,383	—	—	—	9,747	—	—	—
14 Independents Party	—	—	—	—	58,573	53,061	81,134	65,756	44,994	14,360	—
15 Socialist Peoples Party	—	—	—	—	—	—	149,440	151,697	304,437	174,553	262,756
16 Liberal Centre	—	—	—	—	—	—	—	—	69,180	37,407	—
17 Left Socialists	—	—	—	—	—	—	—	—	—	57,184	45,979
18 Christian Peoples Party	—	—	—	—	—	—	—	—	—	—	57,072
Others	55	3,775	—	—	—	71	109	9,325	114	127	919

Source: *Folketingsvalget den 21 Sept. 1971, 1972 : 50-55.*

Table 5.12   DENMARK   Percentage of Votes 1945—1971

	1945	1947	1950	1953 (April)	1953 (Sept.)	1957	1960	1964	1966	1968	1971
Valid Votes	86.0	85.6	81.6	80.5	80.4	83.3	85.6	85.2	88.4	89.0	86.6
Invalid Votes	0.3	0.2	0.2	0.3	0.2	0.4	0.3	0.3	0.3	0.3	0.6
Total Votes	86.3	85.8	81.9	80.8	80.6	83.7	85.8	85.5	88.6	89.3	87.2
Share Invalid	0.3	0.2	0.3	0.3	0.3	0.5	0.3	0.4	0.3	0.4	0.7
PARTY VOTES											
1 Conservatives	18.2	12.4	17.8	17.3	16.8	16.6	17.9	20.1	18.7	20.4	16.7
2 Liberals	23.4	27.6	21.3	22.1	23.1	25.1	21.1	20.8	19.3	18.6	15.6
3 Social Democrats	32.8	40.0	39.6	40.4	41.3	39.4	42.1	41.9	38.3	34.1	37.3
5 Radicals	8.2	6.9	8.2	8.6	7.8	7.8	5.8	5.3	7.3	15.0	14.3
7 Schleswig Party	–	0.4	0.3	0.4	0.4	0.4	0.4	0.4	–	0.2	0.2
8 Communist Party	12.5	6.8	4.6	4.8	4.3	3.1	1.1	1.2	0.8	1.0	1.4
9 Justice Party	1.9	4.5	8.2	5.6	3.5	5.3	2.2	1.3	0.7	0.7	1.7
12 Danish Union	3.1	1.2	–	0.8	–	–	–	0.4	–	–	–
14 Independent Party	–	–	–	–	2.7	2.3	3.3	2.5	1.6	0.5	–
15 Socialist Peoples Party	–	–	–	–	–	–	6.1	5.8	10.9	6.1	9.1
16 Liberal Centre	–	–	–	–	–	–	–	–	2.5	1.3	–
17 Left Socialists	–	–	–	–	–	–	–	–	–	2.0	1.6
18 Christian Peoples Party	–	–	–	–	–	–	–	–	–	–	2.0
Others	0.0	0.2	–	–	–	0.0	0.0	0.4	0.0	0.0	0.0

Table 5.13   DENMARK   Number of Seats won in the Folketing 1945—1971

	1945	1947	1950	1953 (April)	1953 (Sept.)	1957	1960	1964	1966	1968	1971
1 Conservatives	26	17	27	26	30	30	32	36	34	37	31
2 Liberals	38	49	32	33	42	45	38	38	35	34	30
3 Social Democrats	48	57	59	61	74	70	76	76	69	62	70
5 Radical Party	11	10	12	13	14	14	11	10	13	27	27
7 Schleswig Party	–	0	0	0	1	1	1	0	–	0	0
8 Communist Party	18	9	7	7	8	6	0	0	0	0	0
9 Justice Party	3	6	12	9	6	9	0	0	0	0	0
12 Danish Union	4	0	–	0	–	–	–	0	–	–	–
14 Independent Party	–	–	–	–	–	0	6	5	0	0	–
15 Socialist Peoples Party	–	–	–	–	–	–	11	10	20[1]	11	17
16 Liberal Centre	–	–	–	–	–	–	–	–	4	0	–
17 Left Socialists	–	–	–	–	–	–	–	–	–	4	0
18 Christian Peoples Party	–	–	–	–	–	–	–	–	–	–	0
Others	0	0	–	–	–	0	0	0	0	0	0
Total Seats	148	148	149	149	175	175	175	175	175	175	175

[1] The Socialist Peoples Party split on December 17, 1967 when six members resigned to form the Left Socialist Party.

Source: *Folketingsvalget den 21 Sept. 1972: 50—55.*

Table 5.14   DENMARK   Percentage of Seats won in the Folketing 1945—1971

	1945	1947	1950	1953 (April)	1953 (Sept.)	1957	1960	1964	1966	1968	1971
1 Conservatives	17.6	11.5	18.1	17.4	17.1	17.1	18.3	20.6	19.4	21.1	17.7
2 Liberal Party	25.7	33.1	21.5	22.1	24.0	25.7	21.7	21.7	20.0	19.4	17.1
3 Social Democrats	32.4	38.5	39.6	40.9	42.3	40.0	43.4	43.4	39.4	35.4	40.0
5 Radical Party	7.4	6.8	8.1	8.7	8.0	8.0	6.3	5.7	7.4	15.4	15.4
7 Schleswig Party	–	0.0	0.0	0.0	0.6	0.6	0.6	0.6	–	0.0	0.0
8 Communist Party	12.2	6.1	4.7	4.7	4.6	3.4	0.0	0.0	0.0	0.0	0.0
9 Justice Party	2.0	4.1	8.1	6.0	3.4	5.1	0.0	0.0	0.0	0.0	0.0
12 Danish Union	2.7	0.0	–	0.0	–	–	–	0.0	–	–	–
14 Independent Party	–	–	–	–	0.0	0.0	3.4	2.9	0.0	0.0	–
15 Socialist Peoples Party	–	–	–	–	–	–	6.3	5.7	11.4	6.3	9.7
16 Liberal Centre	–	–	–	–	–	–	–	–	2.3	0.0	–
17 Left Socialists	–	–	–	–	–	–	–	–	–	2.3	0.0
18 Christian Peoples Party	–	–	–	–	–	–	–	–	–	–	0.0
Others	0.0	0.0	–	–	–	0.0	0.0	0.0	0.0	0.0	0.0

Chapter 6
FINLAND

Until 1917 Finland was a Grand Duchy under Russian rule. Two major political parties appeared before the end of the nineteenth century: a Finnish nationalist party, which later split into two factions, the Old Finns and the Young Finns and a party representing the Swedish minority, which in 1906 became the Swedish Peoples Party. But apart from the Finnish Labour Party, founded in 1899 and renamed the Social Democratic Party in 1903, no party had developed a strong extra-parliamentary organization until after the electoral reform of 1906. Before this date the Finnish Parliament consisted of a diet of four estates on the Swedish pattern. The Estate of Nobility and the Estate of Burgesses were dominated by the Swedish Party, whereas the Estate of the Clergy and the Estate of Farmers, which had a more popular franchise, had an overwhelmingly Finnish majority. The system of plural voting in the Estates of Burgesses and Farmers and of indirect election in the latter case make detailed analysis of electoral support extremely difficult (Törnudd, 1969: 23-26; Jutikkala, 1961).

In 1906 the four estates were replaced by a single chamber legislature, the Eduskunta. Adult suffrage with a minimum age of 24 (reduced to 21 in 1944) was introduced. Deputies are chosen by secret ballot in multi-member constituencies by the d'Hondt system of proportional representation. Lapland from 1906 until 1938 and the Aland Islands since 1948 have formed single-member constituencies whose representative was chosen by a plurality. The minimum voting age was reduced to 20 in 1969 and 18 in April 1972.

Sources:

Finnish Statistical Yearbook, 1970 (Helsinki: Central Statistical Office, 1970).
Jutikkala, E., "Political parties in the elections of the Finnish Diet of Estates" in *Sitzungsberichte der Finnischen Akademie der Wissenschaften 1960* (Helsinki, 1961) pp. 167-184.
Official Statistics of Finland, Series XXIX A, *Parliamentary Elections, 1907ff.* (Helsinki: Central Statistical Office, 1908ff.).
Törnudd, K., *The Electoral System of Finland* (London: Hugh Evelyn, 1968).
Pesonen, P., "Finland: party support in a fragmented system," in R. Rose (ed.) *Electoral Behavior: a Comparative Handbook* (New York: Free Press, 1973).

Table 6.1
POLITICAL PARTIES IN FINLAND SINCE 1907

	Party Names	Elections contested	Number contested
1	Social Democrats (Suomen Sosialdemokraattinen Puolue	1907ff	26
2	Swedish Peoples Party (Svenska Folkpartiet/ Ruotsalainen Kansanpuolue)	1907ff	26
3	Christian Labour Union (Suomen Kristillinen Työväen Puolue)	1907-1917	8
4	Agrarian Union (Maalaisliitto). Since 1965 the Centre Party (Keskustapuolue)	1907ff	26
5	Young Finnish Party (Nuorsuomalainen Puolue)	1907-1917	8
6	Finnish Party (Suomalainen Puolue)[1]	1907-1917	8
7	Peoples Party (Kansanpuolue)	1917	1
8	National Coalition (Kansallinen Kokomoos)	1919ff	18
9	National Progressive Party (Kansallinen Edistyspuolue). Renamed the Finnish Peoples Party (Suomen Kansanpuolue) in 1951. In 1966 it became the Liberal Peoples Party (Liberaalinen Kansanpuolue)	1919ff	18
10	Socialist Workers Party (Suomen Sosialistinen Työväenpuolue)[2]	1922-1930	5
11	Small Farmers Party (Suomen Pienviljelijäin Puolue)	1929-1951	8
12	Swedish Left Wing (Svenska Vänstern/ Ruotsalainen Vasemmisto)	1939-1945	3
13	Patriotic Peoples Movement (Isanmaallinen Kansanliike)	1933-1939	3
14	Finnish Peoples Democratic Union (Suomen Kansan Demokraattinen Liitto)[3]	1945ff	8
15	Liberal League (Vapaamielisten Liitto)[4]	1951-1962	2
16	Social Democratic League of Workers and Smallholders (Työväen ja Pienviljelijäin Sosialdemokraattinen Liitto)	1958ff	5
17	Finnish Smallholders Party (Suomen Pientalon-poiken Puolue). Since 1966 the Finnish Rural Party (Suomen Maaseudun Puolue)	1962ff	4
18	Christian League (Suomen Kristillinen Liitto)	1966ff	3

[1] Also known as the Old Finns (Vahasuomalaiset).

[2] The Socialist Workers Party—closely connected with the proscribed Finnish Communist Party (Suomen Kommunistinen Puolue)—changed its name several times. It was founded in 1920 as the Socialist Workers Party. Dissolved by the government, it re-emerged as the Finnish Socialist Workers Party (Suomen Sosialistinen Työväen Puolue). Renamed the Finnish Labour Party (Suomen Työväen Puolue) in 1923, it was again banned in the same year. The party was replaced by the Association of

Socialist Workers and Smallholders (Sosialistinen Työväen ja Pienviljelijäin), which was suppressed in 1930.

[3] The Communist Party was legalised in 1944; it contests national elections as part of the Finnish Peoples Democratic Union.

[4] Established in 1951 by former members of the Progressive Party. It merged with the Finnish Peoples Party to form the Liberal Peoples Party in 1966.

Table 6.2
DATES OF ELECTIONS TO THE EDUSKUNTA 1907–1972

1.	15 – 16 March 1907	
2.	1 – 2 July 1908	
3.	1 – 3 May 1909	
4.	1 – 2 February 1910	
5.	2 – 3 January 1911	
6.	1 – 2 August 1913	
7.	1 – 2 July 1916	
8.	1 – 2 October 1917	
9.	1 – 3 March 1919	
10.	1 – 3 July 1922	
11.	1 – 2 April 1924	
12.	1 – 2 July 1927	
13.	1 – 2 July 1929	
14.	1 – 2 October 1930	
15.	1 – 3 July 1933	
16.	1 – 2 July 1936	
17.	1 – 2 July 1939	
18.	17 – 18 March 1945	
19.	1 – 2 July 1948	
20.	2 – 3 July 1951	
21.	7 – 8 March 1954	
22.	6 – 7 July 1958	
23.	4 – 5 February 1962	
24.	20 – 21 March 1966	
25.	15 – 16 March 1970	
26.	2 – 3 January 1972	

Source: Professor Pertti Pesonen, University of Helsinki.

Table 6.3　　FINLAND　　Total Votes 1907–1917

	1907	1908	1909	1910	1911	1913	1916	1917
Electorate	1,272,873	1,269,177	1,305,305	1,324,931	1,350,058	1,430,135	1,442,091	1,441,075
Valid Votes	890,990	809,441	846,471	791,559	802,387	724,304	795,209	992,762
Invalid Votes	8,357	7,896	6,212	5,010	4,707	6,345	5,725	4,903
Total Votes	899,347	817,567	852,683	796,569	807,094	730,649	800,934	997,665
PARTY VOTES								
4 Agrarian Union	51,242	51,756	56,943	60,157	62,885	56,977	71,608	122,900
3 Christian Labour Union	13,790	18,848	23,259	17,344	17,245	12,850	14,626	15,489
6 Finnish Party	243,573	205,892	199,920	174,661	174,177	143,982	139,111	299,516[1]
7 Peoples Party	–	–	–	–	–	–	–	
5 Young Finnish Party	121,604	115,201	122,770	114,291	119,361	102,313	99,419	
1 Social Democrats	329,946	310,826	337,685	316,951	321,201	312,214	376,030	444,670
2 Swedish Peoples Party	112,267	103,146	104,191	107,121	106,810	94,672	93,555	108,190
Others	18,568	3,772	1,703	1,034	708	1,296	860	1,997

[1] An electoral alliance of the Finnish, Young Finnish and Peoples parties.

Sources: Törnudd, 1968 : 146-150; Statistical Yearbook, 1970 : 374; Parliamentary Elections, 1907 : 25.

Table 6.4   FINLAND   Percentage of Votes 1907–1917

	1907	1908	1909	1910	1911	1913	1916	1917
Valid Votes	70.0	63.8	64.8	59.7	59.4	50.6	55.1	68.9
Invalid Votes	0.7	0.6	0.5	0.4	0.3	0.4	0.4	0.3
Total Votes	70.7	64.4	65.3	60.1	59.8	51.1	55.5	69.2
Share Invalid	0.9	1.0	0.7	0.6	0.6	0.9	0.7	0.5
PARTY VOTES								
4 Agrarian Union	5.8	6.4	6.7	7.6	7.8	7.9	9.0	12.4
3 Christian Labour Union	1.5	2.3	2.7	2.2	2.1	1.8	1.8	1.6
6 Finnish Party	27.3	25.4	23.6	22.1	21.7	19.9	17.5	30.2
7 Peoples Party	–	–	–	–	–	–	–	
5 Young Finnish Party	13.6	14.2	14.5	14.4	14.9	14.1	12.5	
1 Social Democrats	37.0	38.4	39.9	40.0	40.0	43.1	47.3	44.8
2 Swedish Peoples Party	12.6	12.7	12.3	13.5	13.3	13.1	11.8	10.9
Others	2.1	0.5	0.2	0.1	0.1	0.2	0.1	0.2

Table 6.5   FINLAND   Number of Seats Won in the Eduskunta 1907–1917

	1907	1908	1909	1910	1911	1913	1916	1917
4 Agrarian Union	9	9	13	17	16	18	19	26
3 Christian Labour Union	2	2	1	1	1	0	1	0
6 Finnish Party	59	54	48	42	43	38	33	24
7 Peoples Party	–	–	–	–	–	–	–	5
5 Young Finnish Party	26	27	29	28	28	28	23	32
1 Social Democrats	80	83	84	86	86	90	103	92
2 Swedish Peoples Party	24	25	25	26	26	26	21	21
Others	0	0	0	0	0	0	0	0
Total Seats	200	200	200	200	200	200	200	200

Source: Törnudd, 1968 : 146-150.

Table 6.6 FINLAND Percentage of Seats Won in the Eduskunta 1907–1917

	1907	1908	1909	1910	1911	1913	1916	1917
4 Agrarian Union	4.5	4.5	6.5	8.5	8.0	9.0	9.5	13.0
3 Christian Labour Union	1.0	1.0	0.5	0.5	0.5	0.0	0.5	0.0
6 Finnish Party	29.5	27.0	24.0	21.0	21.5	19.0	16.5	12.0
7 Peoples Party	–	–	–	–	–	–	–	2.5
5 Young Finnish Party	13.0	13.5	14.5	14.0	14.0	14.0	11.5	16.0
1 Social Democrats	40.0	41.5	42.0	43.0	43.0	45.0	51.5	46.0
2 Swedish Peoples Party	12.0	12.5	12.5	13.0	13.0	13.0	10.5	10.5
Others	0.0	0.0	0.0	0.0	0.0	0.0	0.0	0.0

Table 6.7   FINLAND   Total Votes 1919–1939

	1919	1922	1924	1927	1929	1930	1933	1936	1939
Electorate	1,438,709	1,489,022	1,539,393	1,638,864	1,719,567	1,722,588	1,789,331	1,872,908	1,956,807
Valid Votes	961,101	865,421	878,941	910,191	951,270	1,130,028	1,107,823	1,173,382	1,297,319
Invalid Votes	4,771	5,404	4,884	4,180	5,026	5,517	4,917	5,030	5,029
Total Votes	965,872	870,825	883,825	914,371	956,296	1,135,545	1,112,740	1,178,412	1,302,348
PARTY VOTES									
4 Agrarian Union	189,297	175,401	177,982	205,313	248,762	308,280	249,758	262,917	296,529
3 Christian Labour Union	14,718	–							–
1 Social Democrats	365,046	216,861	255,068	257,572	260,254	386,026	413,551	452,751	515,980
2 Swedish Peoples Party	116,582	107,414	105,733	111,005	108,886	113,318	115,433	131,440	124,720
8 National Coalition	151,018	157,116	166,880	161,450	138,008	203,958	187,527[1]	121,619	176,215
13 Patriotic Peoples Movement	–	–			–	–		97,891	86,219
9 Progressive Party	123,090	79,676	79,937	61,613	53,301	65,830	82,129	73,654	62,387
10 Socialist Workers Party	–	128,181	91,839	109,939	128,164	11,504	–		
11 Small Farmers Party	–	–	–	–	10,154	20,883	37,544	23,159	27,783
12 Swedish Left Wing	–	–	–	–	–	9,271	–		5,980
Others	1,350	772	1,502	3,299	3,741	10,958	21,881[2]	9,951[3]	1,506

[1] An electoral alliance of the Patriotic Peoples Movement and the National Coalition.
[2] Including the Peoples Party (Kansanpuolue) with 9,390 votes.
[3] Including the Peoples Party with 7,449 votes.

Sources: Törnudd, 1968 : 151-158; Statistical Yearbook, 1970 : 374.

Table 6.8   FINLAND   Percentage of Votes 1919–1939

	1919	1922	1924	1927	1929	1930	1933	1936	1939
Valid Votes	66.8	58.1	57.1	55.5	55.3	65.6	61.9	62.7	66.3
Invalid Votes	0.3	0.4	0.3	0.3	0.3	0.3	0.3	0.3	0.3
Total Votes	67.1	58.5	57.4	55.8	55.6	65.9	62.2	62.9	66.6
Share Invalid	0.5	0.6	0.6	0.5	0.5	0.5	0.4	0.4	0.4
PARTY VOTES									
4 Agrarian Union	19.7	20.3	20.2	22.6	26.2	27.3	22.5	22.4	22.9
3 Christian Labour Union	1.5	–	–	–	–	–	–	–	–
1 Social Democrats	38.0	25.1	29.0	28.3	27.4	34.2	37.3	38.6	39.8
2 Swedish Peoples Party	12.1	12.4	12.0	12.2	11.4	10.0	10.4	11.2	9.6
8 National Coalition	15.7	18.2	19.0	17.7	14.5	18.0 }	16.9	10.4	13.6
13 Patriotic Peoples Movement	–	–	–	–	–	–		8.3	6.6
9 Progressive Party	12.8	9.2	9.1	6.8	5.6	5.8	7.4	6.3	4.8
10 Socialist Workers Party	–	14.8	10.4	12.1	13.5	1.0	–	–	–
11 Small Farmers Party	–	–	–	–	1.1	1.8	3.4	2.0	2.1
12 Swedish Left Wing	–	–	–	–	–	0.8	–	–	0.5
Others	0.1	0.1	0.2	0.4	0.4	1.0	2.0	0.8	0.1

Table 6.9   FINLAND   Number of Seats Won in the Eduskunta 1919–1939

		1919	1922	1924	1927	1929	1930	1933	1936	1939
4	Agrarian Union	42	45	44	52	60	59	53	53	56
3	Christian Labour Union	2	–	–	–	–	–	–	–	–
1	Social Democrats	80	53	60	60	59	66	78	83	85
2	Swedish Peoples Party	22	25	23	24	23	20	21	21	18
8	National Coalition	28	35	38	34	28	42	18	20	25
13	Patriotic Peoples Movement	–	–	–	–	–	–	14	14	8
9	Progressive Party	26	15	17	10	7	11	11	7	6
10	Socialist Workers Party	–	27	18	20	23	0	–	–	–
11	Small Farmers Party	–	–	–	–	0	1	3	1	2
12	Swedish Left Wing	–	–	–	–	–	1	–	–	0
	Others	0	0	0	0	0	0	2[1]	1[1]	0
	Total Seats	200	200	200	200	200	200	200	200	200

[1] Peoples Party.

Source: Törnudd, 1968 : 151-158.

Table 6.10   FINLAND   Percentage of Seats Won in the Eduskunta 1919–1939

	1919	1922	1924	1927	1929	1930	1933	1936	1939
4 Agrarian Union	21.0	22.5	22.0	26.0	30.0	29.5	26.5	26.5	28.0
3 Christian Labour Union	1.0	–	–	–	–	–	–	–	–
1 Social Democrats	40.0	26.5	30.0	30.0	29.5	33.0	39.0	41.5	42.5
2 Swedish Peoples Party	11.0	12.5	11.5	12.0	11.5	10.0	10.5	10.5	9.0
8 National Coalition	14.0	17.5	19.0	17.0	14.0	21.0	9.0	10.0	12.5
13 Patriotic Peoples Movement	–	–	–	–	–	–	7.0	7.0	4.0
9 Progressive Party	13.0	7.5	8.5	5.0	3.5	5.5	5.5	3.5	3.0
10 Socialist Workers Party	–	13.5	9.0	10.0	11.5	0.0	–	–	–
11 Small Farmers Party	–	–	–	–	0.0	0.5	1.5	0.5	1.0
12 Swedish Left Wing	–	–	–	–	–	0.5	–	–	0.0
Others	0.0	0.0	0.0	0.0	0.0	0.0	1.0	0.5	0.0

Table 6.11   FINLAND   Total Votes 1945—1972

	1945	1948	1951	1954	1958	1962	1966	1970	1972
Electorate	2,284,249	2,420,287	2,448,239	2,526,969	2,606,258	2,714,838	2,800,461	3,094,359	3,178,169
Valid Votes	1,698,376	1,879,968	1,812,817	2,008,257	1,944,235	2,301,998	2,370,046	2,535,782	2,577,949
Invalid Votes	11,875	13,869	12,962	10,785	10,162	8,092	8,537	8,728	9,111
Total Votes	1,710,251	1,893,837	1,825,779	2,019,042	1,954,397	2,310,090	2,378,583	2,544,510	2,587,060

PARTY VOTES

		1945	1948	1951	1954	1958	1962	1966	1970	1972
4	Agrarian Union/Centre Party	362,662	455,635	421,613	483,958	448,364	528,409	503,047	434,150	423,039
1	Social Democrats	425,948	494,719	480,754	527,094	450,212	448,930	645,339	594,185	664,724
2	Swedish Peoples Party	134,106	145,455	137,171	140,130	130,888	147,655	141,688	144,436	138,079
8	National Coalition	255,394	320,366	264,044	257,025	297,094	346,638	326,928	457,582	453,434
9	Progressive Party[1]	87,868	73,444	102,933	158,323	114,617	146,005	153,259	150,823	132,955
11	Small Farmers Party	20,061	5,378	4,964	–	–	–	–	–	–
12	Swedish Left Wing	8,192	–	–	–	–	–	–	–	–
14	Finnish Peoples Democratic Union	398,618	375,820	391,362	433,528	450,506	507,124	502,635	420,556	438,757
15	Liberal League	–	–	4,936	6,810	6,424	12,000	–	–	–
16	Social Democratic League	–	–	–	–	33,947	100,396	61,274	35,453	25,527
17	Finnish Rural Party	–	–	–	–	–	49,773	24,351	265,939	236,206
18	Christian League	–	–	–	–	–	15,068	10,646	28,547	65,228
	Others	5,527	9,151	5,040	11,389	12,183	15,068	879	4,111	–

[1] From 1951 the Finnish Peoples Party; since 1966 the Liberal Peoples Party.

Sources: Törnudd, 1968 : 159-165; Statistical Yearbook, 1970 : 374; Parliamentary Elections, 1970 : 10-11; and figures provided by the Central Office of Statistics, Helsinki.

118

Table 6.12   FINLAND   Percentage of Votes 1945—1972

	1945	1948	1951	1954	1958	1962	1966	1970	1972
Valid Votes	74.4	77.7	74.0	79.5	74.6	84.8	84.6	81.9	81.1
Invalid Votes	0.5	0.6	0.5	0.4	0.4	0.3	0.3	0.3	0.3
Total Votes	74.9	78.2	74.6	79.9	75.0	85.1	84.9	82.2	81.4
Share Invalid	0.7	0.7	0.7	0.5	0.5	0.4	0.4	0.3	0.4
PARTY VOTES									
4 Agrarian Union/Centre Party	21.4	24.2	23.3	24.1	23.1	23.0	21.2	17.1	16.4
1 Social Democrats	25.1	26.3	26.5	26.2	23.2	19.5	27.2	23.4	25.8
2 Swedish Peoples Party	7.9	7.7	7.6	7.0	6.7	6.4	6.0	5.7	5.4
8 National Coalition	15.0	17.0	14.6	12.8	15.3	15.1	13.8	18.0	17.6
9 Progressive Party	5.2	3.9	5.7	7.9	5.9	6.3	6.5	5.9	5.2
11 Small Farmers Party	1.2	0.3	0.3	–	–	–	–	–	–
13 Swedish Left Wing	0.5	–	–	–	–	–	–	–	–
14 Finnish Peoples Democratic Union	23.5	20.0	21.6	21.6	23.2	22.0	21.2	16.6	17.0
15 Liberal League	–	–	0.3	0.3	0.3	0.5	–	–	–
16 Social Democratic League	–	–	–	–	1.7	4.4	2.6	1.4	1.0
17 Finnish Rural Party	–	–	–	–	–	2.2	1.0	10.5	9.2
18 Christian League	–	–	–	–	–	–	0.4	1.1	2.5
Others	0.3	0.5	0.3	0.1	0.6	0.7	0.0	0.2	–

Table 6.13   FINLAND   Number of Seats Won in the Eduskunta 1945–1972

	1945	1948	1951	1954	1958	1962	1966	1970	1972
4 Agrarian Union/Centre Party	49	56	51	53	48	53	49	37	35
1 Social Democrats	50	54	53	54	48	38	55	51	55
2 Swedish Peoples Party	14	14	15	13	14	14	12	12	10
8 National Coalition	28	33	28	24	29	32	26	37	34
9 Progressive Party[1]	9	5	10	13	8	13	9	8	7
11 Small Farmers Party	0	0	0	–	–	–	–	–	–
13 Swedish Left Wing	1	–	–	–	–	–	–	–	–
14 Finnish Peoples Democratic Union	49	38	43	43	50	47	41	36	37
15 Liberal League	–	–	–	–	0	1	–	–	–
16 Social Democratic League	–	–	–	–	3	2	7	0	0
17 Finnish Rural Party	–	–	–	–	–	0	1	18	18
18 Christian League	–	–	–	0	0	0	0	1	4
Others	0	0	0	0	0	0	0	0	–
Total Seats	200	200	200	200	200	200	200	200	200

[1] From 1951 the Finnish Peoples Party; since 1966 the Liberal Peoples Party.

Sources: Törnudd, 1968 : 159-165; *Parliamentary Elections, 1970* : 12; and figures provided by the Central Office of Statistics, Helsinki.

Table 6.14 FINLAND   Percentage of Seats Won in the Eduskunta 1945–1972

	1945	1948	1951	1954	1958	1962	1966	1970	1972
4 Agrarian Union/Centre Party	24.5	28.0	25.5	26.5	24.0	26.5	24.5	18.5	17.5
1 Social Democrats	25.0	27.0	26.5	27.0	24.0	19.0	27.5	25.5	27.5
2 Swedish Peoples Party	7.0	7.0	7.5	6.5	7.0	7.0	6.0	6.0	5.0
8 National Coalition	14.0	16.5	14.0	12.0	14.5	16.0	13.0	18.5	17.0
9 Progressive Party	4.5	2.5	5.0	6.5	4.0	6.5	4.5	4.0	3.5
11 Small Farmers Party	0.0	0.0	0.0	–	–	–	–	–	–
13 Swedish Left Wing	0.5	–	–	–	–	–	–	–	–
14 Finnish Peoples Democratic Union	24.5	19.0	21.5	21.5	25.0	23.5	20.5	18.0	18.5
15 Liberal League	–	–	–	–	0.0	0.5	–	–	–
16 Social Democratic League	–	–	–	–	1.5	1.0	3.5	0.0	0.0
17 Finnish Rural Party	–	–	–	–	–	0.0	0.5	9.0	9.0
18 Christian League	–	–	–	–	–	–	0.0	0.5	2.0
Others	0.0	0.0	0.0	0.0	0.0	0.0	0.0	0.0	–

Chapter 7

FRANCE

The introduction of universal suffrage in France after the 1848 revolution came long before the development of national political parties. During the Second Empire from 1851 to 1870 democratic forms were retained, but elections were 'managed' more or less successfully by the government. Free elections were restored in 1871. However, until the end of the 19th century party organization outside parliament was rudimentary (Campbell, 1958:25). Parliamentary groups were very ill-defined, and until 1910 deputies were allowed to belong to more than one parliamentary group (Bomier-Landowski, 1951:6). During the twentieth century French party organization has continued to be ill-defined, especially on the Right. The large number of parties, difficulties in assigning party labels to individual candidates, frequent changes in electoral alliances and different alliances in different parts of the country at the same election, wide differences between electoral and parliamentary party groups and considerable instability in the membership of the latter, combine to make analysis particularly difficult. Substantial research is now under way to validate data for elections in the Third Republic (Rosenthal and Padioleau, 1972) and the Fourth and Fifth Republics (Derivry, 1972).

The 1848 revolution replaced a very restrictive *régime censitaire* with adult male suffrage. The electorate increased from 241,000 to 8,221,000. Election to the Constituent and Legislative assemblies of the Second Republic in 1848 and 1849 was by plurality in multi-member constituencies. Each elector had as many votes as there were seats to fill. In order to win a seat a candidate had to receive at least 2,000 votes or, in 1849, the support of one-eighth of the registered electorate. The election to the Constituent Assembly in April, 1848, returned about 300 monarchists, about 100 socialist republicans and, between the two extremes, some 500 moderate republicans.

Three major groups contested the first Legislative Assembly elections. The Party of Order included both monarchist and Catholic supporters of Louis Napoleon; the Constitutional Republicans, the socially conservative but anti-Bonapartist elements who had supported the presidential candidacy of General Cavaignac; and the Democrat-Socialists, the extreme republicans and socialists. (Table 7.a)

Table 7.a **Election to the Assemblée Législative 13—14 May 1849**

	Votes	%	seats
Electorate	9,837,000		
Valid votes	6,594,000	67.0	750

123

	Votes	%	seats
Party of Order	3,310,000	50.2	500
Constitutional Republicans	834,000	12.6	70
Democrat-Socialists	1,955,000	29.6	180
Others	495,000	7.5	

Source: Genique, 1921:34. See also Bouillon, 1936, especially for a critique of Genique's estimate of the Democrat-Socialist vote.

Louis Napoleon's coup d'Etat in December 1851 led to the replacement of the Second Republic by the Second Empire. Government sponsored candidates always won a large majority of the seats in parliament, but their electoral support declined sharply in the elections of 1863 and 1869 (Campbell, 1965:67-68).

The collapse of the Second Empire in 1870 was followed the next year by elections to a National Assembly held under the electoral laws of the Second Republic. The constitutional law of 1875 established the Third Republic. It provided for a two-chamber National Assembly, consisting of a Senate and a Chamber of Deputies. The President was to be elected by the National Assembly for a seven-year term. Members of the Chamber of Deputies were elected in single-member constituencies by the two-ballot system. Except for elections of 1885, 1919 and 1924 this system was employed throughout the Third Republic. A quarter of the Senate's 300 members were elected for life by the 1871 parliament; their successors were to be chosen by the Senate itself. The remaining Senators were chosen by departmental electoral colleges. Because each department chose between three and five Senators the rural departments were heavily over-represented. In 1884 the electoral law was changed. No more life senators were appointed. Vacancies were allotted to the more populous departments and chosen in the same way as the other senators (Campbell, 1965: 139-140).

In the election to the National Assembly in 1871, the monarchists won 415 of the 645 seats; vote totals are not available. At the next five elections the Republicans won a majority of both seats and votes (Table 7.b)

Table 7.b   **Elections to the Chambre des Deputés, 1876—1889**

	1876	1877	1881	1885	1889
Electorate	9,961,000	9,948,000	10,125,000	10,181,000	10,387,000
Conservatives	3,202,000	3,639,000	1,789,000	3,420,000	2,915,000
	(155)	(208)	(96)	(202)	(168)
Republicans	4,028,000	4,340,000	5,128,000	4,373,000	4,353,000
	(371)	(318)	(455)	(367)	(350)
Boulangists	—	—	—	—	709,000
					(42)
Total Votes	7,230,000	7,979,000	6,917,000	7,793,000	7,977,000
Total Seats	(526)	(526)	(541)	(569)	(570)

Source: Campbell, 1965: 73-81 and Lancelot, 1968:14.

The 1885 election was held in multi-member constituencies. Each voter was allowed as many votes as there were seats. Voters were allowed to cast their votes for candidates on different lists. They could cast only one vote per candidate. The provisions for first and second ballots were unaltered. In 1889 the single-member two-ballot system was restored.

It was not until the end of the nineteenth century that organised nation-wide parties began to develop (Campbell, 1965: 24-25). Many monarchists (the Ralliés) now accepted the legitmacy of the republic. Divisions began to appear between moderate republicans and the radicals and radical socialists; support for socialist parties grew rapidly (Table 7.c).

Table 7.c   **Elections to the Chambre des Deputés, 1893—1898**

	1893	**1898**
Electorate	10,446,178	10,635,206
Conservatives	1,178,007(76)	1,011,398(65)
Moderate Republicans	3,187,670(279)	3,347,826(235)
Radicals	1,443,915(143)	1,400,416(98)
Ralliés	458,416(27)	541,576(35)
Socialist Radicals	171,810(10)	748,412(82)
Socialists	598,206(31)	888,385(57)
Others	108,596(0)	—
Totals	**7,146,620(566)**	**7,838,013(572)**

Sources: Lancelot, 1968: 14; Avenel, 1894 and Ibid., 1898.

With the formation of the Radical Socialist Party in 1901 and of the French Socialist Party in 1906 party divisions on the centre and left of the political spectrum became more clearly delineated. The 1902 election is therefore an appropriate date to begin tables of series of election results.

The 1919 electoral law was a mixture of majoritarian and proportional representation procedures. Candidates could stand independently or as part of a list which could have as many names as there were seats in the constituency. Each constituency's seats were distributed in three stages. First, any candidate who received an absolute majority of the valid votes cast was declared elected. Secondly, vacant seats were allotted in proportion to an electoral quotient calculated by dividing the total number of valid votes cast by the number of seats in the constituency. Individuals who were not members of party lists could be elected at this stage, but only so long as no candidate on a party list of more than two members and who had more votes than the independent candidate remained unelected. Lastly, any remaining seats went to the list with the highest average. If that list did not have enough candidates to fill all the empty seats any seats still unfilled went to the list with the next highest average and so on.

For the 1924 election the law was altered to discriminate further against strong candidates who stood independently of party lists. All candidates had to stand as members of a list with as many names as there were seats in a constituency. This was intended to reduce the chances of an independent candidate with only a strong personal following being elected at the highest average stage. Voters were allowed to split their votes between different lists.

When Germany occupied France in 1940 a French-led regime was established at Vichy; political parties were outlawed. After the liberation in 1944 political parties and free elections were restored. Women were given the vote. A purely proportional representation system was introduced for the first time in the 1945 election. Seats were allocated in multi-member constituencies by the d'Hondt highest average system for both the National Assembly and for the Council of the Republic, which replaced the Senate in 1946. The Council of the Republic was indirectly elected by departmental electoral colleges. Sixty-five of its 315 members represented Algerian and the overseas departments and territories. In 1948 the size of the Council was increased to 320, of whom 246 represented mainland France.

In 1951 the electoral system for the National Assembly was altered. In the Paris region the largest remainder system replaced the d'Hondt system. Elsewhere the d'Hondt system was retained, but with an important modification. In each constituency alliances were allowed between national parties, defined as those presenting lists in at least 30 departments. A list or an alliance of lists which won an absolute majority in a particular constituency was awarded every seat. In the case of an alliance of lists the seats were divided between the member parties by the highest average system.

The Fifth Republic, inaugurated in 1958, saw a return to the two-ballot single-member system. To be elected to the Chamber of Deputies on the first ballot an absolute majority of votes and the support of one-quarter of the electorate was required. No new candidates were allowed at the second ballot; a plurality sufficed for election. Candidates winning less than five percent of the vote in the first round were eliminated. In 1967 this minimum was increased to ten per cent of the electorate. The upper house, renamed the Senate, continued to be chosen by departmental electoral colleges.

Major changes were made in the election of the President of the Republic. Fourth Republic presidents, like their predecessors of the Third Republic, were elected by the National Assembly for a seven-year term. The Constitution of the Fifth Republic provided for election by an electoral college. This consisted of members of the National Assembly, members of departmental general councils, representatives of communal councils and representatives of Algeria, the overseas territories and the new states of the French Community. In 1962 a constitutional revision approved by referendum provided for the direct election of the President by universal suffrage. At the first round an absolute majority is required. If no candidate wins an absolute majority a second ballot is held a week later. The second round is limited to the two candidates who obtained the largest number of votes in the first round (Table 7.d).

Table 7.d   **Presidential Elections 1965—1969[1]**

1965	First Round	%	Second Round	%
Electorate	28,233,167	83	28,223,198	
Valid votes	23,557,669	83.4	23,197,512	82.2
Invalid votes	444,292	1.6	665,141	2.4
Total votes	24,001,961	85.0	23,862,653	84.5
De Gaulle (Gaullists)	10,386,734	43.7	12,643,527	54.5
Mitterand (Socialists, Communists and Radicals)	7,658,792	27.1	10,553,985	45.5
Lecanuet (MRP)	3,767,404	13.3		
Tixier-Vignancour (Extreme Right)	1,253,958	4.4		
Marcillacy (Moderate Conservatives)	413,129	1.5		
Barbu (Non-party)	277,652	1.0		

1969	First Round	%	Second Round	%
Electorate	28,774,041		28,761,494	
Valid votes	22,204,687	77.2	18,558,871	64.5
Invalid votes	287,372	1.0	295,216	1.0
Total votes	22,492,059	78.2	18,854,087	65.5
Pompidou (Gaullists)	9,761,297	44.0	10,688,183	57.6
Poher (Centre Democrats and Radicals)	5,201,133	23.4	7,870,688	42.4
Duclos (Communists)	4,779,539	21.5		
Defferre (Socialists)	1,127,733	5.1		
Rocard (United Socialist Party)	814,051	3.7		
Ducatel (Non-party)	284,697	1.3		
Krivine (Trotskyist)	236,237	1.1		

[1] Principal supporters at the first round indicated in brackets after the candidates name (presidential candidates often fight as candidates of an alliance of parties).

Source: Duverger, 1971:432.

The French colonies have been continuously represented in the French parliament since 1871. They were also represented from 1848 to 1852. The number of overseas deputies and the method of their election has varied considerably. Full details are given in Campbell, 1965:136-138. Unless otherwise mentioned all figures given here refer to mainland France only.

The membership of parliamentary groups, including overseas deputies, may be conveniently found in Bomier-Landowski (1951) for the Third Republic and Duverger (1971:428-430) for the Fourth and Fifth Republics. The membership of parliamentary groups often differs considerably from that of the electoral parties described in the following tables.

Sources:

Association Française de Science Politique, *Les élections législatives du mars 1956* (Paris: Armand Colin, 1957).

Ibid., *L'établissement de la Cinquième République: le référendum du septembre et les élections législatives du novembre 1958* (Paris: Armand Colin, 1960).

Avenel, H., *Comment votent la France. Dix-huit ans de suffrage universel* (Paris: Quantin, 1894).

Ibid., *Le nouveau ministère et la nouvelle chambre* (Paris: Flammarion, 1898).

Bomier-Landowski, A., "Les groupes parlementaires de l'Assemblée Nationale et de la Chambre des Deputés de 1871 a 1940" In F. Goguel and G. Dupeux (eds.) *Sociologie Électorale:esquisse d'un bilen, guide de recherche* (Paris: Armand Colin, 1951).

Bouillon, J., "Les démocrates-socialistes aux élections de 1849". *Revue Française de Science Politique 6 : 71-95 (1956)*

Campbell, P., *French Electoral Systems and Elections since 1789* (London: Faber and Faber, 1965).

Derivry, D., "A data-bank of French electoral statistics 1945—1971" *Social Science Information* 11: 309-316 (1972).

Duverger, M., *Constitutions et documents politiques* (6th edition Paris: Presses Universitairies de France, 1971).

Fondation Nationale des Sciences Politiques, *Les élections législatives de mars 1967* (Paris: Armand Colin, 1971).

Genique, G., *L'élection a l'assemblée législative en 1849. Essai d'une répartition géographiques des partis en France* (Paris: F. Rieder, 1921).

Goguel, F., "Le référendum du 28 octobre et les élections des 18-25 novembre 1962" *Revue Française de Science Politique* 13 : 289-314 (1963).

Ibid., "Les élections Législatives des 23 et 30 juin 1968" *Revue Française de Science Politique* 18: 837-853 (1968).

Lancelot, A., *L'abstentionnisme électorale en France* (Paris: Armand Colin, 1968)

Ministère de l'Intérieur, *Les élections législatives du 17 juin 1951* (Paris: La Documentation française, 1953 — subsequent elections are each covered by a volume in this series).

"Le Monde", *Elections et réferéndums des 13 october, 10 et 24 novembre et 8 decembre 1946* (Paris: Le Monde, 1947).

Rémond, R., *La politique en France depuis 1789, Volume 2: 1848—1879* (Paris: Armand Colin, 1969).

Rosenthal, H. and Padioleau, J., "A data-bank of political statistics of the French Third Republic 1871—1940" *Social Science Information* 11: 303-308 (1972).

Zeldin, T., *The political system of Napoleon III* (London: Macmillan, 1958).

Table 7.1
POLITICAL PARTIES IN FRANCE SINCE 1902

	Party Names	Elections contested	Number contested
1	Conservatives I[1]	1902-1936	9
2	Socialists[2]	1902	1
3	Left Republicans (Republicains de Gauche)	1902-1936	7
4	Liberal Popular Action (Action Libérale Populaire)[3]	1902-1914	4
5	Independent Radicals (Radicaux Indépendants)	1902-1936	9
6	Radical Socialist party (Parti Républicain Radical et Radical Socialiste)[4]	1902ff	18
7	Independent Socialists (Socialists Indépendants)	1906-1910; 1919	3
8	Socialist Party (Section Française de l'Internationale Ouvrière—SFIO; literally the French Section of the Workers International)	1906ff	17
9	Republican Union (Union Républicaine)	1910-1936	7
10	Socialist Republicans (Républicains Socialistes)	1914-1936	6
11	Communist Party (Parti Communiste Français—PCF)	1924ff	13
12	Popular Democratic Party (Parti Démocrate Populaire—PDP)	1932-1936	2
13	Conservatives II[5]	1945ff	9
14	Popular Republican Movement (Mouvement Populaire Républicain—MRP)	1945-1962	7
15	Gaullists[6]	1946ff	7
16	Poujadists—Union for the Defence of Traders and Artisans (Union pour la Defence des Commerçants et Artisans—UDCA)[7]	1956-1958	2
17	Union of Democratic Forces (Union des Forces Démocratiques)	1958	1
18	United Socialist Party (Parti Socialiste Unifié—PSU)	1962ff	3
19	Democratic Centre (Centre Démocrate); in 1968 the Centre du Progrés et de la Démocratie Moderne	1967ff	2

[1] Those classified as Conservateurs or Indépendants by Duverger (1971)

[2] Several socialist parties and factions.

[3] Successor to the Ralliés.

[4] Established in 1901 by a merger of Radicals and Radical Socialists. During the IVth Republic includes the Democratic and Socialist Union of the Resistance (Union Démocratique et Socialiste de la Résistance—UDSR).

[5] Includes the Parti Républicain de la Liberté, the Indépendants Républicains, the Parti Paysan, the Centre National des Indépendants et des Paysans, Action Républicaine et Sociale and candidates classified as Moderés.

[6] In 1946 the Union Gaulliste; in 1952 the Rassemblement du Peuple Français (RPF); in 1956 the Républicains Sociaux; in 1956 the Union pour la Nouvelle

Republique (UNR) and various smaller groups: Centre de la Réforme République, Renouveau et Fidelité and independent Gaullist candidates; in 1962 the UNR, the Union Démocratique du Travail (UDT) and the Républicains Independants; in 1967 candidates sponsored by the Comité d'Action pour la Cinquieme République. After the 1967 election the party was renamed the Union des Démocrates pour la Cinquième République (UDVeR). It contested the 1968 election as the Union pour la Defence de la République (UDR) and took the name Union des Démocrates pour la République (UDR) later in the year.

[7]Several lists formed by Pierre Poujade, leader of the UDCA whose successful candidates formed the parliamentary group Union et Fraternité Française.

Table 7.2
DATES OF ELECTIONS
TO THE CHAMBRE DES DEPUTES 1902–1936[1]

1.	27 April 1902	11.	2 June 1946[2]
2.	6 May 1906	12.	10 November 1946
3.	24 April 1910	13.	17 June 1951
4.	26 April 1914	14.	2 January 1956
5.	16 November 1919	15.	23 November 1958
6.	11 May 1924	16.	18 November 1962
7.	22 April 1928	17.	5 December 1965[3]
8.	1 May 1932	18.	5 March 1967
9.	26 April 1936	19.	23 June 1968
10.	21 October 1945[2]	20.	19 June 1969[3]

[1] Since November 1946 the National Assembly.
From 1902 to 1936 and since 1958 the date refers to the first ballot.
[2] Election of a Constituent Assembly.
[3] Presidential Election.

Source: Lancelot, 1968 : 14-16.

Table 7.3 FRANCE Total Votes 1902–1936[1]

	1902	1906	1910	1914	1919	1924	1928	1932	1936
Electorate	11,058,702	11,341,062	11,326,828	11,305,986	11,604,322	11,187,745	11,557,764	11,740,893	11,971,923
Valid Votes	8,412,727	8,812,493	8,445,773	8,431,056	8,148,090	9,026,837	9,469,861	9,579,482	9,847,266
PARTY VOTES									
6 Radical Socialist Party	853,140	2,514,508	1,727,064	1,530,188	1,420,381	3,426,581[2]	1,682,543	1,836,991	1,422,611[3]
10 Socialist Republicans	–	–	–	326,927	283,001	}	432,045	515,176	748,600[3]
8 Socialist Party	–	877,221	1,110,561	1,413,044	1,728,663	–	1,708,972	1,964,384	1,955,306[3/4]
7 Independent Socialists	–	205,081	345,202	–	147,053	–	–	–	–
2 Socialists	875,532	–	–	–	–	–	–	–	–
11 Communist Party	–	–	–	–	–	885,993	1,066,099	796,630	1,502,404[3]
1 Conservatives I	2,383,080	2,571,765	1,602,209	1,297,722	1,139,794	375,806	215,169	582,095	–
4 Liberal Popular Action	385,615	1,238,048	153,231	–	–	–	–	–	–
3 Left Republicans	2,501,429	703,912	1,018,704	819,184	889,177	1,058,193	2,198,243	1,299,936	4,202,298[5]
5 Independent Radicals	1,413,931	692,029	966,407	1,399,830	504,363	3,190,831	2,082,041	955,990	}
9 Republican Union	–	–	1,472,442	1,588,075	1,819,691	–	–	1,233,360	–
12 Popular Democratic Party	–	–	–	–	–	–	–	309,336	–
Others	n.a.	9,924	49,953	56,086	215,967	89,333	86,749	82,524	16,047

[1] Includes Algeria.

[2] The Cartel des Gauches, an electoral alliance of Radicals, Socialists and Socialist Republicans. Also includes the 781,812 votes cast for Socialist candidates who stood independently of the alliance.

[3] Contested the election as part of the Popular Front (Front Populaire) electoral alliance.

[4] Includes other minor socialist parties.

[5] Contested the election as part of the National Front (Front National) electoral alliance.

Sources: Duverger, 1971 : 422-425.

Table 7.4   FRANCE   Percentage of Votes 1902–1936

	1902	1906	1910	1914	1919	1924	1928	1932	1936
Valid Votes	76.1	77.7	74.6	74.6	70.2	80.7	81.9	81.6	82.3
PARTY VOTES									
6 Radical Socialist Party	10.1	28.5	20.4	18.1	17.4	38.0	17.8	19.2	14.4
10 Socialist Republicans	–	–	–	3.9	3.5		4.6	5.4	7.6
8 Socialist Party	–	10.0	13.1	16.8	21.2	–	18.0	20.5	19.9
7 Independent Socialists	–	2.3	4.1	–	1.8	–	–	–	–
2 Socialists	10.4	–	–	–	–	–	–	–	–
11 Communist Party	–	–	–	–	–	9.8	11.3	8.3	15.3
1 Conservatives I	28.3	29.2	19.0	15.4	14.0	4.2	2.3	6.1	–
4 Liberal Popular Action	4.6	14.0	1.8	–	–	–	–	–	
3 Left Republicans	29.7	8.0	12.1	9.7	10.9	11.7	23.2	13.6	42.7
5 Independent Radicals	16.8	7.9	11.4	16.6	6.2	35.3	22.0	10.0	
9 Republican Union	–	–	17.4	18.8	22.3	–	22.0	12.9	
12 Popular Democratic Party	–	–	–	–	–	–	–	3.2	
Others	n.a.	0.1	0.6	0.7	2.7	1.0	0.9	0.9	0.2

Table 7.5 FRANCE Number of Seats Won in the Chambre des Deputés 1902–1936[1]

		1902	1906	1910	1914	1919	1924	1928	1932	1936
6	Radical Socialist Party	75	241	121	140	106	162	120	157	109
10	Socialist Republicans	–	–	–	27	17	–	30	37	56
8	Socialist Party	–	53	78	103	67	104	99	129	149
7	Independent Socialists	–	18	24	–	5	–	–	–	–
2	Socialists	46	–	–	–	–	–	–	–	–
11	Communist Party	–	–	–	–	–	26	14	12	72
1	Conservatives I	147	109	112	73	88	25	26	33	–
4	Liberal Popular Action	18	69	11	–	–	–	–	–	–
3	Left Republicans	180	52	71	57	79	53	74	72	222
5	Independent Radicals	120	39	67	96	51	–	52	62	–
9	Republican Union	–	–	103	96	201	204	182	76	–
12	Popular Democratic Party	–	–	–	–	–	–	–	16	–
	Others	3	0	0	0	2	0	5	11	0
	Total Seats	589[2]	581	587	592	616	574	602	605	608

[1] Including Algerian deputies.
[2] Including deputies from Réunion and the French West Indies.

Source: Duverger, 1971 : 422-425.

Table 7.6   FRANCE   Percentage of Seats Won in the Chambre des Deputés 1902–1936

	1902	1906	1910	1914	1919	1924	1928	1932	1936
6 Radical Socialist Party	12.7	41.5	20.6	23.6	17.2	28.2	19.9	26.0	17.9
10 Socialist Republicans	–	–	–	4.6	2.8	–	5.0	6.1	9.2
8 Socialist Party	–	9.1	13.3	17.4	10.9	18.1	16.4	21.3	24.5
7 Independent Socialists	–	3.1	4.1	–	0.8	–	–	–	–
2 Socialists	7.8	–	–	–	–	–	–	–	–
11 Communist Party	–	–	–	–	–	4.5	2.3	2.0	11.8
1 Conservatives I	25.0	18.8	19.1	12.3	14.3	4.4	4.3	5.5	–
4 Liberal Popular Action	3.1	11.9	1.9	–	–	–	–	–	–
3 Left Republicans	30.6	9.0	12.1	9.6	12.8	9.2	12.3	11.9	36.5
5 Independent Radicals	20.4	6.7	11.4	16.2	8.3	–	8.6	10.2	–
9 Republican Union	–	–	17.5	16.2	32.6	35.5	30.2	12.6	–
12 Popular Democratic Party	–	–	–	–	–	–	–	2.6	–
Others	0.5	0.0	0.0	0.0	0.3	0.0	0.8	1.8	0.0

Table 7.7   FRANCE   Total Votes 1945–1968

	1945	1946 (June)	1946 (Nov.)	1951	1956	1958	1962	1967	1968
Electorate	24,621,000[1]	24,697,000[1]	25,052,000[1]	24,530,523	26,772,255	27,236,491	27,535,019	28,300,936	28,172,635
Valid Votes	19,190,000	19,881,000	19,203,000	19,129,064[2]	21,490,886[2]	20,341,908	18,329,986	22,389,514	22,138,657
Invalid Votes	468,000	334,000	362,000	541,591	647,160	652,889	601,747	512,710	401,086
Total Votes	19,568,000	20,215,000	19,565,000	19,670,655	22,138,046	20,994,797	18,931,733	22,902,224	22,539,743
PARTY VOTES									
6 Radical Socialist Party	2,131,000	2,295,000	2,381,000	1,887,583	3,227,484[3]	1,503,878	1,384,498	4,224,110[7]	3,654,003[7]
8 Socialist Party	4,561,000	4,188,000	3,432,000	2,744,842	3,247,431	3,193,786	2,319,662	5,039,032	4,435,357
11 Communist Party	5,005,000	5,199,000	5,489,000	5,056,505	5,514,403	3,907,763	3,992,431	–	–
17 Union of Democratic Forces	–	–	–	–	–	261,738	–	–	–
18 United Socialist Party	–	–	–	–	–	–	449,743	495,412	874,212
13 Conservatives II	2,546,000	2,540,000	2,466,000	2,657,095	3,257,782	4,502,449	1,742,523[5]	3,651,095[8]	2,700,864[3]
19 Democratic Centre	–	–	–	–	–	–			
14 Popular Republican Movement	4,780,000	5,589,000	5,058,000	2,369,778	2,366,321	2,273,281	1,635,452[6]	–	–
15 Gaullists	–	–	313,000	4,125,492	842,351[4]	4,165,453	6,645,495	8,448,982	10,201,024
16 Poujadists	–	–	–	–	2,483,813	244,958	159,682	510,883	273,197
Others	165,000	70,000	64,000	125,739	359,349	288,693			

[1] The totals are rounded in the original source. [2] The difference between the total party vote and the total valid vote in 1951 and 1956 is the result of *panachage*.
[3] Of which Front Républicain (an electoral alliance of Socialists, some of the Radicals led by Pierre Mendès-France and some of the Social Republicans led by Jacques Chaban-Delmas) 2,389,163 votes and the Centre Right (an alliance of Conservatives, the M.R.P. and some of the Radicals led by Edgar Faure) 244,594 votes.
[4] Of which Front Républicain 256,587 votes. [5] Including 487,806 votes cast for Independents supported by the Comité d'Action pour la Cinquième République.
[6] Including 190,384 votes cast for M.R.P. candidates supported by the Comité d'Action. [7] Federation of the Democratic and Socialist Left (Fédération de la Gauche Démocrate et Socialiste—FGDS). [8] Including Moderés (821,097 votes) who ran independently of the Centre Démocrate. [9] Including Moderés (410,699 votes) who ran independently of the Centre Démocrate.

Table 7.8 FRANCE Percentage of Votes 1945—1968

	1945	1946 (June)	1946 (Nov.)	1951	1956	1958	1962	1967	1968
Valid Votes	77.9	80.5	76.7	78.0	79.7	74.7	66.6	79.1	78.6
Invalid Votes	1.9	1.4	1.4	2.2	2.4	2.4	2.2	1.8	1.4
Total Votes	79.8	81.9	78.1	80.2	82.2	77.1	68.8	80.9	80.0
Share Invalid	2.4	1.7	1.9	2.8	2.9	3.1	3.2	2.2	1.8
PARTY VOTES									
6 Radical Socialist Party	11.1	11.5	12.4	10.0	15.2	7.4	7.6 }	19.0	16.5
8 Socialist Party	23.8	21.1	17.9	14.5	15.2	15.7	12.7 }	—	—
11 Communist Party	26.1	26.2	28.6	26.7	25.9	19.2	21.8	22.5	20.0
17 Union of Democratic Forces	—	—	—	—	—	1.3	—	—	—
18 United Socialist Party	—	—	—	—	—	—	2.5	2.2	3.9
13 Conservatives II	13.3	12.8	12.8	14.0	15.3	22.1	9.5 }	—	—
19 Democratic Centre	—	—	—	—	—	—	—	16.3	12.2
14 Popular Republican Movement	24.9	28.1	26.3	12.5	11.1	11.2	8.9 }	—	—
15 Gaullists	—	—	1.6	21.7	4.0	20.5	36.3	37.7	46.1
16 Poujadists	—	—	—	—	11.7	1.2	—	—	—
Others	0.9	0.4	0.3	0.7	1.7	1.4	0.9	2.3	1.2

Sources: 1945-1946: Le Monde, 1947: 256-257; 1951: Ministère de l'Intérieur, 1953: 42; 1956: Association Française de Science Politique, 1957: 470 and Ministère de l'Intérieur, 1957: 12; 1958: Association Française de Science Politique, 1960: 298; 1962: Goguel, 1963: 300; 1967: Fondation Nationale des Sciences Politiques, 1971: 414-415; 1968: Goguel, 1968: 840.

Table 7.9   FRANCE   Number of Seats Won in the Assembleé Nationale 1945—1968

	1945	1946 (June)	1946 (Nov.)	1951	1956	1958	1962	1967	1968
6 Radical Socialist Party	35	39	55	77	73	23	43	117	57
8 Socialist Party	134	115	90	94	88	44	65	72	33
11 Communist Party	148	146	166	97	147	10	41	–	–
17 Union of Democratic Forces	–	–	–	–	–	0	–	–	0
18 United Socialist Party	–	–	–	–	–	0	2	4	–
13 Conservatives II	62	62	70	87	95	133	48	–	31
19 Democratic Centre	–	–	–	–	–	–	–	45	–
14 Popular Republican Movement	141	160	158	82	71	57	36	–	–
15 Gaullists	–	–	5	107	16	198	229	232	349
16 Poujadists	–	–	–	–	51	0	–	–	–
Others	2	0	0	0	3	0	1	0	0
Total Seats	**522**	**522**	**544**	**544**	**544**	**465**	**465**	**470**	**470**

Sources: 1945 and 1946: *Le Monde*, 1947 : 257; 1951: Ministère de l'Intérieur, 1953 : 43; 1956: Association Française de Science Politique, 1957 : 470; 1958: Ibid, 1960 : 255; 1962 and 1967: Duverger, 1971 : 426-427; 1968: Goguel, 1968 : 841-842.

Table 7.10   FRANCE   Percentage of Seats Won in the Assemblée Nationale 1945—1968

	1945	1946 (June)	1946 (Nov.)	1951	1956	1958	1962	1967	1968
6 Radical Socialist Party	6.7	7.5	10.1	14.2	13.4	4.9	9.2	24.9	12.1
8 Socialist Party	25.7	22.0	16.5	17.3	16.2	9.5	14.0	–	–
11 Communist Party	28.4	28.0	30.5	17.8	27.0	2.2	8.8	15.3	7.0
17 Union of Democratic Forces	–	–	–	–	–	0.0	–	–	–
18 United Socialist Party	–	–	–	–	–	0.0	0.4	0.9	0.0
13 Conservatives II	11.9	11.9	12.9	16.0	17.5	28.6	10.3	–	–
19 Democratic Centre	–	–	–	–	–	–	–	9.6	6.6
14 Popular Republican Movement	27.0	30.7	29.0	15.1	13.1	12.3	7.7	–	–
15 Gaullists	–	–	0.9	19.7	2.9	42.6	49.2	49.4	74.3
16 Poujadists	–	–	–	–	9.4	0.0	–	–	–
Others	0.4	0.0	0.0	0.0	0.6	0.0	0.2	0.0	0.0

Chapter 8

GERMANY

This chapter is confined to developments since the establishment of the German Empire in 1871. It includes elections to the Reichstag of the Empire from 1871 to 1912, the 1919 elections to the Constituent Assembly, elections to the Reichstag of the Weimar Republic from 1920 to 1933 and to the Bundestag of the Federal Republic of Germany since 1949. Major boundary changes occurred at the end of the First and Second World Wars. Other smaller territorial changes should also be noted. Alsace-Lorraine, annexed from France, did not participate in the 1871 election. Voting figures for the Federal Republic before 1957 exclude the Saarland. West Berlin's non-voting representatives in the Bundestag are chosen by its Chamber of Deputies and not by the voters directly. In order to make comparison between Weimar elections and post-1945 elections easier. Tables 8.15-16 show voting figures, 1919–1933 within the territory of what is now the Federal Republic.

Until 1918 elections to the Reichstag were held under a majority system in single-member constituencies. If no candidate received a majority in the first round, a run-off election was held between the two leading candidates. The franchise was limited to men over 25 years. The ballot was secret. For a description of the complex and varied electoral laws employed in elections to the legislatures of the constituent states of the Empire see Urwin (1973).

During the Weimar period a system of direct proportional representation was used. A uniform quota of 60,000 votes was needed to win a seat in one of the 35 constituencies. (In 1919 only the quota was 150,000). Surplus votes were combined in a group of constituencies and a seat awarded to a party list for each 60,000 votes polled. Remaining excess votes were grouped in a national pool. At this stage a minimum of 30,000 votes was needed to win a seat. Universal adult suffrage with a minimum voting age of 20 was introduced.

The first President of the Weimar Republic was chosen by the Constituent Assembly. Subsequent Presidents were elected by popular vote in 1925 and 1932 using a two ballot system.

| | 1925 | | | |
	First Round	%	Second Round	%
Electorate	39,226,136		39,414,316	
Valid votes	26,866,106	68.5	30,351,813	77.0
Invalid votes	150,654	0.4	216,061	0.5
Total votes	27,016,760	68.9	30,567,874	77.6

1925

Candidates	First Round	%	Second Round	%
Hindenburg (Right Wing Parties)	–		14,655,641	48.5
Jarres (DNVP and DVP)	10,416,658	38.8	–	
Held (BVP)	1,007,450	3.7	–	
Ludendorff (Extreme Nationalist)	285,793	1.1	–	
Braun (SPD)	7,802,497	29.0	–	
Marx (Zentrum)	3,887,734	14.5	13,751,605	45.2
Hellpach (DDP)	1,568,398	5.8	–	
Thälman (KPD)	1,871,815	7.0	1,931,151	6.3
Others	25,761	0.1	13,416	0.0

1932

	First Round	%	Second Round	%
Electorate	43,949,681		44,063,959	
Valid votes	37,648,317	85.7	36,490,761	82.8
Invalid votes	242,134	0.6	281,026	0.6
Total votes	37,890,451	86.2	36,771,787	83.5
Candidates				
Hindenburg (SPD and Moderate Parties)	8,651,497	49.6	19,539,983	53.0
Duesterberg (Stahlhelm)	2,557,729	6.8	–	
Hitler (NSDAP)	11,339,446	30.1	13,418,547	36.8
Thälmann (KPD)	4,938,341	13.2	3,706,759	10.2
Others	116,304	0.3	–	

Sources:

Statistik des Deutschen Reichs, Vols. 321 and 427.

The electoral laws of the Federal Republic provide for a mixed proportional representation (d'Hondt) and plurality system. They have been modified several times. The minimum voting age of 21 was reduced to 18 in 1970. In the 1949 election, 60 per cent of the deputies were elected by a plurality in single-member constituencies. The remaining deputies were chosen by proportional representation from Land lists. The overall distribution of seats was made at the Land level on a proportional representation basis. After this initial allocation had been made the constituency seats won by each party were deducted from their total allocation and the remainder chosen from the Land list. A barrier clause eliminated any party which failed either to win at least one constituency seat or five per cent of the vote in the Land concerned. An exception is made for parties specially designated as 'Minority Parties' by the Federal Government. So far only one party, the South Schleswig Voters League, which represents the Danish-speaking minority, has benefited from this provision.

A 1953 law modified the system by reducing the number of constituency elected deputies to one-half the total, and strengthening the barrier clause by making the five per cent vote minimum a national rather than a Land requirement. A 1956 law introduced an initial allocation of seats by the d'Hondt method, at the national level. A second allocation is then made within each Land. The barrier clause was again raised to provide a minimum requirement of five per cent of the vote or three constituency seats. If a party wins more constituency seats than it would be entitled to under the proportional representation distribution (Überhängmandate), it keeps the extra seats. Since 1953 the elector has had two votes, one for the constituency and one for the party list. In 1949 the elector had only one vote, which was counted at both constituency and Land levels.

Sources:

Flechtheim, O.K., *Dokumente zur partei-politischen Entwicklung in Deutschland seit 1945 Vol. VIII* (Berlin: Wendler, 1970).

Milatz, A., *Wähler und Wahlen in der Weimarer Republik* (Bonn: Schriftenreihe der Bundeszentrale für politische Bildung, 1965).

Statistisches Bundesamt, *Bevölkerung und Kultur: Wahl zum 5. Deutschen Bundestag am 19. September, 1965* Series 8, No. 6 (Wiesbaden, 1965).

Ibid. Wahl zum 7. Deuschen Bundestag am 19. November, 1972 Series 8, No. 5 (Wiesbaden, 1972).

Statistisches Reichsamt, "Die Wahl des Reichspräsidenten am 29 Marz und 26 April 1925 *"Statistik des Deutschen Reichs* Volume 321 (Berlin, 1925).

Ibid. "Die Wahl des Reichspräsidenten am 13 Marz und 10 April 1932" *Statistik des Deutschen Reichs* Volume 427 (Berlin, 1932).

Sanger, F. and Liepelt, K. (eds) *Wahlhandbuch, 1965* Frankfurt: Europäische Verlagsanstalt, 1965).

Urwin, D.W., "Continuity and change in German electoral politics" in R. Rose (ed.) *Electoral Behavior: a Comparative Handbook* (New York: Free Press, 1973).

Vogel, B., Nohlen N. and Schultze, R.O., *Wahlen in Deutschland* (Berlin: de Gruyter, 1971).

Table 8.1
POLITICAL PARTIES IN GERMANY SINCE 1871

	Party Names	Elections contested	Number contested
1	Social Democrats (Sozialdemokratische Partei Deutschlands—SPD)	1871ff	29
2	Centre Party (Deutsche Zentrumspartei)[1]	1871-1957; 1969	26
3	Poles (Polen)	1871-1912	13
4	Danes (Dänen)	1871-1912	13
5	Guelph Party (Welfen)	1871-1912	13
6	German Conservatives (Deutsch-Konservative)	1871-1912	13
7	National Liberals (Nationalliberale)	1871-1912	13
8	German Reich Party (Deutsche Reichspartei)	1871-1912	13
9	Progressive Party (Fortschrittspartei)	1871-1881	5
10	German Peoples Party (Deutsche Volkspartei)	1871-1907	12
11	Liberal Reich Party (Liberale Reichspartei)	1871-1874	2
12	Alsatians (Elsässer)	1874-1912	12
13	Liberal Union (Liberale Vereinigung)[2]	1877-1881	3
14	Anti-Semites (Anti-Semiten)[3]	1887-1912	7
15	Freethinking Party (Freisinnige Partei)[4]	1884-1896	3
16	Freethinking Peoples Party (Freisinnige Volkspartei)[5]	1893-1907	4
17	Freethinking Union (Freisinnige Vereinigung)[5]	1893-1907	4
18	Bavarian Farmers League (Bayerische Bauernbund)	1898-1933	13
19	Farmers League (Bund der Landwirte)	1898-1912	4
20	Economic Union (Wirtschafts Vereinigung)	1907-1912	2
21	Progressive Peoples Party (Fortschrittliche Volkspartei)[6]	1912	1
22	Independent Social Democrats (Unabhängige Sozialdemokratische Partei Deutschlands—USPD)	1919-1930	6
23	German National Peoples Party (Deutsch Nationale Volkspartei—DNVP)	1919-1933	9
24	German Peoples Party (Deutsche Volkspartei—DVP)	1919-1933	9
25	German Democratic Party (Deutsche Demokratische Partei—DDP). In 1928 renamed the German State Party (Deutsche Staatspartei)	1919-1933	9
26	Middle Class Party (Reichspartei des Deutschen Mittelstands-Wirtschaftspartei)	1919-1932	8
27	Hanoverian Party (Deutsch Hannoversche Partei)	1919-1933	9
28	Communist Party (Kommunistische Partei Deutschlands—KPD)[7]	1920-1953; 1972	11
29	Bavarian Peoples Party (Bayerische Volkspartei—BVP)	1920-1933	8
30	National Socialists/Nazi Party (Nationalsozialistische Deutsche Arbeiterpartei—NSDAP)	1924-1933	7

	Party Names	Elections contested	Number contested
31	Land League (Landbund)[8]	1924-1933	7
32	Peoples Land Party (Landvolkpartei)	1928-1932	4
33	Farmers Party (Deutsche Bauernpartei)	1928-1933	5
34	Peoples Rights Party (Volksrechtspartei)	1928-1932	4
35	Christian Peoples Service (Christlich-sozialer Volksdienst)	1930-1933	4
36	Christian Democratic Union/Christian Social Union (Christlich Demokratische Union/ Christlich Soziale Union—CDU/CSU)[9]	1949ff	7
37	Free Democrats (Freie Demokratische Partei—FDP)	1949ff	7
38	German Party (Deutsche Partei—DP)	1949-1957	3
39	Bavarian Party (Bayernpartei—BP)	1949-1957; 1969	4
40	Economic Reconstruction League (Wirtschaftliche Aufbauvereinigung)	1949	1
41	South Schleswig Voters League (Südschleswigscher Wählerverbund)	1949-1961	4
42	German Reich Party (Deutsche Reichspartei—DRP)	1949-1961	4
43	All-German Peoples Party (Gesamtdeutsche Volkspartei)	1953	1
44	Refugee Party (Gesamtdeutscher Block/Bund der Heimatvertriebenen und Entrechteten)	1953-1957	2
45	Federal Union (Föderalistische Union)[10]	1957	1
46	German Freedom Union (Deutsche Friedensunion—DFU)	1961-1965	2
47	All-German Party (Gesamtdeutsche Partei—GDP)[11]	1961; 1969	2
48	National Democratic Party (Nationaldemokratische Partei Deutschlands—NPD)	1965ff	3
49	Action for Democratic Progress (Aktion Demokratischer Fortschritt)[12]	1969	1

[1] In 1919 only the Christian Peoples Party (Christliche Volkspartei—CVP). Since 1949 the minority of the former Zentrum which decided not to join the CDU.

[2] The Liberale Vereinigung was a splinter of the Nationalliberale.

[3] A group of parties including the Christlich-Soziale and Deutsche Reform parties for which separate figures are not available.

[4] The Freisinnige Partei was a merger of the Fortschrittspartei and the Liberale Vereinigung.

[5] The Freisinnige Partei split in 1892 to form the Freisinnige Vereinigung and the Freisinnige Volkspartei.

[6] A merger of the Freisinnige Vereinigung, the Freisinnige Volkspartei and the Deutsche Volkspartei.

[7] In 1956 the Communist Party (KPD) was banned by the Constitutional Court. In 1968 a Communist party was reformed under the name Deutsche Kommunistische Partei (DKP).

[8] An electoral alliance of regional farmers' parties, of which by far the largest was the Württemberg Farmers and Winegrowers Association (Württembergischer Bauren-und Weingärtnerbund).

[9] The Bavarian CSU forms a parliamentary group in the Bundestag with the CDU.

[10] An electoral alliance of four regionally based parties: the Bayernpartei, the Zentrum, the Deutsche Hannoversche Partei (DHP) and the Schleswig-Holsteinische Landespartei (SHL) (Flechtheim, 1970 : 465).

[11] A merger of the Deutsche Partei and the Refugee Party.

[12] Formed by the DFU and the DKP.

Table 8.2
DATES OF ELECTIONS TO THE REICHSTAG 1871–1933[1]
AND TO THE BUNDESTAG 1949–1972

1.	3 March 1871	16.	4 May 1924
2.	10 February 1874	17.	7 December 1924
3.	10 January 1877	18.	20 May 1928
4.	30 July 1878	19.	14 September 1930
5.	27 October 1881	20.	31 July 1932
6.	28 October 1884	21.	6 November 1932
7.	21 February 1887	22.	5 March 1933
8.	20 February 1890	23.	14 August 1949
9.	15 June 1893	24.	6 September 1953
10.	16 June 1898	25.	15 September 1957
11.	16 June 1903	26.	17 September 1961
12.	25 January 1907	27.	19 September 1965
13.	12 January 1912	28.	28 September 1969
14.	19 January 1919	29.	19 November 1972
15.	6 June 1920		

[1] Election dates up to 1912 refer to the date of the first ballot. In 1919 the election was for a Constituent Assembly.

Source: Vogel, 1971 : 290-297, 306-308.

Table 8.3 GERMANY Total Votes 1871–1887

	1871	1874	1877	1878	1881	1884	1887
Electorate	7,656,200	8,523,400	8,943,000	9,128,300	9,088,300	9,383,100	9,769,800
Valid Votes	3,892,200	5,190,300	5,401,000	5,760,900	5,097,800	5,663,000	7,540,900
Invalid Votes	255,800	29,600	21,600	20,000	20,600	18,700	29,800
Total Votes	4,148,000	5,219,900	5,422,600	5,780,900	5,118,400	5,681,700	7,570,700

PARTY VOTES

		1871	1874	1877	1878	1881	1884	1887
2	Centre Party	700,400	1,446,000	1,341,300	1,328,100	1,182,900	1,282,000	1,516,200
6	German Conservatives	549,700	360,000	526,000	749,500	830,800	861,100	1,147,200
10	German Peoples Party	18,700	21,700	44,900	66,100	103,400	95,900	88,800
8	German Reich Party	346,900	375,500	426,600	785,800	379,300	387,700	736,400
11	Liberal Reich Party	273,900	53,900	–	–	–	–	–
7	National Liberals	1,176,600	1,542,500	1,604,300	1,486,800	746,600	997,000	1,678,000
13	Liberal Union	–		–	–	429,000	–	–
9	Progressive Party	342,400	447,500	417,800	385,100	649,300	–	–
1	Social Democrats	124,700	352,000	493,300	437,100	312,000	550,000	763,100
12	Alsatians	–	234,500	200,000	178,900	153,000	165,600	233,700
4	Danes	18,200	19,900	17,300	16,100	14,400	14,400	12,400
5	Guelph Party	85,300	92,100	97,200	102,600	86,700	96,400	112,800
3	Poles	176,300	198,400	216,200	210,100	194,900	203,200	220,000
14	Anti-Semites	–	–	–	–	–	–	11,600
15	Free Thinking Party	–	–	–	–	–	997,000	973,100
	Others	79,100	46,300	16,100	14,700	15,300	12,700	47,600

Source: Vogel et al., 1971 : 290-291.

148

Table 8.4   GERMANY   Percentage of Votes 1871–1887

	1871	1874	1877	1878	1881	1884	1887
Valid Votes	50.8	60.9	60.4	63.1	56.1	60.4	77.2
Invalid Votes	3.3	0.3	0.2	0.2	0.2	0.2	0.2
Total Votes	54.2	61.2	60.6	63.3	56.3	60.6	77.5
Share Invalid	6.2	0.6	0.4	0.3	0.4	0.3	0.4
PARTY VOTES							
2 Centre Party	18.0	27.9	24.8	23.1	23.2	22.6	20.1
6 German Conservatives	14.1	6.9	9.7	13.0	16.3	15.2	15.2
10 German Peoples Party	0.5	0.4	0.8	1.1	2.0	1.7	1.2
8 German Reich Party	8.9	7.2	7.9	13.6	7.4	6.8	9.8
11 Liberal Reich Party	7.0	1.0	–	–	–	–	–
7 National Liberals	30.2	29.7	29.7	25.8	14.6	17.6	22.3
13 Liberal Union	–	–	–	–	8.4	–	–
9 Progressive Party	8.8	8.6	7.7	6.7	12.7	–	–
1 Social Democrats	3.2	6.8	9.1	7.6	6.1	9.7	10.1
12 Alsatians	–	4.5	3.7	3.1	3.0	2.9	3.1
4 Danes	0.5	0.4	0.3	0.3	0.3	0.3	0.2
5 Guelph Party	2.2	1.8	1.8	1.8	1.7	1.7	1.5
3 Poles	4.5	3.8	4.0	3.6	3.8	3.6	2.9
14 Anti-Semites	–	–	–	–	–	–	0.2
15 Free Thinking Party	–	–	–	–	–	17.6	12.9
Others	2.0	0.9	0.3	0.3	0.3	0.2	0.6

149

Table 8.5 GERMANY Number of Seats Won in the Reichstag 1871–1887

	1871	1874	1877	1878	1881	1884	1887
2 Centre Party	61	91	93	94	100	99	98
6 German Conservatives	57	22	40	59	50	78	80
10 German Peoples Party	1	1	4	3	9	7	0
8 German Reich Party	37	33	38	57	28	28	41
11 Liberal Reich Party	30	3	–	–	–	–	–
7 National Liberals	125	155	128	99	47	51	99
13 Liberal Union	–	–	13	10	46	–	–
9 Progressive Party	46	49	35	26	60	–	–
1 Social Democrats	2	9	12	9	12	24	11
12 Alsatians	–	15	15	15	15	15	15
4 Danes	1	1	1	1	2	1	1
5 Guelph Party	9	4	10	4	10	11	4
3 Poles	13	14	14	14	18	16	13
14 Anti-Semites	–	–	–	–	–	–	1
15 Free Thinking Party	–	–	–	–	–	67	32
Others	0	0	0	0	0	0	2
Total Seats	**382**	**397**	**397**	**397**	**397**	**397**	**397**

Source: Vogel et al., 1971 : 290-291

Table 8.6 GERMANY Percentage of Seats Won in the Reichstag 1871–1887

		1871	1874	1877	1878	1881	1884	1887
2	Centre Party	16.0	22.9	23.4	23.7	25.2	24.9	24.7
6	German Conservatives	14.9	5.5	10.1	14.9	12.6	19.6	20.2
10	German Peoples Party	0.3	0.3	1.0	0.8	2.3	1.8	0.0
8	German Reich Party	9.7	8.3	9.6	14.4	7.1	7.1	10.3
11	Liberal Reich Party	7.9	0.8	–	–	–	–	–
7	National Liberals	32.7	39.0	32.2	24.9	11.8	12.8	24.9
13	Liberal Union	–	–	3.3	2.5	11.6	–	–
9	Progressive Party	12.0	12.3	8.8	6.5	15.1	–	–
1	Social Democrats	0.5	2.3	3.0	2.3	3.0	6.0	2.8
12	Alsatians	–	3.8	3.8	3.8	3.8	3.8	3.8
4	Danes	0.3	0.3	0.3	0.3	0.5	0.3	0.3
5	Guelph Party	2.4	1.0	1.0	2.5	2.5	2.8	1.0
3	Poles	3.4	3.5	3.5	3.5	4.5	4.0	3.3
14	Anti-Semites	–	–	–	–	–	–	0.3
15	Free Thinking Party	–	–	–	–	–	16.9	8.1
	Others	0.0	0.0	0.0	0.0	0.0	0.0	0.5

Table 8.7 GERMANY   Total Votes 1890–1912

	1890	1893	1898	1903	1907	1912
Valid Votes	10,145,900	10,628,300	11,441,100	12,531,200	13,352,900	14,441,400
Invalid Votes	7,228,500	7,674,000	7,752,700	9,489,000	11,253,400	12,207,500
Total Votes	33,100	28,300	34,000	44,800	50,100	53,100
Share Invalid	7,261,600	7,702,300	7,786,700	9,533,800	11,303,500	12,260,600
PARTY VOTES						
2 Centre Party	1,342,100	1,468,500	1,455,100	1,875,300	2,179,800	1,996,800
1 German Conservatives	895,100	1,038,300	859,200	948,500	1,060,200	1,126,300
10 German Peoples Party	147,600	166,800	108,500	91,200	138,600	–
8 German Reich Party	482,300	438,400	343,600	333,400	471,900	367,200
7 National Liberals	1,177,800	997,000	971,300	1,317,400	1,630,600	1,662,700
1 Social Democrats	1,427,300	1,786,700	2,107,100	3,010,800	3,259,000	4,250,400
2 Alsatians	101,100	114,700	107,400	101,900	103,600	162,000
4 Danes	13,700	14,400	15,400	14,800	15,400	17,300
5 Guelph Party	112,700	101,800	105,200	94,300	78,200	84,600
3 Poles	246,800	229,500	244,100	347,800	453,900	441,600
14 Anti-Semites	47,500	263,900	284,300	244,500	248,500	51,900
15 Free Thinking Party	1,159,900	–	–	–	–	–
16 Free Thinking Peoples Party	–	666,400	558,300	538,200	736,000	–
17 Free Thinking Union	–	258,500	195,700	243,200	359,300	–
18 Bavarian Farmers League	–	66,300	140,300	111,400	75,300	48,200
19 Farmers League	–	–	110,400	118,800	119,400	29,800
20 Economic Union	–	–	–	–	104,600	304,600
21 Progressive Peoples Party	–	–	–	–	–	1,497,000
Others	74,600	62,800	146,800	97,500	219,100	167,100

Source: Vogel et al., 1971 : 291-293

Table 8.8 GERMANY Percentage of Votes 1890–1912

	1890	1893	1898	1903	1907	1912
Valid Votes	71.2	72.2	67.8	75.7	84.3	84.5
Invalid Votes	0.3	0.3	0.3	0.4	0.4	0.4
Total Votes	71.6	72.5	68.1	76.1	84.7	84.9
Share Invalid	0.5	0.4	0.4	0.5	0.4	0.4
PARTY VOTES						
2 Centre Party	18.6	19.1	18.8	19.8	19.4	16.4
1 German Conservative	12.4	13.5	11.1	10.0	9.4	9.2
10 German Peoples Party	2.0	2.2	1.4	1.0	1.2	–
8 German Reich Party	6.7	5.7	4.4	3.5	4.2	3.0
7 National Liberals	16.3	13.0	12.5	13.9	14.5	13.6
1 Social Democrats	19.7	23.3	27.2	31.7	29.0	34.8
2 Alsatians	1.4	1.5	1.4	1.1	0.9	1.3
4 Danes	0.2	0.2	0.2	0.2	0.1	0.1
5 Guelph Party	1.6	1.3	1.4	1.0	0.7	0.7
3 Poles	3.4	3.0	3.1	3.7	4.0	3.6
14 Anti-Semites	0.7	3.4	3.7	2.6	2.2	0.5
15 Free Thinking Party	16.0	–	–	–	–	–
16 Free Thinking Peoples Party	–	8.7	7.2	5.7	6.5	–
17 Free Thinking Union	–	3.4	2.5	2.6	3.2	–
18 Bavarian Farmers League	–	0.9	1.8	1.2	0.7	0.4
19 Farmers League	–	–	1.4	1.3	1.1	0.2
20 Economic Union	–	–	–	–	0.9	2.5
21 Progressive Peoples Party	–	–	–	–	–	12.3
Others	1.0	0.8	1.9	1.0	1.9	1.4

Table 8.9 GERMANY   Number of Seats won in the Reichstag 1890–1912

		1890	1893	1898	1903	1907	1912
2	Centre Party	106	96	102	100	105	91
1	German Conservatives	73	72	56	54	60	43
10	German Peoples Party	10	11	8	6	7	–
8	German Reich Party	20	28	23	21	24	14
7	National Liberals	42	53	46	51	54	45
1	Social Democrats	35	44	56	81	43	110
12	Alsatians	10	8	10	9	7	9
4	Danes	1	1	1	1	1	1
5	Guelph Party	11	7	9	6	1	5
3	Poles	16	19	14	16	20	18
14	Anti-Semites	5	16	13	11	16	3
15	Free Thinking Party	66	–	–	–	–	–
16	Free Thinking Peoples Party	–	24	29	21	28	–
17	Free Thinking Union	–	13	12	9	14	–
18	Bavarian Farmers League	–	4	5	4	1	2
19	Farmers League	–	–	–	4	8	2
20	Economic Union	–	–	–	–	5	10
21	Progressive Peoples Party	–	–	–	–	–	42
	Others	2	1	7	3	3	2
	Total Seats	397	397	397	397	397	397

Source: Vogel *et al.*, 1971 : 291-293

Table 8.10 GERMANY   Percentage of Seats won in the Reichstag 1890–1912

	1890	1893	1898	1903	1907	1912
2 Centre Party	26.7	24.2	25.7	25.2	26.4	22.9
1 German Conservatives	18.4	18.1	14.1	13.6	15.1	10.8
10 German Peoples Party	2.5	2.8	2.0	1.5	1.8	–
8 German Reich Party	5.0	7.1	5.8	5.3	6.0	3.5
7 National Liberals	10.6	13.4	11.6	12.8	13.6	11.3
1 Social Democrats	8.8	11.1	14.1	20.4	10.8	27.7
12 Alsatians	2.5	2.0	2.5	2.3	1.8	2.3
4 Danes	0.3	0.3	0.3	0.3	0.3	0.3
5 Guelph Party	2.8	1.8	2.3	1.5	0.3	1.3
3 Poles	4.0	4.8	3.5	4.0	5.0	4.5
14 Anti-Semites	1.3	4.0	3.3	2.8	4.0	0.8
15 Free Thinking Party	16.6	–	–	–	–	–
16 Free Thinking Peoples Party	–	6.0	7.3	5.3	7.1	–
17 Free Thinking Union	–	3.3	3.0	2.3	3.5	–
18 Bavarian Farmers League	–	1.0	1.3	1.0	0.3	0.5
19 Farmers League	–	–	1.5	1.0	2.0	0.5
20 Economic Union	–	–	–	–	1.3	2.5
21 Progressive Peoples Party	–	–	–	–	–	10.6
Others	0.5	0.3	1.8	0.8	0.8	0.5

Table 8.11 GERMANY Total Votes 1918—1933

	1919[1]	1920[3]	1924 (May)	1924 (Dec.)	1928	1930	1932 (July)	1932 (Nov.)	1933[4]
Electorate	37,362,100	35,949,800	38,374,400	38,987,400	41,224,700	42,957,700	44,211,200	44,374,100	44,664,800
Valid Votes	30,400,300	28,196,300	29,281,800	30,311,900	30,753,200	34,960,900	36,882,400	35,470,800	39,343,300
Invalid Votes	124,500	267,300	427,600	391,700	412,600	264,900	279,700	287,500	315,000
Total Votes	30,524,800	28,463,600	29,709,400	30,703,600	31,165,800	35,225,800	37,162,100	35,758,300	39,658,300
PARTY VOTES									
2 Centre Party	5,760,900	3,845,000	3,914,400	4,120,900	3,712,200	4,127,900	4,589,400	4,230,500	4,425,000
1 Social Democrats	11,509,000	6,104,400	6,008,900	7,886,300	9,152,900	8,577,700	7,959,700	7,247,900	7,181,300
25 German Democratic Party	5,641,800	2,333,700	1,655,100	1,921,300	1,505,700	1,322,400	371,800	336,400	334,300
23 German Nat. Peoples Party	3,121,500	4,249,100	5,696,500	6,209,200	4,381,600	2,458,200	2,177,400	2,959,100	3,136,900
24 German Peoples Party	1,345,600	3,919,400	2,694,400	3,051,300	2,679,700	1,578,200	436,000	660,900	432,200
27 Hanoverian Party	296,100[2]	319,100	319,800	262,800	195,600	144,300	46,900	63,900	47,700
22 Ind. Social Democrats	2,317,300	5,046,800	235,100	99,200	20,800	11,900	–	–	–
26 Middle Class Party	275,800	218,600	693,600	1,006,300	1,397,100	1,362,300	146,900	110,300	–
29 Bavarian Peoples Party	–	1,238,600	946,600	1,135,100	945,600	1,059,100	1,192,700	1,095,400	1,073,600
28 Communist Party	–	589,500	3,693,300	2,711,800	3,264,800	4,592,100	5,355,300	5,980,200	4,847,900
31 Land League	–	–	574,900	499,600	199,500	193,900	96,900	105,200	83,800
30 National Socialists/Nazi Party	–	–	1,918,300	907,900	810,100	6,409,600	13,745,700	11,737,000	17,277,300
33 Farmers Party	–	–	–	–	481,300	339,600	137,100	149,000	114,100
32 Peoples Land Party	–	–	–	–	581,800	1,108,700	90,600	46,400	–
34 Peoples Rights Party	–	–	–	–	483,200	271,400	40,800	46,200	–
35 Christian Peoples Service	–	–	–	–	–	870,100	364,500	403,700	383,900
Others	131,800	332,100	930,800	500,100	941,300	532,800	130,700	298,500	5,000

[1] Elections to the Constituent Assembly.
[2] Includes votes cast for a joint list with the Christliche Volkspartei.
[3] Includes elections held in East Prussia and Schleswig Holstein on 20 February 1921 and in Oppeln, Silesia, on 19 November 1922. Elections were postponed in these areas pending referenda on whether they wished to be part of Germany.
[4] This election was held after Hitler became Chancellor in January 1933.

Table 8.12 GERMANY   Percentage of Votes 1918–1933

	1919	1920	1924 (May)	1924 (Dec.)	1928	1930	1932 (July)	1932 (Nov.)	1933
Valid Votes	81.4	78.4	76.3	77.7	74.6	81.4	83.4	79.9	88.1
Invalid Votes	0.3	0.7	1.1	1.0	1.0	0.6	0.6	0.6	0.7
Total Votes	81.7	79.2	77.4	78.8	75.6	82.0	84.1	80.6	88.8
Share Invalid	0.4	0.9	1.4	1.3	1.3	0.8	0.8	0.8	0.8
PARTY VOTES									
2 Centre Party	19.0	13.6	13.4	13.6	12.1	11.8	12.4	11.9	11.2
1 Social Democrats	37.9	21.6	20.5	26.0	29.8	24.5	21.6	20.4	18.3
25 German Democratic Party	18.6	8.3	5.7	6.3	4.9	3.8	1.0	0.9	0.8
23 German National Peoples Party	10.3	15.1	19.5	20.5	14.2	7.0	5.9	8.3	8.0
24 German Peoples Party	4.4	13.9	9.2	10.1	8.7	4.5	1.2	1.9	1.1
27 Hanoverian Party	1.0	1.1	1.1	0.9	0.6	0.4	0.1	0.2	0.1
22 Independent Social Democrats	7.6	17.9	0.8	0.3	0.1	0.0	–	–	–
26 Middle Class Party	0.9	0.8	2.4	3.3	4.5	3.9	0.4	0.3	–
29 Bavarian Peoples Party	–	4.4	3.2	3.7	3.1	3.0	3.2	3.1	2.7
28 Communist Party	–	2.1	12.6	8.9	10.6	13.1	14.5	16.9	12.3
31 Land League	–	–	2.0	1.6	0.6	0.6	0.3	0.3	0.2
30 National Socialists/Nazi Party	–	–	6.6	3.0	2.6	18.3	37.3	33.1	43.9
33 Farmers Party	–	–	–	–	1.6	1.0	0.4	0.4	0.3
32 Peoples Land Party	–	–	–	–	1.9	3.2	0.2	0.1	–
34 Peoples Rights Party	–	–	–	–	1.6	0.8	0.1	0.1	–
35 Christian Peoples Service	–	–	–	–	–	2.5	1.0	1.1	1.0
Others	0.4	1.2	3.2	1.6	3.1	1.5	0.4	0.8	0.0

Source: Vogel et al., 1971 : 296-297

Table 8.13   GERMANY   Number of Seats Won in the Reichstag 1918–1933

		1919	1920	1924 (May)	1924 (Dec.)	1928	1930	1932 (July)	1932 (Nov.)	1933
2	Centre Party	91	64	65	69	62	68	75	70	74
1	Social Democrats	163	102	100	131	153	143	133	121	120
25	German Democratic Party	75	39	28	32	25	20	4	2	5
23	German National Peoples Party	44	71	95	103	73	41	37	52	52
24	German Peoples Party	19	65	45	51	45	30	7	11	2
27	Hanoverian Party	1	5	5	4	3	3	0	1	0
22	Independent Social Democrats	22	84	0	0	0	0	–	–	–
26	Middle Class Party	4	4	10	17	23	23	2	1	–
29	Bavarian Peoples Party	–	21	16	19	16	19	22	20	18
28	Communist Party	–	4	62	45	54	77	89	100	81
31	Land League	–	–	10	8	3	3	2	2	1
30	National Socialists/Nazi Party	–	–	32	14	12	107	230	196	288
33	Farmers Party	–	–	–	–	8	6	2	3	2
32	Peoples Land Party	–	–	–	–	10	19	1	0	–
34	Peoples Rights Party	–	–	–	–	2	0	1	0	–
35	Christian Peoples Service	–	–	–	–	–	14	3	5	4
	Others	2	0	4	0	2	4	0	0	0
	Total Seats	421	459	472	493	491	577	608	584	647

Source: Vogel et al., 1971 : 296-297

Table 8.14   GERMANY   Percentage of Seats Won in the Reichstag 1918–1933

		1919	1920	1924 (May)	1924 (Dec.)	1928	1930	1932 (July)	1932 (Nov.)	1933
2	Centre Party	21.6	13.9	13.8	14.0	12.6	11.8	12.3	12.0	11.4
1	Social Democrats	38.7	22.2	21.2	26.6	31.2	24.8	21.9	20.7	18.5
25	German Democratic Party	17.8	8.5	5.9	6.5	5.1	3.5	0.7	0.3	0.8
23	German National Peoples Party	10.5	15.5	20.1	20.9	14.9	7.1	6.1	8.9	8.0
24	German Peoples Party	4.5	14.2	9.5	10.3	9.2	5.2	1.2	1.9	0.3
27	Hanoverian Party	0.2	1.1	1.1	0.8	0.5	0.5	0.0	0.2	0.0
22	Independent Social Democrats	5.2	18.3	0.0	0.0	0.0	0.0	–	–	–
26	Middle Class Party	1.0	0.9	2.1	3.4	4.7	4.0	0.3	0.2	–
29	Bavarian Peoples Party	–	4.6	3.4	3.9	3.3	3.3	3.6	3.4	2.8
28	Communist Party	–	0.9	13.1	9.1	11.0	13.3	14.6	17.1	12.5
31	Land League	–	–	2.1	1.6	0.6	0.5	0.3	0.3	0.2
30	National Socialists/Nazi Party	–	–	6.8	2.8	2.4	18.5	37.8	33.6	44.5
33	Farmers Party	–	–	–	–	1.6	1.0	0.3	0.5	0.3
32	Peoples Land Party	–	–	–	–	2.0	3.3	0.2	0.0	–
34	Peoples Rights Party	–	–	–	–	0.4	0.0	0.2	0.0	–
35	Christian Peoples Service	–	–	–	–	–	2.4	0.5	0.9	0.6
	Others	0.5	0.0	0.8	0.0	0.4	0.7	0.0	0.0	0.0

Table 8.15   GERMANY   Total Votes (Territory of the Federal Republic only) 1919—1933

	1919	1920	1924 (May)	1924 (Dec.)	1928	1930	1932 (July)	1932 (Nov.)	1933
Valid Votes	16,471,992	15,520,920	16,013,107	16,688,377	16,875,044	19,569,100	20,832,021	19,868,144	22,238,560
PARTY VOTES									
2 Centre Party	4,610,370	3,173,451	3,158,552	3,310,902	2,964,017	3,301,679	3,674,187	3,366,488	3,515,537
1 Social Democrats	5,828,347	3,275,754	2,987,776	3,919,780	4,539,569	4,291,604	3,984,743	3,584,321	3,665,721
25 German Democratic Party	2,659,923	1,275,300	877,509	1,031,367	804,872	771,046	210,317	199,248	178,100
23 German Nat. Peoples Party	975,381	1,643,143	2,098,777	2,469,717	1,649,902	787,812	965,812	1,310,275	1,363,023
24 German Peoples Party	1,004,518	1,924,636	1,429,083	1,637,398	1,471,204	898,039	254,428	393,763	256,862
27 Hanoverian Party	296,076	318,858	311,546	262,132	195,266	166,573	46,927	63,219	47,133
22 Ind. Social Democrats	703,353	2,138,870	112,310	60,221	9,792	4,731	–	–	–
29 Bavarian Peoples Party	–	1,173,344	946,648	1,135,131	945,844	1,059,141	1,192,684	1,094,597	1,073,551
28 Communist Party	–	276,187	1,934,443	1,317,119	1,449,936	2,185,888	2,699,387	3,044,781	2,409,636
30 National Socialists/Nazi Party	–	–	1,048,472	441,437	641,446	3,429,321	7,186,582	6,132,403	9,283,370
35 Christian Peoples Service	–	–	–	–	–	576,241	273,545	306,090	251,293
Others[1]	393,024	321,377	1,107,991	1,101,173	2,203,206	2,097,025	343,894	372,959	194,334

[1] Includes the Land League, the Farmers Party, the Peoples Land Party and the Peoples Rights Party.

Source: Sanger and Liepelt, 1965 : 3.31.

160

Table 8.16 GERMANY   Percentage of Votes (Territory of the Federal Republic only) 1919—1933

		1919	1920	1924 (May)	1924 (Dec.)	1928	1930	1932 (July)	1932 (Nov.)	1933
2	Centre Party	27.9	20.4	19.7	19.8	17.6	16.9	17.7	17.0	15.8
1	Social Democrats	35.4	21.1	18.7	23.5	26.9	21.9	19.1	18.0	16.5
25	German Democratic Party	16.2	8.2	5.5	6.2	4.8	3.9	1.0	1.0	0.8
23	German National Peoples Party	5.9	10.5	13.0	14.8	9.8	4.0	4.6	6.6	6.1
24	German Peoples Party	6.1	12.4	8.9	9.8	8.7	4.6	1.2	2.0	1.2
27	Hanoverian Party	1.8	2.1	1.9	1.6	1.1	0.9	0.2	0.3	0.2
22	Independent Social Democrats	4.3	13.8	0.8	0.4	0.0	0.0	–	–	–
29	Bavarian Peoples Party	–	7.6	5.9	6.8	5.6	5.4	5.7	5.5	4.8
28	Communist Party	–	1.8	12.1	7.9	8.6	11.2	13.0	15.3	10.8
30	National Socialists/Nazi Party	–	–	6.5	2.6	3.3	17.5	34.5	30.9	41.8
35	Christian Peoples Service	–	–	–	–	–	3.0	1.3	1.5	1.1
	Others	2.4	2.1	6.9	6.6	13.6	10.7	1.7	1.9	0.9

Table 8.17 GERMANY   Total Votes 1949–1972[1]

	1949	1953	1957	1961	1965	1969	1972
Electorate	31,207,620	33,202,287	35,400,923	37,440,715	38,510,395	38,677,325	41,446,302
Valid Votes	23,732,398	27,551,272	29,905,428	31,550,901	32,620,442	32,966,024	37,459,750
Invalid Votes	763,216	928,278	1,167,466	1,298,723	795,765	557,040	301,839
Total Votes	24,495,614	28,479,550	31,072,894	32,849,624	33,416,207	33,523,064	37,761,589

PARTY VOTES

	1949	1953	1957	1961	1965	1969	1972
1 Social Democrats	6,934,975	7,944,943	9,495,571	11,427,355	12,813,186	14,065,716	17,175,169
28 Communist Party	1,361,706	607,860	–	–	–	49,694	113,891
39 Bavarian Party	986,478	465,641	–	–	–	15,933	–
2 Centre Party	727,505	217,078	–	–	–	–	–
36 Christian Democratic Union[2]	7,359,084	12,443,981	15,008,399	14,298,372	15,524,068	15,195,187	16,806,020
40 Economic Reconstruction League	681,888	–	–	–	–	–	–
37 Free Democrats	2,829,920	2,629,163	2,307,135	4,028,766	3,096,739	1,903,422	3,129,982
38 German Party	939,934	896,128	1,007,282	–	–	–	–
42 German Reich Party	429,031	295,739	308,564	262,977	–	–	–
41 South Schleswig Voters League	75,388	44,585	32,262	25,449	–	–	–
44 Refugee Party	–	1,616,953	1,374,066	–	–	–	–
43 All-German Peoples Party	–	318,475	–	–	–	–	–
45 Federal Union	–	–	254,322	–	–	–	–
46 German Freedom Union	–	–	–	609,918	434,182	–	–
47 All-German Party	–	–	–	870,756	–	–	–
48 National Democratic Party	–	–	–	–	664,193	1,422,010	207,465
49 Action for Democratic Progress	–	–	–	–	–	197,331	–
Others	1,406,489	70,726	117,827	27,308	88,074	71,330	27,223

[1] West Berlin does not participate in federal elections.
[2] Includes the Christian Social Union.

Table 8.18 GERMANY Percentage of Votes 1949—1972

	1949	1953	1957	1961	1965	1969	1972
Valid Votes	76.0	83.0	84.5	84.3	84.7	85.2	90.4
Invalid Votes	2.4	2.8	3.3	3.5	2.1	1.4	0.7
Total Votes	78.5	85.8	87.8	87.7	86.8	86.7	91.1
Share Invalid	3.1	3.3	3.8	4.0	2.4	1.7	0.8
PARTY VOTES							
1 Social Democrats	29.2	28.8	31.8	36.2	39.3	42.7	45.8
28 Communist Party	5.7	2.2	–	–	–	–	0.3
39 Bavarian Party	4.2	1.7	–	–	–	0.2	–
2 Centre Party	3.1	0.8	–	–	–	0.0	–
36 Christian Democratic Union	31.0	45.2	50.2	45.3	47.6	46.1	44.9
40 Economic Reconstruction League	2.9	–	–	–	–	–	–
37 Free Democrats	11.9	9.5	7.7	12.8	9.5	5.8	8.4
38 German Party	4.0	3.3	3.4	–	–	–	–
42 German Reich Party	1.8	1.1	1.0	0.8	–	–	–
41 South Schleswig Voters League	0.3	0.2	0.1	0.1	–	–	–
44 Refugee Party	–	5.9	4.6	–	–	–	–
43 All-German Peoples Party	–	1.2	–	–	–	–	–
45 Federal Union	–	–	0.9	–	–	–	–
46 German Freedom Union	–	–	–	1.9	1.3	0.1	–
47 All-German Party	–	–	–	2.8	–	–	–
48 National Democratic Party	–	–	–	–	2.0	4.3	0.6
49 Action for Democratic Progress	–	–	–	–	–	0.6	–
Others	5.9	0.3	0.4	0.1	0.3	0.2	0.1

Source: Statistisches Bundesamt, 1965 : 6-10; *ibid.*, 1972 : 4-5

Table 8.19 GERMANY — Number of Seats Won in the Bundestag 1949–1972[1]

		1949	1953	1957	1961	1965	1969	1972
1	Social Democrats	131	151	169	190	202	224	230
28	Communist Party	15	0	–	–	–	–	0
39	Bavarian Party	17	0	–	–	–	0	–
2	Centre Party	10	3	–	–	–	0	–
36	Christian Democratic Union[2]	139	243	270	242	245	242	225
40	Economic Reconstruction League	12	–	–	–	–	–	–
37	Free Democrats	52	48	41	67	49	30	41
38	German Party	17	15	17	–	–	–	–
42	German Reich Party	5	0	0	0	–	–	–
41	South Schleswig Voters League	1	0	0	0	–	–	–
44	Refugee Party	–	27	0	–	–	–	–
43	All-German Peoples Party	–	0	–	–	–	–	–
45	Federal Union	–	–	0	0	0	–	–
46	German Freedom Union	–	–	–	0	–	0	–
47	All-German Party	–	–	–	–	–	0	–
48	National Democratic Party	–	–	–	0	0	0	0
49	Action for Democratic Progress	–	–	–	–	–	0	–
	Others	3	0	0	0	0	0	0
	Total Seats	**402**	**487**	**497**	**499**	**496**	**496**	**496**

[1] Excluding the non-voting representatives of West Berlin.
[2] Includes the Christian Social Union.

Sources: Vogel et al., 1971: 306-308; Statistisches Bundesamt, 1972 : 26.

Table 8.20 GERMANY Percentage of Seats Won in the Bundestag 1949–1972

		1949	1953	1957	1961	1965	1969	1972
1	Social Democrats	32.6	31.0	34.0	38.1	40.7	45.2	46.4
28	Communist Party	3.7	0.0	–	–	–	–	0.0
39	Bavarian Party	4.2	0.0	–	–	–	0.0	–
2	Centre Party	2.5	0.6	–	–	–	0.0	–
36	Christian Democratic Union	34.6	49.9	54.3	48.5	49.4	48.8	45.4
40	Economic Reconstruction League	3.0	–	–	–	–	–	–
37	Free Democrats	12.9	9.9	8.2	13.4	9.9	6.0	8.3
38	German Party	4.2	3.1	3.4	–	–	–	–
42	German Reich Party	1.2	0.0	0.0	0.0	–	–	–
41	South Schleswig Voters League	0.2	0.0	0.0	0.0	–	–	–
44	Refugee Party	–	5.5	0.0	–	–	–	–
43	All-German Peoples Party	–	0.0	–	–	–	–	–
45	Federal Union	–	–	0.0	–	–	–	–
46	German Freedom Union	–	–	–	0.0	0.0	–	–
47	All-German Party	–	–	–	0.0	–	0.0	–
48	National Democratic Party	–	–	–	–	0.0	0.0	0.0
49	Action for Democratic Progress	–	–	–	–	–	0.0	–
	Others	0.7	0.0	0.0	0.0	0.0	0.0	0.0

Chapter 9
ICELAND

Organized political groups began to compete in Icelandic elections in 1897. They reflected major differences within the country about its future constitutional relations with Denmark. But these groups lacked stability and cohesion (Grimsson, 1970: 272-273). The establishment of the Progressive and Social Democratic parties in 1916 marked the beginning of an effective party system in Iceland. No figures on party divisions are given in official sources before the election of that year.

The Constitutional Law of 1915 provided for direct and secret elections to the Althingi by universal adult suffrage. Six members, the landskjör, were elected by the country as a whole for a twelve year period, half of them being up for election every six years. The landskjör were elected by proportional representation, using the d'Hondt method; 34 members were elected by plurality, 18 in two-member and the remainder in single-member constituencies. The landskjör and eight of the constituency members formed the upper house of the parliament. All citizens over 25 who were not in receipt of communal assistance were entitled to vote for the constituency representatives; for the elections of the landskjör the minimum age was 35. In 1920 the term of office of the landskjör was reduced to eight years and the number of constituency representatives increased to 36. Of these, four were elected by proportional representation in the capital, Reykjavik, and the remainder by plurality, 12 in two-member and the remainder in single-member constituencies.

In 1934 the landskjör were abolished. Since then one third of the Althingi have been chosen by the Parliament as a whole to form the upper house. Persons in receipt of public assistance were enfranchised and the voting age was reduced to 21. Eleven additional seats were created in order to achieve greater proportionality. They were to be allotted to the parties which had the highest average ratio of votes to representatives. In order to be included in this division a party must already have won at least one constituency seat.

In 1942 the number of seats in the Althingi was increased to 52. Of these 20 were elected by proportional representation, eight in the capital and 12 in two-member constituencies, 21 were elected by plurality in single-member constituencies and the 11 additional seats were distributed as before. In 1959 proportional representation was introduced in all constituencies. The 11 additional seats were retained. Twelve representatives are elected in the capital, which forms a single constituency, 25 in five-member and 12 in six-member constituencies.

Sources:

Central Bureau of Statistics, *Althingiskosningar,* 1949ff (Reykjavik, 1950ff).

Central Bureau of Statistics, *Statistical Abstract of Iceland, 1967*
(Reykjavik, 1967).

Grimsson, O.R., "Iceland" in S. Rokkan and J. Meyriat (eds.) *International
Guide to Electoral Statistics* (Paris: Mouton, 1969) pp. 183-194.

Grimsson, O.R., *Political Power in Iceland prior to the Period of Class Politics,
1845–1918* (University of Manchester, PhD Thesis, 1970).

Table 9.1
POLITICAL PARTIES IN ICELAND SINCE 1916

	Party Names	Elections contested	Number contested
1	Home Rule Party (Heimastjórnarmenn)	1916-1919	2
2	Independence Party I (Sjálfstaedisflokkur)	1916-1919	2
3	Hardline Independence Party (Sjálfstaedis-flokkur 'thversum')	1916	1
4	Moderate Independence Party (Sjálfstaedis-flokkur 'langsum')	1916	1
5	Social Democrats (Althýduflokkur)	1916ff	19
6	Farmers Party I (Baendaflokkur)	1916	1
7	Independent Farmers Party (Óhádir Baendur)	1916	1
8	Progressive Party (Framsóknarflokkur)	1919ff	18
9	Citizens Party (Borgaraflokkur)	1923	1
10	Liberal Party (Frjálslyndi Flokkurinn)	1927	1
11	Conservative Party (Íhaldsflokkur)	1927	1
12	Independence Party II (Sjálfstaedisflokkur)[1]	1931ff	15
13	Farmers Party II (Baendaflokkur)	1934-1937	2
14	Communist Party (Kommúnistaflokkur)[2]; latterly United Socialist Party and Peoples Alliance[2]	1931ff	15
15	Commonwealth Party (Thjodveldismenn)	1942	2
16	Republic Party (Lýdveldisflokkur)	1953	
17	National Preservation Party (Thjodvarnar-flokkur)	1953-1959	4
18	Independent Democratic Party (Ohádi Lýdraedisflokkurin)	1967	1
19	Union of Liberals and Leftists (Samtök Frjálslyndra og Vinstri Manna)[3]	1967ff	2
20	Independent Party (Frambodsflokkur)	1971	1

[1] A merger of the Liberal and Conservative Parties.

[2] In 1938 the Communist Party merged with a Social Democrat splinter group to form the United Socialist Party (Sosialistaflokkur). in 1956 the Peoples Alliance (Althýdubandalag) was formed by the United Socialist Party and some Social Democrats.

[3] In 1967 a dissident Peoples Alliance list led by Hannibal Valdermarsson, who formed the Union of Liberals and Leftists in 1970.

Table 9.2
DATES OF ELECTIONS TO THE ALTHINGI 1916–1971

1.	21 October 1916	11.	30 June 1946
2.	15 November 1919	12.	23 October 1949
3.	27 October 1923	13.	28 June 1953
4.	9 July 1927	14.	24 June 1956
5.	12 June 1931	15.	28 June 1959
6.	16 July 1933	16.	25 October 1959
7.	24 June 1934	17.	9 June 1963
8.	20 June 1937	18.	11 June 1967
9.	5 July 1942	19.	13 June 1971
10.	18 October 1942		

Sources: *Althingiskosningar 1969* and *1971; Statistical Abstract of Iceland,* 1967: 340-341.

Table 9.3 ICELAND Total Votes 1916–1942

	1916	1919	1923	1927	1931	1933	1934	1937	1942 (July)	1942 (Oct.)
Electorate	28,529	31,870	43,932	46,047	50,617	52,465	64,338	67,195	73,440	73,560
Valid Votes	13,350	14,035	30,362	32,009	38,544	35,680	51,929	58,415	58,131	59,668
Invalid Votes	680	429	784	919	1,064	1,091	516	681	809	908
Total Votes	14,030	14,464	31,146	32,928	39,608	36,771	52,445	59,096	58,940	60,576
PARTY VOTES										
1 Home-Rule Party	5,333	4,120	–	–	–	–	–	–	–	–
2 Independence Party I	1,014	1,563	–	–	–	–	–	–	–	–
3 Hardline Independence Party	2,097	–	–	–	–	–	–	–	–	–
4 Moderate Independence Party	938	–	–	–	–	–	–	–	–	–
6 Farmers Party I	1,173	–	–	–	–	–	–	–	–	–
7 Independent Farmers Party	554	–	–	–	–	–	–	–	–	–
5 Social Democrats	903	949	4,912	6,097	6,197	6,864	11,269	11,084	8,979	8,455
8 Progressive Party	–	1,873	8,062	9,532	13,844	8,530	11,377	14,556	16,033	15,869
9 Citizens Party	–	–	16,272	–	–	–	–	–	–	–
11 Conservative Party	–	–	–	13,616	–	–	–	–	–	–
12 Independence Party II	–	–	–	–	16,891	17,131	21,974	24,132	22,975	23,001
10 Liberal Party	–	–	–	1,858	–	–	–	–	–	–
14 Communist Party/United Socialist Party	–	–	–	–	1,165	2,673	3,098	4,932	9,423	11,059
13 Farmers Party II	–	–	–	–	–	–	3,348	3,578	–	–
15 Commonwealth Party	–	–	–	–	–	–	862	–	618	–
Others	1,336	5,528	1,115	904	446	480	862	131	103	1,284

Sources: *Statistical Abstract of Iceland, 1967* : 340-341; *Althingiskosningar, 1949* : 5, 12.

Table 9.4   ICELAND   Percentage of Votes 1916–1942

	1916	1919	1923	1927	1931	1933	1934	1937	1942 (July)	1942 (Oct.)
Valid Votes	46.8	44.0	69.1	69.5	76.1	68.0	80.7	86.9	79.2	81.1
Invalid Votes	2.4	1.3	1.8	2.0	2.1	2.1	0.8	1.0	1.1	1.2
Total Votes	49.2	45.4	70.9	71.5	78.3	70.1	81.5	87.9	80.3	82.3
Share Invalid	4.8	3.0	2.5	2.8	2.7	3.0	1.0	1.2	1.4	1.5

PARTY VOTES

	1916	1919	1923	1927	1931	1933	1934	1937	1942 (July)	1942 (Oct.)
1 Home-Rule Party	40.0	29.4	–	–	–	–	–	–	–	–
2 Independence Party I	7.6	11.1	–	–	–	–	–	–	–	–
3 Hardline Independence Party	15.7	–	–	–	–	–	–	–	–	–
4 Moderate Independence Party	7.0	–	–	–	–	–	–	–	–	–
6 Farmers Party I	8.8	–	–	–	–	–	–	–	–	–
7 Independent Farmers Party	4.2	–	–	–	–	–	–	–	–	–
5 Social Democrats	6.8	6.8	16.2	19.0	16.1	19.2	21.7	19.0	15.4	14.2
8 Progressive Party	–	13.3	26.6	29.8	35.9	23.9	21.9	24.9	27.6	26.6
9 Citizens Party	–	–	53.6	–	–	–	–	–	–	–
11 Conservative Party	–	–	–	42.5	–	–	–	–	–	–
12 Independence Party II	–	–	–	–	43.8	48.0	42.3	41.3	39.5	38.5
10 Liberal Party	–	–	–	5.8	–	–	–	–	–	–
14 Communist Party/United Socialist Party	–	–	–	–	3.0	7.5	6.0	8.4	16.2	18.5
13 Farmers Party II	–	–	–	–	–	–	6.4	6.1	–	–
15 Commonwealth Party	–	–	–	–	–	–	–	–	1.1	2.2
Others	10.0	39.4	3.7	2.8	1.2	1.3	1.7	0.2	0.2	–

Table 9.5 ICELAND Number of Seats Won in the Althingi 1916—1942

	1916	1919	1923	1927	1931	1933	1934	1937	1942 (July)	1942 (Oct.)
1 Home-Rule Party	12	9	—	—	—	—	—	—	—	—
2 Independence Party I	3	7	—	—	—	—	—	—	—	—
3 Hardline Independence Party	7	—	—	—	—	—	—	—	—	—
4 Moderate Independence Party	3	—	—	—	—	—	—	—	—	—
6 Farmers Party I	5	—	—	—	—	—	—	—	—	—
7 Independent Farmers Party	1	—	—	—	—	—	—	—	—	—
5 Social Democrats	1	0	1	4	3	4	10	8	6	7
8 Progressive Party	—	6	13	17	21	14	15	19	20	15
9 Citizens Party	—	—	21	—	—	—	—	—	—	—
11 Conservative Party	—	—	—	13	—	—	—	—	—	—
12 Independence Party II	—	—	—	—	12	17	20	17	17	20
10 Liberal Party	—	—	1	1	0	—	—	—	—	—
14 Communist Party/United Socialist Party	—	—	—	—	0	0	0	3	6	10
13 Farmers Party II	—	—	—	—	—	—	3	2	0	—
15 Commonwealth Party	—	—	—	—	—	—	1	0	0	0
Others[1]	2	12	—	1	—	1	—	—	—	—
Total Seats	**34**	**34**	**36**	**36**	**36**	**36**	**49**	**49**	**49**	**52**

[1] All non-party.

Source: *Statistical Abstract of Iceland, 1967 : 340-341*

Table 9.6   ICELAND   Percentage of Seats Won in the Althingi 1916—1942

	1916	1919	1923	1927	1931	1933	1934	1937	1942 (July)	1942 (Oct.)
1 Home-Rule Party	35.3	26.5	—	—	—	—	—	—	—	—
2 Independence Party I	8.8	20.6	—	—	—	—	—	—	—	—
3 Hardline Independence Party	20.6	—	—	—	—	—	—	—	—	—
4 Moderate Independence Party	8.8	—	—	—	—	—	—	—	—	—
6 Farmers Party I	14.7	—	—	—	—	—	—	—	—	—
7 Independent Farmers Party	2.9	—	—	—	—	—	—	—	—	—
5 Social Democrats	2.9	0.0	2.8	11.1	8.3	11.1	20.4	16.3	12.2	13.5
8 Progressive Party	—	17.6	36.1	47.2	58.3	38.9	30.6	38.8	40.8	28.8
9 Citizens Party	—	—	58.3	—	—	—	—	—	—	—
11 Conservative Party	—	—	—	36.1	—	—	—	—	—	—
12 Independence Party II	—	—	—	—	33.3	47.2	40.8	34.7	34.7	38.5
10 Liberal Party	—	—	—	2.8	—	—	—	—	—	—
14 Communist Party/United Socialist Party	—	—	—	—	0.0	0.0	0.0	6.1	12.2	19.2
13 Farmers Party II	—	—	—	—	—	—	6.1	4.1	—	—
15 Commonwealth Party	—	—	—	—	0.0	—	—	0.0	0.0	0.0
Others	5.9	35.3	2.8	2.8	0.0	2.8	2.0	0.0	0.0	—

Table 9.7 ICELAND   Total Votes 1946–1971

	1946	1949	1953	1956	1959 (June)	1959 (Oct.)	1963	1967	1971
Electorate	77,670	82,481	87,601	91,618	95,050	95,637	99,798	107,101	118,289
Valid Votes	66,913	72,219	77,410	82,678	84,788	85,095	89,352	96,090	105,395
Invalid Votes	982	1,213	1,344	1,677	1,359	1,331	1,606	1,765	1,580
Total Votes	67,895	73,432	78,754	84,355	86,147	86,426	90,958	97,855	106,975
PARTY VOTES									
5 Social Democrats	11,914	11,937	12,093	15,153	10,632	12,909	12,697	15,059	11,020
8 Progressive Party	15,429	17,659	16,959	12,925	23,061	21,882	25,217	27,029	26,645
12 Independence Party II	26,428	28,546	28,738	35,027	36,029	33,800	37,021	36,036	38,170
14 United Socialist Party/ Peoples Alliance	13,049	14,077	12,422	15,859	12,929	13,621	14,274	13,403	18,055
17 National Preservation Party	–	–	4,667	3,706	2,137	2,883	–	–	–
16 Republic Party	–	–	2,531	–	–	–	–	–	–
18 Independent Democratic Party	–	–	–	–	–	–	–	1,043	–
19 Union of Liberals and Leftists	–	–	–	–	–	–	–	3,520	9,395
20 Independent Party	–	–	–	–	–	–	–	–	2,110
Others	93	–	–	8	–	–	143	–	–

Sources: *Statistical Abstract of Iceland, 1967* : 340–341; *Althingiskosningar*, 1949ff.

Table 9.8   ICELAND   Percentage of Votes 1946—1971

	1946	1949	1953	1956	1959 (June)	1959 (Oct.)	1963	1967	1971
Valid Votes	86.2	87.6	88.4	90.2	89.2	89.0	89.5	89.7	89.1
Invalid Votes	1.3	1.5	1.5	1.8	1.4	1.4	1.6	1.6	1.3
Total Votes	87.4	89.0	89.9	92.1	90.6	90.4	91.1	91.4	90.4
Share Invalid	1.4	1.7	1.7	2.0	1.6	1.5	1.8	1.8	1.5
PARTY VOTES									
5 Social Democrats	17.8	16.5	15.6	18.3	12.5	15.2	14.2	15.7	10.5
8 Progressive Party	23.1	24.5	21.9	15.6	27.2	25.7	28.2	28.1	25.3
12 Independence Party II	39.5	39.5	37.1	42.4	42.5	39.7	41.4	37.5	36.2
14 United Socialist Party/ Peoples Alliance	19.5	19.5	16.0	19.2	15.2	16.0	16.0	13.9	17.1
17 National Preservation Party	–	–	6.0	4.5	2.5	3.4	–	–	–
16 Republic Party	–	–	3.3	–	–	–	–	–	–
18 Independent Democratic Party	–	–	–	–	–	–	–	1.1	–
19 Union of Liberals and Leftists	–	–	–	–	–	–	–	3.7	8.9
20 Independent Party	–	–	–	–	–	–	–	–	2.0
Others	0.1	–	–	0.0	–	–	0.2	–	–

Table 9.9   ICELAND   Number of Seats Won in the Althingi 1946—1971

	1946	1949	1953	1956	1959 (June)	1959 (Oct.)	1963	1967	1971
5 Social Democrats	9	7	6	8	6	9	8	9	6
8 Progressive Party	13	17	16	17	19	17	19	18	17
12 Independence Party II	20	19	21	19	20	24	24	23	22
14 United Socialist Party/ Peoples Alliance	10	9	7	8	7	10	9	9	10
17 National Preservation Party	–	–	2	0	0	0	–	–	–
16 Republic Party	–	–	0	–	–	–	–	–	–
18 Independent Democratic Party	–	–	–	–	–	–	–	0	–
19 Union of Liberals and Leftists	–	–	–	–	–	–	–	1	5
20 Independent Party	–	–	–	0	–	–	0	–	0
Others	0	–	–	0	–	–	0	–	–
Total Seats	52	52	52	52	52	60	60	60	60

Sources: *Statistical Abstract of Iceland, 1967* : 340; *Althingiskosningar,* 1949ff.

Table 9.10   ICELAND   Percentage of Seats Won in the Althingi 1946—1971

	1946	1949	1953	1956	1959 (June)	1959 (Oct.)	1963	1967	1971
5 Social Democrats	17.3	13.5	11.5	15.4	11.5	15.0	13.3	15.0	10.0
8 Progressive Party	25.0	32.7	30.8	32.7	36.5	28.3	31.7	30.0	28.3
12 Independence Party II	38.5	36.5	40.4	36.5	38.5	40.0	40.0	38.3	36.7
14 United Socialist Party/ Peoples Alliance	19.2	17.3	13.5	15.4	13.5	16.7	15.0	15.0	16.7
17 National Preservation Party	–	–	3.8	0.0	0.0	0.0	–	–	–
16 Republic Party	–	–	0.0	–	–	–	–	–	–
18 Independent Democratic Party	–	–	–	–	–	–	–	0.0	–
19 Union of Liberals and Leftists	–	–	–	–	–	–	–	1.7	8.3
20 Independent Party	–	–	–	–	–	–	–	–	0.0
Others	0.0	–	–	0.0	–	–	0.0	–	–

179

Chapter 10

IRELAND

The Irish Free State, which became the Republic of Ireland in 1949, was established in 1922. However the first republican parliament was constituted by Sinn Féin MPs elected to the United Kingdom parliament in December 1918. The elections in the 26 counties which later became the Free State were held under existing British electoral law. Voting was in single-member constituencies and election was by a plurality. Two MPs were returned by Dublin University and one by the National University. The former were chosen by Single Transferable Vote. The vote was confined to men over 21 years old and women over 30. Plural voting rights were granted to occupiers of business premises and university graduates. The results were:—

1918 Election	Votes	Percent	Seats
Irish Parliamentary Party	183,252	27.6	2
Sinn Féin 1	428,781	64.6[1]	71
Unionists	40,568	6.1	3
Others	11,601	1.7	0
Totals	664,202	100.0	76
Electorate	1,374,509		

[1] 25 Sinn Féin candidates were returned unopposed.

Source: Calculated from figures provided by Political Reference Publications.

The second and third Irish parliaments were elected under the same suffrage law, but elections were held under the Single Transferable Vote system in multi-member constituencies. In the election of May 1921, a time of guerrilla war, there were no contests; 124 Sinn Féin MPs and four Unionist MPs representing Dublin University were returned unopposed. The election of 1923 was the first to take place under an Irish election law. Universal adult suffrage, with a minimum age requirement of 21, was introduced. Plural voting was abolished. A two chamber parliament, the Oireachtas, which consists of an upper house, Seanad Éirann, and a lower house, Dáil Éirann, was established. Separate university representation in the Dáil was continued until 1936, when the university seats were transferred to a reformed Seanad. The Single Transferable Vote system was retained. In December 1972 a referendum approved the lowering of the voting age to 18. Under the 1937 Constitution, constitutional changes must be submitted to a referendum.

Sources:

Chubb, B., *The Government and Politics of Ireland*
(London: Oxford University Press, 1971).

Craig, F.W.S., *British Parliamentary Election Statistics 1918–1970*
(Chichester: Political Reference Publications, 1971).

Farrell, B., "Labour and the Irish political party system: a suggested approach
to analysis", *The Economic and Social Review* 1 : 477-501 (1970).

Manning, M., *Irish Political Parties: an Introduction*
(Dublin: Gill & Macmillan, 1972).

Pyne, P., "The third Sinn Féin party 1923–1926", *The Economic and Social
Review* 1 : 29-50 and 229-258 (1969 & 1970).

Figures provided by Professor Basil Chubb, Trinity College, Dublin derived
from *Annual Reports of the Department of Local Government; Election
Results and Transfer of Votes* (for elections from 1948 onwards), W.J. Flynn,
Oireachtas Companion and *Irish Parliamentary Handbooks* (published in
1928, 1929, 1932, 1933, 1939 and 1945); newspapers and other sources. Up
to 1948 details of the counts, constituency by constituency, were not published officially. Up to 1965 party affiliations were not shown on the ballot
papers. There are, therefore, no completely authoritative figures for the total
party vote at elections up to that date. Conflicting figures are to be found in
various publications.

Table 10.1

POLITICAL PARTIES IN IRELAND SINCE 1918

	Party Names	Elections contested	Number contested
1	Irish Parliamentary Party	1918	1
2	Sinn Féin I (Ourselves Alone)	1918-1921; 1927 (June)	3
3	Unionist Party	1918-1921	2
4	Pro-Treaty Party[1]	1922	1
5	Republican Party[1]	1922-1923	2
6	Cumann na nGaedheal (The League of Gaels)[2]	1923-1933	5
7	Irish Labour Party[3]	1922ff	17
8	Fianna Fáil (The Warriors of Destiny)[4]	1927 (June)ff	15
9	Farmers Union	1922-1932	5
10	National League	1927	2
11	National Centre Party	1933	1
12	Fine Gael/United Ireland Party (The Tribe of Gaels)[5]	1937ff	11
13	Clann na Talmhan (The People of the Land)	1943-1961	7
14	National Labour[6]	1944-1948	2
15	Clann na Poblachta (Republican Party)	1948-1965	6
16	Sinn Féin II	1957-1961	2

[1] The Pro-Treaty and Republican (Anti-Treaty) parties were the outcome of a split in Sinn Féin. The Republicans also called themselves Sinn Féin in the 1923 election.

[2] Formerly the Pro-Treaty Party.

[3] The Irish Labour Party was founded in 1912. Because it did not participate in the 1918 United Kingdom or the 1921 Irish election, its electoral history dates from 1922.

[4] Incorporating Republican and Sinn Féin elements.

[5] Established by the merger of the Cumann na nGaedheal and National Centre parties and members of the banned National League in 1933. Until the 1940s usually referred to as the United Ireland Party.

[6] A splinter party from the Labour Party formed in 1944. The two parties were reunited in 1950.

Table 10.2
DATES OF ELECTIONS TO THE DAIL 1918–1969

1.	14 December 1918	11.	22 June 1943
2.	24 May 1921	12.	30 May 1944
3.	16 June 1922	13.	4 February 1948
4.	27 August 1923	14.	30 May 1951
5.	9 June 1927	15.	18 April 1954
6.	15 September 1927	16.	5 March 1957
7.	16 February 1932	17.	4 October 1961
8.	24 January 1933	18.	7 April 1965
9.	1 July 1937	19.	16 June 1969
10.	17 June 1938		

Table 10.3 IRELAND Total Votes 1922–1944[1]

	1922	1923	1927 (June)	1927 (Sept.)	1932	1933	1937	1938	1943	1944
Electorate	1,430,104	1,785,436	1,730,426	1,728,340	1,691,933	1,724,420	1,775,055	1,697,323	1,816,142	1,816,142
Valid Votes	627,574	1,053,426	1,146,433	1,170,761	1,274,026	1,386,558	1,324,449	1,286,259	1,331,709	1,217,349
Invalid Votes	23,126	40,047	31,337	21,886	20,850	14,750	27,824	15,811	16,198	12,790
Total Votes	650,700	1,093,996	1,177,797	1,192,755	1,294,870	1,401,300	1,352,273	1,302,070	1,347,907	1,230,139

PARTY VOTES

	1922	1923	1927 (June)	1927 (Sept.)	1932	1933	1937	1938	1943	1944
7 Labour Party	132,583	114,707	143,987	106,170	98,286	79,221	135,758	128,945	208,812	139,499[3]
14 National Labour	—	—	—	—	—	—	—	—	}	}
4 Pro-Treaty	243,758	—	—	—	—	—	—	—	—	—
6 Cumann na nGaedheal	—	410,814	314,712	453,013	449,506	422,495	—	—	—	—
12 Fine Gael	—	—	—	—	—	—	461,171	428,633	307,490	249,329
5 Republican Party	136,358	288,603	—	—	—	—	—	—	—	—
2 Sinn Féin I	—	—	41,436	—	—	—	—	—	—	—
8 Fianna Fáil	—	—	299,616	411,841	566,498	689,054	599,040	667,996	557,525	595,259
9 Farmers Union	48,717	127,798	101,473	74,520	39,727	—	—	—	—	—
10 National League	—	—	83,548	18,990	—	—	—	—	—	—
11 Centre Party	—	—	—	—	—	126,906	—	—	—	—
13 Clann na Talmhan	—	—	—	—	—	—	—	—	150,938	141,241
Others	66,158	111,504	161,661[2]	106,227	120,009	68,882	128,480	60,685	106,944	92,021

[1] All voting figures refer to first preferences.

[2] Including Clann Eirann, 5,567 votes.

[3] Separate figures not available. There were 29 Labour and 9 National Labour candidates.

Source: Figures provided by Professor Basil Chubb, Trinity College, Dublin.

Table 10.4　　IRELAND　　Percentage of Votes 1922–1944

	1922	1923	1927 (June)	1927 (Sept.)	1932	1933	1937	1938	1943	1944
Valid Votes	43.9	59.0	66.3	67.7	75.3	80.4	74.6	75.8	73.3	67.0
Invalid Votes	1.6	2.2	1.8	1.3	1.2	0.9	1.6	0.9	0.9	0.7
Total Votes	45.5	61.2	68.1	69.0	76.5	81.3	76.2	76.7	74.2	67.7
Share Invalid	3.6	3.7	2.7	1.8	1.6	1.1	2.1	1.2	1.2	1.0
PARTY VOTES										
7 Labour Party	21.1	10.9	12.6	9.1	7.7	5.7	10.3	10.0	15.7 ⎫	11.5
14 National Labour	–	–	–	–	–	–	–	–	⎭	–
4 Pro-Treaty	38.8	–	–	–	–	–	–	–	–	–
6 Cumann na nGaedheal	–	39.0	27.5	38.7	35.3	30.5	–	–	–	–
12 Fine Gael	–	–	–	–	–	–	34.8	33.3	23.1	20.5
5 Republican Party	21.7	27.4	–	–	–	–	–	–	–	–
2 Sinn Féin I	–	–	3.6	–	–	–	–	–	–	–
8 Fianna Fáil	–	–	26.1	35.2	44.5	49.7	45.2	51.9	41.9	48.9
9 Farmers Union	7.8	12.1	8.9	6.4	3.1	–	–	–	–	–
10 National League	–	–	7.3	1.6	–	–	–	–	–	–
11 Centre Party	–	–	–	–	–	9.2	–	–	–	–
13 Clann na Talmhan	–	–	–	–	–	–	–	–	11.3	11.6
Others	10.5	10.6	14.1	9.1	9.4	5.0	9.7	4.7	8.0	7.6

Table 10.5   IRELAND   Number of Seats Won in the Dáil 1922–1944

		1922	1923	1927 (June)	1927 (Sept.)	1932	1933	1937	1938	1943	1944
7	Labour Party	17	14	22	13	7	8	13	9	17	8
14	National Labour	–	–	–	–	–	–	–	–	–	4
4	Pro-Treaty	58	–	–	–	–	–	–	–	–	–
6	Cumann na nGaedheal	–	63	47	62	57	48	–	–	–	–
12	Fine Gael	–	–	–	–	–	–	48	45	32	30
5	Republican Party	35	44	–	–	–	–	–	–	–	–
2	Sinn Féin I	–	–	5	–	–	–	–	–	–	–
8	Fianna Fáil	–	–	44	57	72	77	69	77	67	76
9	Farmers Union	7	15	11	6	4	–	–	–	–	–
10	National League	–	–	8	2	–	–	–	–	–	–
11	Centre Party	–	–	–	–	–	11	–	–	–	–
13	Clann na Talmhan	–	–	–	–	–	–	–	–	14	11
	Others	11	17	16	13	13	9	8	7	8	9
	Total Seats	128	153	153	153	153	153	138	138	138	138
	Unopposed Returns	38	3	0	3	3	3	0	6	0	3

Source: Chubb, 1971 : 333.

Table 10.6   IRELAND   Percentage of Seats Won in the Dáil 1922–1944

		1922	1923	1927 (June)	1927 (Sept.)	1932	1933	1937	1938	1943	1944
7	Labour Party	13.3	9.2	14.4	8.5	4.6	5.2	9.4	6.5	12.3	5.8
14	National Labour	–	–	–	–	–	–	–	–	–	2.9
4	Pro-Treaty	45.3	–	–	–	–	–	–	–	–	–
6	Cumann na nGaedheal	–	41.2	30.7	40.5	37.3	31.4	–	–	–	–
12	Fine Gael	–	–	–	–	–	–	34.8	32.6	23.2	21.7
5	Republicans	27.3	28.8	–	–	–	–	–	–	–	–
2	Sinn Féin I	–	–	3.3	–	–	–	–	–	–	–
8	Fianna Fáil	–	–	28.8	37.3	47.1	50.3	50.0	55.8	48.6	55.1
9	Farmers Union	5.5	9.8	7.2	3.9	2.6	–	–	–	–	–
10	National League	–	–	5.2	1.3	–	–	–	–	–	–
11	Centre Party	–	–	–	–	–	7.2	–	–	–	–
13	Clann na Talmhan	–	–	–	–	–	–	–	–	10.1	8.0
	Others	8.6	11.1	10.5	8.5	8.5	5.9	5.8	5.1	5.8	6.5
	Unopposed Returns	29.7	2.0	0.0	2.0	2.0	2.0	0.0	4.3	0.0	2.2

Table 10.7   IRELAND   Total Votes 1948—1969[1]

	1948	1951	1954	1957	1961	1965	1969
Electorate	1,800,210	1,785,144	1,763,209	1,738,278	1,670,860	1,683,019	1,735,388
Valid Votes	1,323,443	1,331,573	1,335,202	1,227,019	1,168,404	1,253,122	1,318,953
Invalid Votes	13,185	12,043	12,730	11,540	11,334	11,544	16,010
Total Votes	1,336,628	1,343,616	1,347,932	1,238,559	1,179,738	1,264,666	1,334,963
PARTY VOTES							
7 Labour Party	115,073	151,828	161,034	111,747	136,111	192,740	224,498
14 National Labour	34,015	–	–	–	–	–	–
8 Fianna Fáil	553,914	616,212	578,960	592,994	512,073	597,414	602,234
12 Fine Gael	262,393	342,922	427,037	326,699	374,099	427,081	449,749
13 Clann na Talmhan	72,937	38,872	41,249	28,905	17,693	–	–
15 Clann na Poblachta	175,699	54,210	51,069	20,632	14,474	9,427	–
16 Sinn Féin II	–	–	–	65,640	35,092	–	–
Others	109,412	127,529	75,853	80,402	78,862[2]	26,460	42,472

[1] All voting figures refer to first preferences.
[2] Including National Progressive Democratic Party with 11,490 votes.

Source: Figures provided by Professor Basil Chubb, Trinity College, Dublin.

Table 10.8 IRELAND Percentage of Votes 1948—1969

	1948	1951	1954	1957	1961	1965	1969
Valid Votes	73.5	74.6	75.7	70.6	69.9	74.5	76.0
Invalid Votes	0.7	0.7	0.7	0.7	0.7	0.7	0.9
Total Votes	74.2	75.3	76.4	71.3	70.6	75.1	76.9
Share Invalid	1.0	0.9	0.9	0.9	1.0	0.9	1.2
PARTY VOTES							
7 Labour Party	8.7	11.4	12.1	9.1	11.6	15.4	17.0
14 National Labour	2.6	–	–	–	–	–	–
8 Fianna Fail	41.9	46.3	43.4	48.3	43.8	47.7	45.7
12 Fine Gael	19.8	25.8	32.0	26.6	32.0	34.1	34.1
13 Clann na Talmhan	5.5	2.9	3.1	2.4	1.5	–	–
15 Clann na Poblachta	13.3	4.1	3.8	1.7	1.2	0.8	–
16 Sinn Féin II	–	–	–	5.3	3.0	–	–
Others	8.3	9.6	5.7	6.6	6.7	2.1	3.2

Table 10.9 IRELAND Number of Seats Won in the Dáil 1948—1969

		1948	1951	1954	1957	1961	1965	1969
7	Labour Party	14	16	19	12	16	22	18
14	National Labour	5	–	–	–	–	–	–
8	Fianna Fáil	68	69	65	78	70	72	75
12	Fine Gael	31	40	50	40	47	47	50
13	Clann na Talmhan	7	6	5	3	2	–	–
15	Clann na Poblachta	10	2	3	1	1	1	–
16	Sinn Féin II	–	–	–	4	0	–	–
	Others	12	14	5	9	8[1]	2	1
	Total Seats	147	147	147	147	144	144	144

[1] Of which National Progressive Democratic Party, 2.

Source: Chubb, 1971 : 333; and figures provided by the Irish Embassy, London.

Table 10.10   IRELAND   Percentage of Seats Won in the Dáil 1948–1969

	1948	1951	1954	1957	1961	1965	1969
7 Labour Party	9.5	10.9	12.9	8.2	11.1	15.3	12.5
14 National Labour	3.4	–	–	–	–	–	–
8 Fianna Fáil	46.3	46.9	44.2	53.1	48.6	50.0	52.1
12 Fine Gael	21.1	27.2	34.0	27.2	32.6	32.6	34.7
13 Clann na Talmhan	4.8	4.1	3.4	2.0	1.4	–	–
15 Clann na Poblachta	6.8	1.4	2.0	0.7	0.7	0.7	–
16 Sinn Féin II	–	–	–	2.7	0.0	–	–
Others	8.2	9.5	3.4	6.1	5.6	1.4	0.7

Chapter 11

ISRAEL

Under the British mandate the Jewish community in Palestine enjoyed a high degree of communal self-government, including the right of taxation. In 1920 an elected parliament called the Assembly of the Elected, Asefhat Ha'Nivharim, was established. The Israeli party system developed from the system of the mandate period. "Every single Jewish party elected to the second Knesset (1951) had been in existence before the establishment of the state" (Akzin, 1955 : 513). In elections to the Assembly the Mapai had already achieved a dominant position:

	1920	1925	1931	1944[2]
Achdut Ha'avoda	70	54	—	—
Mapai	—	—	31	63
Hapoel Hatzair	41	30	—	—
Poalei Zion	—	—	1	—
Communists	—	6	2	21
Yemenites	12	20	3	—
Other Oriental Lists[1]	64	20	—	—
Religious Parties	60	19	5	17
Revisionists	—	15	15	—
Various Middle Class Lists	67	44	14	—
League for Womens Rights	—	13	—	—
Aliyah Hadassah	—	—	—	18
	314	221	71	119
Registered Voters	28,755	64,714	89,656	303,000

[1] Including the Sephardim.
[2] The 1944 election was boycotted by the Sephardim, General Zionists and Revisionists.

Source: Etzioni, 1959 : 200.

Since the establishment of the State of Israel in 1948 the country's unicameral parliament, the Knesset, has been elected by universal adult suffrage under a system of proportional representation. The ballot is secret. Every citizen aged over 18 on December 31 of the year preceding the election is entitled to vote. In 1949 seats were allocated according to the d'Hondt system of P.R. In 1951 this was replaced by the largest remainder system. Since 1951 a party must win at least one per cent of the total valid votes in order to be included in the division of seats in the Knesset.

195

Sources:

Akzin, B., "The role of parties in Israeli democracy" *Journal of Politics* 17, 1955 : 507-545.

Arazi, A., *Le système électoral israélien* (Geneva: Droz, 1963).

Etzioni, A., "Alternative ways to democracy: the example of Israel." *Political Science Quarterly* 1959 : 196-214.

Inspector General of Elections, *Results of Elections to the Seventh Knesset and to Local Authorities* (Jerusalem: Central Bureau of Statistics, 1970).

Table 11.1
POLITICAL PARTIES IN ISRAEL SINCE 1949

	Party Names	Elections contested	Number contested
1	Labour Party (Mifleget Poalei Eretz Israel—Mapai)[1]	1949ff	7
2	General Zionists (Zionim Klalim)	1949-1959	4
3	Progressive Party (Miflaga Progresivit)	1949-1959	4
4	Freedom Party (Herut)	1949-1961	5
5	Communist Party (Miflaga Kommunistit Isre'elit—Maki)	1949ff	7
6	Minority Lists[2]	1949ff	7
7	United Workers Party (Mifleget Ha'poalim Hameuhedet—Mapam)[3]	1949ff	7
8	Orthodox Religion Party (Agudat Israel)[4]	1949ff	7
9	Orthodox Workers Party (Poalei Agudat Israel)[5]	1949ff	7
10	Mizrachi[6]	1949-1951	2
11	Workers Mizrachi Party (Hapoel Ha'mizrachi)[7]	1949-1951	2
12	Sephardim Party	1949-1951	2
13	Yemenite Party	1949-1951	2
14	Womens International Zionist Organization (WIZO)	1949	1
15	Fighters for Israel's Freedom	1949	1
16	National Religious Party (Miflaga Datit Leumit—Mafdal)[8]	1955ff	5
17	Unity of Labour (Achdut Ha'avoda Poalei Zion)[9]	1955-1965	4
18	Liberal Party (Miflaga Haliberalit)[10]	1961	1
19	Independent Liberal Party (Miflaga Haliberalit Haamatzmahit)[11]	1965ff	2
20	Freedom—Liberal Block (Gerush Herut-Liberaliim—Gahal)[12]	1965ff	2
21	New Communist List (Reshima Kommunistit Hadasha—Rakah)	1965ff	2
22	New Force (Haolem Hazeh)	1965ff	2
23	Workers List (Reshima Poalei Zion—Rafi)[13]	1965	1
24	National List (Reshima Mamlachit)[14]	1969	1
25	Free Centre (Hamerkaz Hahofshi)[15]	1969	1

[1] Mapai was established in 1929 by a merger of Achdut Ha'avoda (Unity of Labour) and Hapoel Hatzair (the Young Worker). In 1948 Achdut Ha'avoda broke away from Mapai. It was reunited with Mapai and Rafi to form the Israel Labour Party (Mifleget Ha'avoda Ha'israe'elit) in 1968. The new party contested the 1969 election as part of an electoral alliance, the Labour Alignment (Ma'arach) with Mapam.

[2] Parties representing the Arab and Druze minorities. Most of these parties have been affiliated with Mapai.

[3] Mapam was established in 1948 by Achdut Ha'avoda, which had broken away from Mapai, Hashomer Hatzair (which had remained independent when other socialist groups merged to form Mapai in 1929) and Poalei Zion Smol (Left Workers of Zion).

[4] Founded in Poland in 1913. In 1949 part of the United Religious Front. In 1955 and 1959 part of the Torah Religious Front, with Poalei Agudat Israel.

[5] Founded in Poland in 1922 as the Labour Wing of Agudat Israel. In 1949 part of the United Religious Front. In 1955 and 1959 part of the Torah Religious Front.

[6] Established in Palestine in 1918. In 1949 formed part of the National Religious Front.

[7] Established by former members of Mizrachi in 1922. In 1949 formed part of the National Religious Front.

[8] A merger of Mizrachi and Hapoel Ha'mizrachi.

[9] Split from Mapam in 1954. In 1965 formed an electoral alliance with Mapai, and in 1968 merged with Mapai to form part of the Israel Labour Party.

[10] A merger of the Progressive Party and the General Zionists.

[11] Part of the Liberal Party which refused to join Gahal.

[12] An alliance of the Liberal and Freedom parties.

[13] A splinter from Mapai, led by David Ben Gurion, formed in 1965. Reunited with the Israel Labour Party in 1968.

[14] Founded in 1969 by former members of Rafi.

[15] Established in 1967 following a split in Herut.

Table 11.2
DATES OF ELECTIONS
TO THE KNESSET 1949–1969

1. 25 January 1949
2. 30 July 1951
3. 26 July 1955
4. 3 July 1959
5. 15 August 1961
6. 2 November 1965
7. 28 October 1969

Source: Central Bureau of Statistics 1970 : xiii.

Table 11.3 ISRAEL Total Votes 1949—1969

	1949	1951	1955	1959	1961	1965	1969
Electorate	506,567	924,885	1,057,795	1,218,483	1,274,280	1,449,709	1,758,685
Valid Votes	434,684	687,492	853,219	969,337	1,006,964	1,206,728	1,367,743
Invalid Votes	5,411	7,515	22,866	24,969	30,066	37,978	60,238
Total Votes	440,095	695,007	876,085	994,306	1,037,030	1,244,706	1,427,981
PARTY VOTES							
1 Labour Party	155,274	256,456	274,735	370,585	349,330	443,379	–
17 Unity of Labour	–	–	62,401	69,468	75,654	79,985	632,035[3]
7 United Workers Party	64,018	86,095	69,475	58,043	66,170	–	–
23 Workers List	–	–	–	–	–	95,328	–
4 Freedom Party	49,782	45,651	107,190	130,515	138,599	–	–
2 General Zionists	22,661	111,394	87,099	59,700	–	–	–
20 Gahal	–	–	–	–	–	256,957	296,294
18 Liberal Party	–	–	–	–	137,255	–	–
3 Progressive Party	17,786	22,171	37,661	44,889	–	–	–
8 Orthodox Religion Party	–	13,799	39,836[2]	45,569[2]	37,178	39,795	44,002
9 Orthodox Workers Party	–	11,194			22,066	22,066	24,968
10 Mizrachi	52,982[1]	10,383	–	–	–	–	–
16 National Religious Party	–		77,936	95,581	98,786	107,966	133,238
11 Workers Mizrachi Party	–	46,347					
5 Communist Party	15,148	27,334	38,492	27,374	42,111	13,617	15,712
15 Fighters for Israel's Freedom	5,363	–	–	–	–	–	–
12 Sephardim Party	15,287	12,002	–	–	–	–	–
14 W.I.Z.O.	5,173	–	–	–	–	–	–

		A	B	C	D	E	F	G
13	Yemenite Party	4,399	7,965	—	—	—	—	—
19	Independent Liberal Party	—	—	—	—	—	45,299	43,933
21	New Communist List	—	—	—	—	—	27,413	38,827
22	New Force	—	—	—	—	—	14,124	16,853
25	Free Centre	—	—	—	—	—	—	16,393
24	National List	—	—	—	—	—	—	42,654
6	Minority Lists	13,413	32,288	42,261	46,191	39,272	45,430	47,989
	Others	13,398	4,413	16,133	21,422	3,181	15,369	14,845

[1] United Religious Front.
[2] Torah Religious Front.
[3] Labour Alignment (Ma'arach).

Source: Inspector General of Elections, 1970 : xiii.

Table 11.4 ISRAEL

Percentage of Votes 1949—1969

	1949	1951	1955	1959	1961	1965	1969
Valid Votes	85.8	74.3	80.7	79.6	79.0	83.2	77.8
Invalid Votes	1.1	0.8	2.2	2.0	2.4	2.6	3.4
Total Votes	86.9	75.1	82.8	81.6	81.4	85.9	81.2
Share Invalid	1.2	1.1	2.6	2.5	2.9	3.1	4.2
PARTY VOTES							
1 Labour Party	35.7	37.3	32.2	38.2	34.7	36.7	46.2
17 Unity of Labour	–	–	7.3	7.2	7.5		
7 United Workers Party	14.7	12.5	8.1	6.0	6.6	6.6	–
23 Workers List	–	–	–	–	–	7.9	–
4 Freedom Party	11.5	6.6	12.6	13.5	13.8	–	–
2 General Zionists	5.2	16.2	10.2	6.2	–	–	–
20 Gahal	–	–	–	–	–	21.3	21.7
18 Liberal Party	–	–	–	–	13.6	–	–
3 Progressive Party	4.1	3.2	4.4	4.6			
8 Orthodox Religion Party	–	2.0	4.7	4.7	3.7	3.3	3.2
9 Orthodox Workers Party	–	1.6			1.9	1.8	1.8
10 Mizrachi	12.2	1.5	9.1	9.9	9.8	8.9	9.7
16 National Religious Party	–						
11 Workers Mizrachi Party	–	6.7					
5 Communist Party	3.5	4.0	4.5	2.8	4.2	1.1	1.1
15 Fighters for Israel's Freedom	1.2	–	–	–	–	–	–
12 Sephardim Party	3.5	1.7	–	–	–	–	–
14 W.I.Z.O.	1.2	–	–	–	–	–	–

13 Yemenite Party	1.0	1.2	–	–	–	–	–
19 Independent Liberal Party	–	–	–	–	–	–	–
21 New Communist List	–	–	–	–	–	2.3	2.8
22 New Force	–	–	–	–	–	1.2	1.2
25 Free Centre	–	–	–	–	–	–	1.2
24 National List	–	–	–	–	–	–	3.1
6 Minority Lists	3.1	4.7	5.0	4.8	3.9	3.8	3.5
Others	3.1	0.6	1.9	2.2	0.3	1.3	1.1

Table 11.5   ISRAEL

Number of Seats Won in the Knesset 1949–1969

		1949	1951	1955	1959	1961	1965	1969
1	Labour Party	46	45	40	47	42	45	—
17	Unity of Labour	—	—	9	9	8	8	56[3]
7	United Workers Party	19	15	10	7	9	10	—
23	Workers List	—	—	—	—	—	—	—
4	Freedom Party	14	8	15	17	17	—	—
2	General Zionists	7	20	13	8	—	—	—
20	Gahal	—	—	—	—	—	26	26
18	Liberal Party	—	—	—	—	17	—	—
3	Progressive Party	5	4	5	6	—	—	—
8	Orthodox Religion Party	—	3	6[2]	6[2]	4	4	4
9	Orthodox Workers Party	—	2	—	—	2	2	2
10	Mizrachi	16[1]	2	—	—	—	—	—
16	National Religious Party	—	—	11	12	12	11	12
11	Workers Mizrachi Party	—	8	—	—	—	—	—
5	Communist Party	4	5	6	3	5	1	1
15	Fighters for Israel's Freedom	1	—	—	—	—	—	—
12	Sephardim Party	4	2	—	—	—	—	—
14	W.I.Z.O.	1	—	—	—	—	—	—
13	Yemenite Party	1	1	—	—	—	—	—
19	Independent Liberal Party	—	—	—	—	—	5	4
21	New Communist List	—	—	—	—	—	3	3
22	New Force	—	—	—	—	—	1	2

25 Free Centre	—	—	—	—	—	2
24 National List	—	—	—	—	—	4
6 Minority Lists	2	5	5	5	4	4
Others	0	0	0	0	0	0
Total Seats	**120**	**120**	**120**	**120**	**120**	**120**

[1] United Religious Front.
[2] Torah Religious Front.
[3] Labour Alignment (Ma'arach).

Source: Inspector General of Elections, 1970 : xiv.

Table 11.6   ISRAEL

Percentage of Seats Won in the Knesset 1949—1969

		1949	1951	1955	1959	1961	1965	1969
1	Labour Party	38.3	37.5	33.3	39.2	35.0	37.5	—
17	Unity of Labour	—	—	7.5	7.5	6.7	6.7	46.7
7	United Workers Party	15.8	12.5	8.3	5.8	7.5	8.3	—
23	Workers List	—	—	—	—	—		—
4	Freedom Party	11.7	6.7	12.5	14.2	14.2	—	—
2	General Zionists	5.8	16.7	10.8	6.7	—	—	—
20	Gahal	—	—	—	—	—	21.7	21.7
18	Liberal Party	—	—	—	—	14.2	—	—
3	Progressive Party	4.2	3.3	4.2	5.0	—	—	—
8	Orthodox Religion Party	—	2.5	5.0	5.0	3.3	3.3	3.3
9	Orthodox Workers Party	—	1.7	—	—	1.7	1.7	1.7
10	Mizrachi	13.3	1.7	—	—	—	—	—
16	National Religious Party	—	—	9.2	10.0	10.0	9.2	10.0
11	Workers Mizrachi Party	—	6.7	—	—	—	—	—
5	Communist Party	3.3	4.2	5.0	2.5	4.2	0.8	0.8
15	Fighters for Israel's Freedom	0.8	—	—	—	—	—	—
12	Sephardim Party	3.3	1.7	—	—	—	—	—
14	W.I.Z.O.	0.8	—	—	—	—	—	—
13	Yemenite Party	0.8	0.8	—	—	—	—	—
19	Independent Liberal Party	—	—	—	—	—	4.2	3.3
21	New Communist List	—	—	—	—	—	2.5	2.5
22	New Force	—	—	—	—	—	0.8	1.7

25 Free Centre	—	—	—	—	—	—	1.7
24 National List	—	—	—	—	—	—	3.3
6 Minority Lists	1.7	4.2	4.2	4.2	3.3	3.3	3.3
Others	0.0	0.0	0.0	0.0	0.0	0.0	0.0

Chapter 12
ITALY

The unification of Italy was largely completed by the occupation of Rome in 1870. The constitution of the new Kingdom of Italy was closely modelled on the 1848 Piedmontese constitution. This provided for a nominated Senate (Senato) and a directly elected Chamber of Deputies (Camera dei Deputati). The franchise was very restricted. Only men aged over 25 who were literate and also met either minimum tax-payment or office holding qualifications could vote, about 2.4 per cent of the total population. A two-ballot single-member constituency system was used. If no candidate won an absolute majority of the vote a run-off election was held between the two leading candidates. Apart from a brief experiment with a multi-member constituency plurality system from 1882 to 1891, the two-ballot system remained in use until 1919. In 1882 the voting age was reduced to 21. Property qualifications were reduced and the vote given to all men who had completed primary education. The percentage of the population entitled to vote increased to 6.9 per cent. In 1912 all men aged over 30 were enfranchised. Illiterates aged under 30 could also vote if they had completed their military service. Adult male suffrage and the d'Hondt system of Proportional Representation were introduced in 1919.

Political parties were very slow to develop. Until the foundation of the Socialist Party in 1892 there were no organized nationwide parties. During the period of unification the Chamber was divided into two more or less distinct groups, the Destra (Right) and the Sinistra (Left). Governments were frequently formed by members of both groups and by the 1880s they had in effect coalesced into a "broad liberal party of the centre, which monopolised political and public life" (Seton-Watson, 1967:51). Deputies from Southern Italy, where electoral corruption and interference by government officials were endemic, always provided a solid bloc of support for the government. The growth of electoral support for the Socialist Party caused the Vatican to modify its initial opposition to Catholic participation in national politics. Beginning with the 1904 election the Church ceased to oppose voting in certain constituencies. But although Catholic organizations were mobilized in support of moderate and, in a very few constituencies, specifically Catholic, candidates the formation of a Catholic political party was not sanctioned by the Vatican until the establishment of the Popular Party in 1919.

In 1922 Benito Mussolini became Prime Minister at the head of a cabinet of Liberals, Nationalists and Fascists. Because of widespread violence and intimidation by the Government the election of 1924 cannot be considered a free one. The non-fascist parties gained 35 per cent of the vote (Schepis,

1958: 55-57). During the next two years the non-fascist parties were suppressed; a one party state established. The fall of Mussolini in 1943 was followed by the re-emergence of the political parties. In 1946 a referendum abolished the monarchy. At the same time a Constituent Assembly was elected.

The new Constitution provided for a two-chamber parliament consisting of a Senate and Chamber of Deputies directly elected by universal adult suffrage. The minimum voting age for the Chamber is 21. Deputies are chosen by proportional representation using the Imperiali system. If all the seats in the Chamber have not been allocated at the constituency level, surplus votes are collected into a national pool where a second distribution takes place using the largest remainder method. In the single-member Val d'Aosta constituency the pre-1919 two-ballot majority system is retained.

Before the 1953 election an electoral law was passed which provided that any party or alliance of parties which won more than half of the total vote should be awarded 380 of the 590 seats in the Chamber. The Christian Democrats and their allies narrowly failed to win half the votes, and in 1956 the former electoral law was restored.

Sources:

Focardi, O., "I partiti politici alle elezioni generali del 1895." Giornale degli Economisti 11: 133-180 (1895).

Ministero dell'Interno, Compendio dei Risultati delle Elezioni Politiche dal 1848 al 1958 (Rome: Istituto Poligrafico dello Stato, 1963).

Ibid., Elezione della Camera dei Deputati, 1948ff. (Rome; Failli, 1949; subsequent volumes Istituto Poligrafico dello Stato).

Schepis, G., Le Consultazioni Popolari in Italia dal 1848 al 1957:Profilo Storico-statistico (Empoli: Editrice Caparrini, 1958).

Schiavi, A., "Le ultime elezioni politiche italiane". La Riforma Sociale 14: 979-988 (1904) and 15: 127-160 (1905).

Ibid. Come Hanno Votati gli Elettori Italiani (Milan: Avanti! 1914)

Seton-Watson, C., Italy from Liberalism to Fascism (London:Methuen, 1967).

Torresin, A., "Statistica delle elezioni generali politiche del giugno 1900." La Riforma Sociale 10: 788-831 (1900).

Table 12.1
POLITICAL PARTIES IN ITALY 1895–1972

	Party Names	Elections contested	Number contested
1	Ministerial and Opposition Liberals[1]	1895-1921	8
2	Radical Party (Partito Radicale)	1895-1919	7
3	Socialist Party (Partito Socialista Italiano)[2]	1895-1963; 1972	14
4	Republican Party (Partito Repubblicano Italiano)	1895ff	15
5	Catholics (Cattolici and Conservatori Cattolici)[3]	1904-1913	3
6	Independent Socialists (Socialisti Independenti)	1913-1921	3
7	Reformist Socialist Party (Socialisti Riformisti)	1913-1919	2
8	Economic Party (Partito Economico)	1919-1921	2
9	Ex-Servicemen (Combattenti)	1919-1921	2
10	Popular Party (Partito Popolare Italiano)	1919-1921	2
11	Communist Party (Partito Comunista Italiano—PCI)	1921ff	8
12	Fascist Party (Partito Nazionale Fascista)	1921	1
13	Slavs and Germans[4]	1921	1
14	Action Party (Partito d'Azione—Pd'A)	1946	1
15	Christian Democrats (Democrazia Cristiana—DC)	1946ff	7
16	Common Man Front (Fronte dell'Uomo Qualunque)	1946	1
17	Liberal Party (Partito Liberale Italiano—PLI)[5]	1946ff	7
18	Monarchist Party[6]	1946ff	7
19	Sardinian Action Party (Partito Sardo d'Azione—PSd'A)	1946-1953; 1963	4
20	Sicilian Independence Movement (Movimento per l'Independenza della Sicilia)	1946	1
21	Social Democrats (Partito Socialista Democra Democratico Italiano—PSDI)[7]	1948-1963; 1972	
22	Italian Social Movement (Movimento Sociale Italiano—MSI)	1948-1969	5
23	South Tyrol Peoples Party (Südtiroler Volkspartei—SVP)	1948ff	6
24	Community Front (Communità)	1958	1
25	Popular Monarchist Party (Partito Monarchico Popolare—PMP)[9]	1958	1
26	Val d'Aosta Union (Union Valdôtaine)	1958-1968	3
27	United Monarchist Party (Partito Democratico Italiano di Unità Monarchica—PDIUM)[10]	1963-1968	2
28	Left Socialist Party (Partito Socialista Italiano di Unità Proletaria—PSIUP)	1968ff	2
29	United Socialist Party (Partito Socialista Unitario—PSU)[11]	1968	1
30	National Right (Destra Nazionale)[12]	1972	1

[1] This *tendance* includes all the variously named liberal parliamentary groups. For details of the individual groups see Schepis, 1958.

[2] In 1945 known as the Partito Socialista Italiano di Unità Proletaria—PSIUP.

[3] A *tendance* including different Catholic groups.

[4] Representatives of the ethnic minorities living in territory annexed by Italy after the First World War.

[5] In 1946 the Unione Democratica Nazionale. In 1948 the Blocco Nazionale.

[6] In 1946 the Blocco Nazionale della Libertà. In 1948 the Partito Nazionale Monarchico and the Alleanza Democratica del Lavoro. From 1953 the Partito Nazionale Monarchico.

[7] Formed by former members of the PSI. In 1948 known as Unità Socialista. The party was reunited with the PSI in 1968 but a split occurred again in 1969, leading to the re-establishment of the PSDI.

[8] Concentrazione della Cultura, degli Operaii e dei Contadini d'Italia — an electoral alliance formed by several regional groups including the PSd'A.

[9] A breakaway group from the Partito Nazionale Monarchico.

[10] A merger of the Partito Nazionale Monarchico and the Partito Popolare Monarchico.

[11] A merger, which did not last, of the Partito Socialista Italiano and the PSDI.

[12] A merger of the MSI and the PDIUM.

Table 12.2
DATES OF ELECTIONS
TO THE CAMERA DEI DEPUTATI 1895–1972[1]

1.	26 May, 2 June 1895	9.	2 June 1946
2.	21, 28 March 1897	10.	18 April 1948
3.	3, 10 June 1900	11.	7 June 1953
4.	6, 13 November 1904	12.	25 May 1958
5.	7, 14 March 1909	13.	28 April 1963
6.	26 October, 2 November 1913	14.	19 May 1968
7.	16 November 1919	15.	7 May 1972
8.	15 May 1921		

[1] From 1895 to 1913 the pair of dates refer to the first and second ballots.

Sources: Ministero dell'Interno, 1963 : 2-5; and Keesings Contemporary Archives.

Table 12.3 ITALY Total Votes 1895–1921

	1895	1897	1900	1904	1909	1913	1919	1921
Electorate	2,121,185	2,120,909	2,248,509	2,541,327	2,930,473	8,443,205	10,239,326	11,477,210
Valid Votes	1,221,598	1,208,140	1,269,061	1,527,180	1,827,865	5,014,921	5,684,833	6,608,141
Invalid Votes	34,646	33,346	41,419	66,706	75,822	85,694	108,674	93,355
Total Votes	1,256,244	1,241,486	1,310,480	1,593,886	1,903,687	5,100,615	5,793,507	6,701,496
PARTY VOTES								
1 Ministerial and Opposition Liberals	979,958	994,083	935,116	989,929	1,144,532	2,804,165	2,016,889	2,846,745[2]
2 Radical Party	142,356	51,207	89,872	128,002	181,242	588,193	110,697	–
3 Socialist Party	82,523	108,086	164,946	326,016	347,615	883,409	1,834,792	1,631,435
4 Republican Party	–	54,764	79,127	75,225	81,461	173,666	53,197	124,924
5 Catholics	–	–	–	8,008	73,015	301,949	–	–
6 Independent Socialists	–	–	–	–	–	67,133	33,938	37,892
7 Reformist Socialists	–	–	–	–	–	196,406	82,172	–
8 Economic Party	–	–	–	–	–	–	87,450	53,382
9 Ex-Servicemens Party	–	–	–	–	–	–	232,923	113,839
10 Popular Party	–	–	–	–	–	–	1,167,354	1,347,305
11 Communist Party	–	–	–	–	–	–	–	304,719
12 Fascist Party	–	–	–	–	–	–	–	n.a.
13 Slavs and Germans	–	–	–	–	–	–	–	88,648
Others	16,761	–	–	–	–	–	65,412[1]	59,252[3]

[1] An electoral alliance of radicals, republicans, socialists and ex-servicemen.

[2] Including 1,260,007 votes cast for the National Bloc (Blocco Nazionale) an electoral alliance of liberals, nationalists and fascists.

[3] Including 29,545 votes cast for a dissident fascist list.

Sources: Ministero dell'Interro, 1963 : 4-5, 46-57, 114-119; Torresin, 1900 : 819, 826.

214

Table 12.4   ITALY   Percentage of Votes 1895—1921

	1895	1897	1900	1904	1909	1913	1919	1921
Valid Votes	57.6	57.0	56.4	60.1	62.4	59.4	55.5	57.6
Invalid Votes	1.6	1.6	1.8	2.6	2.6	1.0	1.1	0.8
Total Votes	59.2	58.5	58.3	62.7	65.0	60.4	56.6	58.4
Share Invalid	2.8	2.7	3.2	4.2	4.0	1.7	1.9	1.4
PARTY VOTES								
1 Ministerial and Opposition Liberals	80.2	82.3	73.7	64.8	62.6	55.9	35.5	43.1
2 Radical Party	11.7	4.2	7.1	8.4	9.9	11.7	1.9	–
3 Socialist Party	6.8	8.9	13.0	21.3	19.0	17.6	32.3	24.7
4 Republican Party	–	4.5	6.2	4.9	4.5	3.5	0.9	1.9
5 Catholics	–	–	–	0.5	4.0	6.0	–	–
6 Independent Socialists	–	–	–	–	–	1.3	0.6	0.6
7 Reformist Socialists	–	–	–	–	–	3.9	1.4	–
8 Economic Party	–	–	–	–	–	–	1.5	0.8
9 Ex-Servicemens Party	–	–	–	–	–	–	4.1	1.7
10 Popular Party	–	–	–	–	–	–	20.5	20.4
11 Communist Party	–	–	–	–	–	–	–	4.6
12 Fascist Party	–	–	–	–	–	–	–	n.a.
13 Slavs and Germans	–	–	–	–	–	–	–	1.3
Others	1.4	–	–	–	–	–	1.2	0.9

Table 12.5   ITALY   Number of Seats Won in the Camera dei Deputati 1895—1921

	1895	1897	1900	1904	1909	1913	1919	1921
1 Ministerial and Opposition Liberals	438	437	412	415	382	310	197	221
2 Radical Party	47	29	34	37	45	73	12	–
3 Socialist Party	15	16	33	29	41	52	156	123
4 Republican Party	–	26	29	24	24	17	4	6
5 Catholics	–	–	–	3	16	29	–	–
6 Independent Socialists	–	–	–	–	–	8	1	1
7 Reformist Socialists	–	–	–	–	–	19	6	–
8 Economic Party	–	–	–	–	–	–	7	5
9 Ex-Servicemens Party	–	–	–	–	–	–	20	10
10 Popular Party	–	–	–	–	–	–	100	108
11 Communist Party	–	–	–	–	–	–	–	15
12 Fascist Party	–	–	–	–	–	–	–	35[2]
13 Slavs and Germans	–	–	–	–	–	–	5[1]	9
Others	8	–	–	–	–	–	–	2[3]
Total Seats	**508**	**508**	**508**	**508**	**508**	**508**	**508**	**535**

[1] Seats won by an electoral alliance of radicals, republicans, socialists and ex-servicemen.
[2] Elected as members of the Blocco Nazionale.
[3] Seats won by dissident fascist lists.

Sources: Ministero dell'Interno, 1963 : 71-77, 136-139; Torresin, 1900 : 824.

Table 12.6   ITALY   Percentage of Seats Won in the Camera dei Deputati 1895–1921

	1895	1897	1900	1904	1909	1913	1919	1921
1 Ministerial and Opposition Liberals	86.2	86.0	81.1	81.7	75.2	61.0	38.8	41.3
2 Radical Party	9.3	5.7	6.7	7.3	8.9	14.4	2.4	–
3 Socialist Party	3.0	3.1	6.5	5.7	8.1	10.2	30.7	23.0
4 Republican Party	–	5.1	5.7	4.7	4.7	3.3	0.8	1.1
5 Catholics	–	–	–	0.6	3.1	5.7	–	–
6 Independent Socialists	–	–	–	–	–	1.6	0.2	0.2
7 Reformist Socialists	–	–	–	–	–	3.7	1.2	–
8 Economic Party	–	–	–	–	–	–	1.4	0.9
9 Ex-Servicemens Party	–	–	–	–	–	–	3.9	1.9
10 Popular Party	–	–	–	–	–	–	19.7	20.2
11 Communist Party	–	–	–	–	–	–	–	2.8
12 Fascist Party	–	–	–	–	–	–	–	6.5
13 Slavs and Germans	–	–	–	–	–	–	–	1.7
Others	1.6	–	–	–	–	–	1.0	0.4

Table 12.7 ITALY — Total Votes 1946–1972

	1946	1948	1953	1958	1963	1968	1972
Electorate	28,005,449	29,117,554	30,267,080	32,436,022	34,201,660	35,566,681	37,039,769
Valid Votes	23,016,464	26,268,912	27,092,743	29,560,269	30,758,031	31,803,253	33,384,492
Invalid Votes	1,930,723	585,291	1,318,108	839,439	1,008,027	1,199,996	1,106,705
Total Votes	24,947,187	26,854,203	28,410,851	30,399,708	31,766,058	33,003,249	34,491,197
PARTY VOTES							
11 Communist Party	4,358,243	8,137,305[2]	6,121,922	6,704,454	7,768,228	8,557,404	9,085,927
3 Socialist Party	4,765,665		3,441,305	4,206,726	4,257,300	–	3,209,503
29 United Socialist Party	–		–	–	–	4,605,832	–
21 Social Democrats	–	1,858,346	1,223,251	1,345,447	1,876,409	–	1,716,197
28 Left Socialist Party	–	–	–	–	–	1,414,544	648,368
15 Christian Democrats	8,102,828	12,741,299	10,864,282	12,520,207	11,745,262	12,441,553	12,943,675
14 Action Party	334,877	–	–	–	–	–	–
16 Common Man Front	1,210,021	–	–	–	–	–	–
17 Liberal Party	1,560,037	1,004,889	816,267	1,047,081	2,143,954	1,851,060	1,300,074
18 Monarchist Party	636,330	729,174	1,855,842	659,997	536,991	–	–
27 United Monarchist Party	–	–	–	–	536,991	414,423	–
25 Popular Monarchist Party	–	–	–	776,919	–	–	–
4 Republican Party	1,100,776[1]	652,477	437,988	405,782	420,419	626,567	953,681
19 Sardinian Action Party	78,554	61,919	27,228	–	–	27,228	–
20 Sicilian Independence Movement	171,201	–	–	–	–	–	–
22 Social Movement–MSI	–	526,670	1,580,293	1,407,718	1,569,815	1,414,794	–
23 South Tyrol Peoples Party	–	124,385	122,792	135,491	135,458	152,954	153,759
24 Community Front	–	–	–	173,227	–	–	–
26 Val d'Aosta Union	–	–	–	30,596	31,844	31,557	–
30 National Right	–	–	–	–	–	–	2,894,789
Others	697,932	432,706	601,573	146,624	272,351	265,337	478,519

[1] Including 97,690 votes cast for the Concentrazione Democratica Repubblicana. [2] The PCI and PSI formed an electoral alliance the Fronte Democratico Popolare.

Table 12.8 ITALY Percentage of Votes 1946—1972

	1946	1948	1953	1958	1963	1968	1972
Valid Votes	82.2	90.2	89.5	91.1	89.9	89.4	90.1
Invalid Votes	6.9	2.0	4.4	2.6	2.9	3.4	3.0
Total Votes	89.1	92.2	93.9	93.7	92.9	92.8	93.1
Share Invalid	7.7	2.2	4.6	2.8	3.2	3.6	3.2
PARTY VOTES							
11 Communist Party	18.9 ⎤	31.0	22.6	22.7	25.3	26.9	27.2
3 Socialist Party	20.7 ⎦		12.7	14.2	13.8	–	9.6
29 United Socialist Party	–	–	–	–	–	14.5	–
21 Social Democrats	–	7.1	4.5	4.6	6.1	–	5.1
28 Left Socialist Party	–	–	–	–	–	4.4	1.9
15 Christian Democrats	35.2	48.5	40.1	42.4	38.2	39.1	38.8
14 Action Party	1.5	–	–	–	–	–	–
16 Common Man Front	5.3	–	–	–	–	–	–
17 Liberal Party	6.8	3.8	3.0	3.5	7.0	5.8	3.9
18 Monarchist Party	2.8	2.8	6.8	2.2	–	–	–
27 United Monarchist Party	–	–	–	–	1.7	1.3	–
25 Popular Monarchist Party	–	–	–	2.6	–	–	–
4 Republican Party	4.8	2.5	1.6	1.4	1.4	2.0	2.9
19 Sardinian Action Party	0.3	0.2	0.1	–	–	0.1	–
20 Sicilian Independence Movement	0.7	–	–	–	–	–	–
22 Social Movement—MSI	–	2.0	5.8	4.8	5.1	4.4	–
23 South Tyrol Peoples	–	0.5	0.5	0.5	0.4	0.5	0.5
24 Community Front	–	–	–	0.6	–	–	–
26 Val d'Aosta Union	–	–	–	0.1	0.1	0.1	–
30 National Right	–	–	–	–	–	–	8.7
Others	3.0	1.6	2.2	0.5	0.9	0.8	1.4

Sources: Ministero dell'Interno, 1963 : 4, 183, Elezione della Camera dei Deputati, 1948 ff.

Table 12.9 ITALY   Number of Seats Won in the Camera dei Deputati 1946–1972

	1946	1948	1953	1958	1963	1968	1972
11 Communist Party	104	131	143	140	166	177	179
3 Socialist Party	115	52	75	84	87	91	61
29 United Socialist Party	–	–	–	–	–	–	–
21 Social Democrats	–	33	19	22	32	23	29
28 Left Socialist Party	–	–	–	–	–	–	0
15 Christian Democrats	207	305	263	273	260	266	267
14 Action Party	7	–	–	–	–	–	–
16 Common Man Front	30	–	–	–	–	–	–
17 Liberal Party	41	19	13	17	40	31	21
18 Monarchist Party	16	14	40	11	8	–	–
27 United Monarchist Party	–	–	–	14	–	6	–
25 Popular Monarchist Party	–	–	–	–	–	–	14
4 Republican Party	25[1]	9	5	6	6	9	14
19 Sardinian Action Party	2	1	0	–	–	0	–
20 Sicilian Independence Movement	4	–	–	–	–	–	–
22 Social Movement—MSI	–	6	29	24	27	24	–
23 South Tyrol Peoples	–	3	3	3	3	3	3
24 Community Front	–	–	–	1	–	–	–
26 Val d'Aosta Union	–	–	–	1	1	0	–
30 National Right	–	–	–	–	–	–	56
Others	5	1	0	0	0	0	0
Total Seats	**556**	**574**	**590**	**596**	**630**	**630**	**630**

[1] Including 2 seats won by the Concentrazione Democratica Repubblicana, whose deputies later joined the Republican Party.

Sources: Ministero dell'Interno, 1963 : 483; *Elezione della Camera dei Deputati*, 1948 ff.

Table 12.10   ITALY   Percentage of Seats Won in the Camera dei Deputati 1946—1972

		1946	1948	1953	1958	1963	1968	1972
11	Communist Party	18.7	22.8	24.2	23.5	26.3	28.1	28.4
3	Socialist Party	20.7	9.1	12.7	14.1	13.8	–	9.7
29	United Socialist Party	–	–	–	–	–	14.4	–
21	Social Democrats	–	5.7	3.2	3.7	5.1	–	4.6
28	Left Socialist Party	–	–	–	–	–	3.7	0.0
15	Christian Democrats	37.2	53.1	44.6	45.8	41.3	42.2	42.4
14	Action Party	1.3	–	–	–	–	–	–
16	Common Man Front	5.4	–	–	–	–	–	–
17	Liberal Party	7.4	3.3	2.2	2.9	6.3	4.9	3.3
18	Monarchist Party	2.9	2.4	6.8	1.8	–	–	–
27	United Monarchist Party	–	–	–	–	1.3	1.0	–
25	Popular Monarchist Party	–	–	–	2.3	–	–	–
4	Republican Party	4.5	1.6	0.8	1.0	1.0	1.4	2.2
19	Sardinian Action Party	0.4	0.2	0.0	–	–	0.0	–
20	Sicilian Independence Movement	0.7	–	–	–	–	–	–
22	Social Movement—MSI	–	1.0	4.9	4.0	4.3	3.8	–
23	South Tyrol Peoples Party	–	0.5	0.5	0.5	0.5	0.5	0.5
24	Community Front	–	–	–	0.2	–	–	–
26	Val d'Aosta Union	–	–	–	0.2	0.2	0.0	–
30	National Right	–	–	–	–	–	–	8.9
	Others	0.9	0.2	0.0	0.0	0.0	0.0	0.0

Chapter 13

JAPAN

A party system began to develop in Japan following the granting of the Meiji constitution in 1889. The Constitution established a two-chamber parliament consisting of a House of Peers and a directly elected House of Representatives. The suffrage was initially very restricted. Only men aged over 25 who paid a direct national tax of at least 15 yen were entitled to vote. The tax requirements limited the electorate to about 100,000 in a nation of thirty million. The tax requirement was gradually reduced and finally abolished in 1925. Elections were held in multi-member constituencies using the single non-transferable vote system. Twenty elections were held from 1890 to 1937. In 1940 all political parties were dissolved.

Nationwide, but highly factionalized political parties developed rapidly after 1890. Their electoral strength was based on connections with influential local families and support from local officeholders. For a discussion of pre-war elections see Scalapino, 1968; its Appendix gives the distribution of seats in the House of Representatives for most elections from 1890 to 1937.

Following the American occupation of Japan at the end of the Second World War, new elections were held for the House of Representatives in 1946. The franchise was extended to women and the minimum voting age reduced to 20. The election was held in multi-member constituencies using the limited vote system (Lakeman, 1970 : 80-84). Constituencies returned four to 14 deputies. Each elector was allowed to cast two or, in larger constituencies, three votes. In 1947 the pre-war electoral system, which employed much smaller constituencies, was restored. Multi-member constituencies are used, except for the district of Anami Oshina which elects one member only. The ballot is secret. The 1947 Constitution replaced the House of Peers with an elected House of Councillors of 250 members. There are 150 councillors elected from multi-member constituencies; the remaining 100 are chosen by the electorate as a whole, the entire country forming a single constituency.

Sources:

Lakeman, E., *How Democracies Vote* (London: Faber and Faber, 1970).
Mason, R.H.P., *Japan's First General Election* (Cambridge: Cambridge University Press, 1969).
Scalapino, R.A., 'Elections and political modernization in prewar Japan.' In R.E. Ward (ed.) *Political Development of Modern Japan* (Princeton: Princeton University Press, 1968) pp.249-291.

Scalapino, R.A. and Masumi, J., *Parties and Politics in Contemporary Japan* (Berkeley and Los Angeles: University of California Press, 1962).
Ward, R.E., *Japan's Political System* (Englewood Cliffs, N.J.: Prentice-Hall, 1967).

Table 13.1
POLITICAL PARTIES IN JAPAN SINCE 1946

	Party Names	Elections contested	Number contested
1	Liberal Party (Jiyuto)[1]	1946-1952	4
2	Progressive Party (Shimpoto)[2]	1946-1953	5
3	Communist Party (Kyosanto)	1946ff	12
4	Socialist Party (Shakaito)[3]	1946-1949; 1958ff	9
5	Peoples Co-operative Party (Kokomin Kyodoto)	1946-1949	3
6	Labour-Farmer Party (Ronoto)	1949-1955	4
7	Left-Wing Socialist Party (Saha Shakaito)	1952-1955	3
8	Right-Wing Socialist Party (Uha Shakaito)	1952-1955	3
9	Hatoyama Liberal Party (Hatoyama Jiyuto)	1953	1
10	Yoshida Liberal Party (Yoshida Jiyuto)	1953-1955	2
11	Democratic Party (Minshuto)[4]	1955	1
12	Liberal Democratic Party (Jiyu Minshuto)[5]	1958ff	6
13	Democratic Socialist Party (Minshu Shakaito)[6]	1960ff	5
14	Fair Play Party (Komeito)	1967ff	3

[1] From March 1948 to March 1950 known as the Democratic Liberal Party (Minshu Jiyuto). In 1953 split into two factions led by Hatoyama and Yoshida.

[2] In 1947 and 1949 the Democratic Party (Minshuto). Merged with the Peoples Co-operative Party and renamed the Reform Party (Kaishinto) in 1952.

[3] The Socialist Party split into right and left-wing factions in 1951. They were re-united in 1955.

[4] A merger of the Reform Party and the Hatoyama Liberals.

[5] A merger of the Democratic Party and the Yoshida Liberals.

[6] A right-wing splinter from the Socialist Party.

Table 13.2
DATES OF ELECTIONS
TO THE HOUSE OF REPRESENTATIVES 1946–1972

1.	10 April 1946		7.	22 May 1958
2.	25 April 1947		8.	20 November 1960
3.	23 January 1949		9.	21 November 1963
4.	1 October 1952		10.	29 January 1967
5.	9 April 1953		11.	27 December 1969
6.	27 February 1955		12.	10 December 1972

Source: Keesings *Contemporary Archives*.

Table 13.3 JAPAN — Total Votes 1946–1953

	1946	1947	1949	1952	1953
Electorate	36,878,420	40,907,493	42,105,300	46,772,584	47,090,167
Valid Votes	26,100,175	27,361,657	30,592,519	35,336,705	34,602,445
Invalid Votes	482,000	436,091	583,376	413,018	345,563
Total Votes	26,582,175[1]	27,797,748	31,175,895	35,749,723	34,948,008
PARTY VOTES					
3 Communist Party	2,135,757	1,002,903	2,984,780	896,765	655,990
2 Progressive Party	10,350,530	6,839,646	4,798,352	6,429,450	6,186,232
9 Hatoyama Liberal Party	–	–	–	–	3,054,688
1 Liberal Party	13,505,746	7,356,321	13,420,269	16,938,221	13,476,428
10 Yoshida Liberal Party	–	–	–	3,398,597	4,516,715
7 Left-Wing Socialist Party	9,858,408	7,175,939	4,129,794	4,108,274	4,677,833
4 Socialist Party					
8 Right-Wing Socialst Party	–	–	606,840	261,190	358,773
6 Labour-Farmer Party	1,799,764	1,915,947	1,041,879	–	–
5 Peoples Co-operative Party	17,798,674	3,070,901	3,610,605	3,304,208	1,675,786
Others					

[1] The total number of electors who voted. Each voter had two, or in larger constituencies three, votes.

Sources: Scalapino and Masumi, 1962 : 157-159; Ward, 1967 : 60-61.

Table 13.4   JAPAN   Percentage of Votes 1946—1953

	1946	1947	1949	1952	1953
Valid Votes	70.8	66.9	72.7	75.6	73.5
Invalid Votes	1.3	1.1	1.4	0.9	0.7
Total Votes	72.1	68.0	74.0	76.4	74.2
Share Invalid	1.8	1.6	1.9	1.2	1.0
PARTY VOTES					
3 Communist Party	3.9	3.7	9.8	2.5	1.9
2 Progressive Party	18.7	25.0	15.7	18.2	17.9
9 Hatoyama Liberal Party	–	–	–	–	8.8
1 Liberal Party	24.4	26.9	43.9	47.9	–
10 Yoshida Liberal Party	–	–	–	–	38.9
7 Left-Wing Socialist Party	–	–	–	9.6	13.1
4 Socialist Party	17.8	26.2	13.5	–	–
8 Right-Wing Socialist Party	–	–	–	11.6	13.5
6 Labour-Farmer Party	–	–	2.0	0.7	1.0
5 Peoples Co-operative Party	3.2	7.0	3.4	–	–
Others	32.1	11.2	11.8	9.4	4.8

Table 13.5　JAPAN　　Number of Seats Won in the House of Representatives 1946–1953

		1946	1947	1949	1952	1953
3	Communist Party	5	4	35	0	1
2	Progressive Party	94	121	69	85	76
9	Hatoyama Liberal Party	–	–	–	–	35
1	Liberal Party	140	131	264	240	–
10	Yoshida Liberal Party	–	–	–	–	199
7	Left-Wing Socialist Party	–	–	–	54	72
4	Socialist Party	92	143	48	–	–
8	Right-Wing Socialist Party	–	–	–	57	66
6	Labour-Farmer Party	–	–	7	4	5
5	Peoples Co-operative Party	14	29	14	–	–
	Others	119	38	29	26	12
	Total Seats	464	466	466	466	466

Sources: Scalapino and Masumi, 1962 : 159; Ward 1967 : 60-61.

Table 13.6 JAPAN

Percentage of Seats Won in the House of Representatives 1946–1953

		1946	1947	1949	1952	1953
3	Communist Party	1.1	0.9	7.5	0.0	0.2
2	Progressive Party	20.3	26.0	14.8	18.2	16.3
9	Hatoyama Liberal Party	–	–	–	–	7.5
1	Liberal Party	30.2	28.1	56.7	51.5	–
10	Yoshida Liberal Party	–	–	–	–	42.7
7	Left-Wing Socialist Party	–	–	–	11.6	19.1
4	Socialist Party	19.8	30.7	10.3	–	–
8	Right-Wing Socialist Party	–	–	–	12.2	14.2
6	Labour-Farmer Party	–	–	1.5	0.9	1.1
5	Peoples Co-operative Party	3.0	6.2	3.0	–	–
	Others	25.6	8.2	6.2	5.6	2.6

Table 13.7   JAPAN   Total Votes 1955—1972

	1955	1958	1960	1963	1967	1969	1972
Electorate	49,235,375	52,013,529	54,312,993	58,281,678	62,992,796	69,260,424	74,149,161
Valid Votes	37,014,837	39,751,661	39,509,123	41,016,540	46,006,570	46,989,890	52,423,477
Invalid Votes	323,184	293,450	414,346	446,011	599,470	459,819	786,466[2]
Total Votes	37,338,021	40,045,111	39,923,469	41,462,551	46,606,040	47,449,709	53,209,943[2]

PARTY VOTES

	1955	1958	1960	1963	1967	1969	1972
3 Communist Party	733,121	1,012,035	1,156,723	1,646,477	2,190,563	3,199,031	5,496,697
11 Democratic Party[1]	13,536,044	–	–	–	–	–	–
12 Liberal Democratic Party	–	22,976,846	22,740,272	22,423,915	22,447,838	22,381,570	24,563,078
10 Yoshida Liberal Party	9,849,457	–	–	–	–	–	–
7 Left-Wing Socialist Party	5,683,312	–	–	–	–	–	–
4 Socialist Party	–	13,093,993	10,887,134	11,906,766	12,826,103	10,074,100	11,478,600
8 Right-Wing Socialist Party	5,129,594	–	–	–	–	–	–
6 Labour-Farmer Party	357,611	–	–	–	–	–	–
13 Democratic Socialist Party	–	–	3,464,148	3,023,302	3,404,463	3,636,590	3,659,922
14 Fair Play Party	–	–	–	–	2,472,371	5,124,666	4,436,631
Others	1,725,695	2,668,786	1,260,846	2,616,078	2,665,232	2,573,933	2,788,549

[1] A merger of the Reform Party and the Hatoyama Liberals
[2] Estimates

Sources: Scalapino and Masumi, 1962 : 157-159; Ward, 1967 : 60-61; and figures provided by the Japanese Embassy, London.

Table 13.8 JAPAN   Percentage of Votes 1955–1972

	1955	1958	1960	1963	1967	1969	1972
Valid Votes	75.2	76.4	72.7	70.4	73.0	67.8	70.7
Invalid Votes	0.7	0.6	0.8	0.8	1.0	0.7	1.0
Total Votes	75.8	77.0	73.5	71.1	74.0	68.5	71.7
Share Invalid	0.9	0.7	1.0	1.1	1.3	1.0	1.5
PARTY VOTES							
3 Communist Party	2.0	2.5	2.9	4.0	4.8	6.8	10.5
11 Democratic Party	36.6	–	–	–	–	–	–
12 Liberal Democratic Party	–	57.8	57.6	53.9	48.8	47.6	46.9
10 Yoshida Liberal Party	26.6	–	–	–	–	–	–
7 Left-Wing Socialist Party	15.4	–	–	–	–	–	–
4 Socialist Party	–	32.9	27.6	28.6	27.9	21.4	21.9
8 Right-Wing Socialist Party	13.9	–	–	–	–	–	–
6 Labour-Farmer Party	1.0	–	–	–	–	–	–
13 Democratic Socialist Party	–	–	8.8	7.3	7.4	7.7	7.0
14 Fair Play Party	–	–	–	–	5.4	10.9	8.5
Others	4.7	6.7	3.2	6.3	5.8	5.5	5.3

233

Table 13.9 JAPAN

Number of Seats Won in the House of Representatives 1955–1972

		1955	1958	1960	1963	1967	1969	1972
3	Communist Party	2	1	3	5	5	14	38
11	Democratic Party	185	–	–	–	–	–	–
12	Liberal Democratic Party	–	287	296	183	277	288	271
10	Yoshida Liberal Party	112	–	–	–	–	–	–
7	Left-Wing Socialist Party	89	–	–	–	–	–	–
4	Socialist Party	–	166	145	144	140	90	118
8	Right-Wing Socialist Party	67	–	–	–	–	–	–
6	Labour-Farmer Party	4	–	–	–	–	–	–
13	Democratic Socialist Party	–	–	17	23	30	31	19
14	Fair Play Party	–	–	–	–	25	47	29
	Others	8	13	6	12	9	16	16
	Total Seats	467	467	467	467	486	486	491

Sources: Scalapino and Masumi, 1962 : 159; Ward, 1967 : 60-61; and figures provided by the Japanese Embassy, London.

234

Table 13.10   JAPAN   Percentage of Seats Won in the House of Representatives 1955–1972

	1955	1958	1960	1963	1967	1969	1972
3 Communist Party	0.4	0.2	0.6	1.1	1.0	2.9	7.7
11 Democratic Party	39.6	–	–	–	–	–	–
12 Liberal Democratic Party	–	61.5	63.4	60.6	57.0	59.3	55.2
10 Yoshida Liberal Party	24.0	–	–	–	–	–	–
7 Left-Wing Socialist Party	19.1	–	–	–	–	–	–
4 Socialist Party	–	35.5	31.0	30.8	28.8	18.5	24.0
8 Right-Wing Socialist Party	14.3	–	–	–	–	–	–
6 Labour-Farmer Party	0.9	–	–	–	–	–	–
13 Democratic Socialist Party	–	–	3.6	4.9	6.2	6.4	3.9
14 Fair Play Party	–	–	–	–	5.1	9.7	5.9
Others	1.7	2.8	1.3	2.6	1.9	3.3	3.3

Chapter 14

LUXEMBOURG

Luxembourg was established as an autonomous state under the Dutch crown in 1815; *de facto* it was administered as an integral part of the Netherlands. From 1830 to 1839 it formed part of newly independent Belgium. In 1839 the territory of the Grand Duchy was divided. Half the population remained part of Belgium. Sovereignty over the remaining territory was restored to the King of the Netherlands, who granted the country its own indirectly elected assembly.

In 1868 a directly elected parliament, the Chambre des Deputés, was introduced. The electorate was limited to men more than 25 years old who met a minimum tax qualification. Initially, the qualification was 30 francs a year; this was reduced by stages to 10 francs in 1902. The percentage of the population enfranchised increased from 2.9 per cent in 1871 to about 12.7 per cent in 1902 (Nohlen, 1969:814-815). The 1902 percentage is calculated from the 1900 Census figures (*Annuaire Statistique,* 1962:10). A two-ballot majority system in multi-member constituencies was used. If sufficient candidates did not win an absolute majority on the first ballot, a second ballot was held, limited to twice as many candidates as there were vacant seats. Each parliamentary term lasted for six years, with half the deputies retiring every three years. General elections were held only when the Chamber was dissolved. The secret ballot was introduced in 1879.

Until the end of the nineteenth century political parties were organized only in Parliament. The Chamber was dominated by the Liberals, who formed all the governments from 1867 until 1915 (Fusilier, 1960:614). A Socialist party appeared in 1896. The Liberals formed their first national organization, the Ligue Liberale, in 1904. The Catholics were slower to establish their own political party. The Parti de la Droite was not established until January, 1914 (Heiderscheid, 1961, 222-224).

The new constitution of 1918 extended the franchise to all adults aged 21 or over. Voting was made compulsory. The country is divided into four multi-member constituencies. Each elector has as many votes as there are seats in his constituency. He may cast up to two votes for a single candidate and may divide his votes between candidates of different parties. Seats are allocated at the constituency level by the Hagenbach-Bischoff method. In 1956 an amendment to the constitution provided for a general election every five years, instead of a parliamentary term of six years with partial elections every three years. In 1972 the voting age was reduced to 18.

No official election statistics are available for elections before 1928. Secondary sources provide figures for some elections from 1918.

Sources:

Fusilier, R., *Les monarchies parlementaires* (Paris: Editions Ouvrières 1960).

Heiderscheid, A., *Aspects de la sociologie religieuse du diocèse de Luxembourg* (Luxembourg: Editions de l'Imprimerie St. Paul, 1961).

Ministère de l'Economie Nationale, *Annuaire statistique 1969* (Luxembourg: Service Centrale de la Statistique et des Etudes Economiques, 1969).

Ibid., *Annuaire statistique rétrospectif 1960* (Luxembourg 1962).

D. Nohlen, "Luxemburg." in D. Sternberger and B. Vogel (eds.) *Die Wahl der Parlamente* (Berlin: de Gruyter, 1969) pp. 809-831.

Table 14.1
POLITICAL PARTIES IN LUXEMBOURG SINCE 1919

	Party Names	Elections contested	Number contested
1	Party of the Right (Parti de la Droite); the Christian Social Party since 1945 (Parti Chrétien Social)	1919ff	14
2	Radical-Liberal Party 1919-1925 Parti Libéral; in 1928 and 1931 the Parti Radical; from 1934 the Parti Libéral Radical[1]	1919-1937	7
3	Socialist Party (Parti Social Démocrate); since 1924 the Socialist Workers Party (Parti Ouvrier Socialiste Luxembourgeois)	1919ff	14
4	Independent National Party (Parti Indépendant National)	1919-1925	3
5	Independent Popular Party (Parti Indépendant Populaire)	1919	1
6	Communist Party (Parti Communiste Luxembourgeois)	1922ff	13
7	Independent Right Party (Parti Indépendant de Droite)	1925	1
8	Left Party (Parti de Gauche)	1925	1
9	Radical Socialist Party (Parti Radical-Socialiste)	1925-1931	2
10	Independents (Indépendants)	1928-1934	3
11	List of Left Independents (Liste des Indépendants de Gauche)	1928	1
12	Farmers and Middle Class Party (Parti des Agriculteurs et des Classes Moyennes)	1931	1
13	Progressive Democrats of the North (Progressistes Démocrates du Nord)	1931	1
14	Independents of the East (Indépendants de l'Est)	1934-1945	2
15	Democratic List (Liste Démocratique)	1937	1
16	Free List of Peasants, the Middle Class and Workers (Liste Libre des Paysans, Classes Moyennes et Ouvriers)	1937	1
17	Liberal Party (Parti Libéral)	1937-1945	2
18	Party of Peasants and the Middle Class (Parti des Paysans et des Classes Moyennes)	1937	1
19	Democratic Party (Parti Démocratique); 1945 to 1951, Groupement Patriotique et Démocratique; in 1954 Groupement Démocratique)	1945ff	7
20	Middle Class Party (Parti des Classes Moyennes)	1954	1
21	Popular Independent Movement (Mouvement Populaire Indépendant)[2]	1964	1

[1] This grouping follows Heiderscheid, 1961 : 233.

[2] The Popular Independent Movement merged with the Democratic Party before the 1968 election. One of the Movement's two deputies stood in the 1968 election as a candidate of the Parti de la Solidarité.

239

Table 14.2
DATES OF ELECTIONS
TO THE CHAMBRE DES DEPUTES 1919—1968

1.	28 September 1919	8.	21 October 1945
2.	28 May 1922 (P)	9.	6 June 1948 (P)
3.	1 March 1925	10.	3 June 1951 (P)
4.	3 June 1928 (P)	11.	30 May 1954
5.	7 June 1931 (P)	12.	1 February 1959
6.	3 June 1934 (P)	13.	7 June 1964
7.	6 June 1937 (P)	14.	15 December 1968

(P) indicates a partial election

Sources: Ministère de l'Economie Nationale, 1963 : 574-575 and *Ibid.*, 1969 : 170-171.

Table 14.3   LUXEMBOURG   Total Votes 1919–1937

	1919[1]	1922[2]	1925[1]	1928[3]	1931[4]	1934[3]	1937[5]
Electorate	126,000	n.a.	n.a.	n.a.	n.a.	n.a.	n.a.
Valid Votes	n.a.	n.a.	n.a.	57,884	106,776	66,416	73,801
Invalid Votes	n.a.	n.a.	n.a.	2,559	7,568	3,207	3,819
Total Votes	n.a.	n.a.	n.a.	60,443	114,344	69,623	78,220

PARTY VOTES

	1919[1]	1922[2]	1925[1]	1928[3]	1931[4]	1934[3]	1937[5]
1 Party of the Right	654,000	n.a.	n.a.	340,545	379,289	407,838	408,773
2 Radical-Liberal Party	210,000	n.a.	n.a.	67,791	65,861	141,695	99,029
3 Socialist Party	240,000	n.a.	n.a.	352,970	189,749	404,729	238,655
4 Independent National Party	72,000	n.a.	–	–	–	–	–
5 Independent Popular Party	69,000	–	–	–	–	–	–
6 Communist Party	–	n.a.	n.a.	–	10,807	70,940	–
7 Independent Right Party	–	–	n.a.	–	–	–	–
8 Left Party	–	–	n.a.	–	89,347	–	–
9 Radical Socialists	–	–	n.a.	–	40,569	25,694	–
10 Independents	–	–	–	56,629	–	–	–
11 List of Left Independents	–	–	–	36,773	–	–	–
12 Farmers and Middle Class Party	–	–	–	–	46,446	–	–
13 Progressive Democrats of the North	–	–	–	–	35,702	50,707	–
14 Independents of the East	–	–	–	–	–	–	–

15	Democratic List	—	—	—	—	—	102,013
16	Free List of Peasants, the Middle Class and Workers	—	—	—	—	—	32,265
17	Liberal Party	—	—	—	—	—	27,621
18	Peasants and Middle Class Party	—	—	—	—	—	19,634
	Others	—	—	—	—	793	—

[1] General Election.
[2] Figures for the 1922 partial and the 1925 General Election are not available.
[3] Partial election in the South and East constituencies.
[4] Partial election in the Centre and North constituencies. Includes votes cast in the South constituency where a special election was held to choose the two extra deputies allocated to the constituency as a result of the 1931 census.
[5] Partial election in the Central and North constituencies.

243

Table 14.4   LUXEMBOURG   Percentage of Votes 1919—1937

	1919	1922	1925	1928	1931	1934	1937
Share Invalid	n.a.	n.a.	n.a.	4.2	6.6	4.6	4.9
PARTY VOTES							
1 Party of the Right	52.5	n.a.	n.a.	39.8	44.2	37.0	44.0
2 Radical-Liberal Party	16.9	n.a.	n.a.	7.9	7.7	12.9	10.7
3 Socialist Party	19.3	n.a.	n.a.	41.3	22.1	36.7	25.7
4 Independent National Party	5.8	n.a.	n.a.	—	—	—	—
5 Independent Popular Party	5.5	—	—	—	—	—	—
6 Communist Party	—	n.a.	n.a.	—	1.3	6.4	—
7 Independent Right Party	—	—	n.a.	—	—	—	—
8 Left Party	—	—	n.a.	—	—	—	—
9 Radical Socialists	—	—	n.a.	—	10.4	—	—
10 Independents	—	—	—	6.6	4.7	2.3	—
11 List of Left Independents	—	—	—	4.3	—	—	—
12 Farmers and Middle Class Party	—	—	—	—	5.4	—	—
13 Progressive Democrats of the North	—	—	—	—	4.2	—	—
14 Independents of the East	—	—	—	—	—	4.6	—

15	Democratic List	—	—	—	—	—	11.0
16	Free List of Peasants, the Middle Class and Workers	—	—	—	—	—	3.5
17	Liberal Party	—	—	—	—	—	3.0
18	Peasants and Middle Class Party	—	—	—	—	—	2.1
	Others	—	—	—	—	0.1	—

Table 14.5   LUXEMBOURG   Number of Seats Won in the Chambre des Deputés 1919–1937

		1919	1922	1925	1928	1931	1934	1937
1	Party of the Right	27	13	22	12	14	12	13
2	Radical-Liberal Party	7	6	4	2	2	3	2
3	Socialist Party	9	2	8	10	5	10	7
4	Independent National Party	3	4	4	–	–	–	–
5	Independent Popular Party	2	–	–	–	–	–	–
6	Communist Party	–	0	0	–	0	1	–
7	Independent Right Party	–	–	1	–	–	–	–
8	Left Party	–	–	2	–	–	–	–
9	Radical Socialists	–	–	5	–	2	–	–
10	Independents	–	–	–	1	1	0	–
11	List of Left Independents	–	–	–	2	–	–	–
12	Farmers and Middle Class Party	–	–	–	–	2	–	–
13	Progressive Democrats of the North	–	–	–	–	1	–	–
14	Independents of the East	–	–	–	–	–	3	–
15	Democratic List	–	–	–	–	–	–	2
16	Free List of Peasants, the Middle Class and Workers	–	–	–	–	–	–	1
17	Liberal Party	–	–	–	–	–	–	1
18	Peasants and Middle Class Party	–	–	–	–	–	0	0
	Others	–	–	–	–	–	0	–
	Total Seats	**48**	**25**	**46**	**27**	**27**	**29**	**26**

Sources: Nohlen, 1969 : 820; *Annuaire statistique, 1960* : 575.

Table 14.6 LUXEMBOURG Percentage of Seats Won in the Chambre des Deputés 1919–1937

	1919	1922	1925	1928	1931	1934	1937
1 Party of the Right	56.3	52.0	47.8	44.4	51.9	41.4	50.0
2 Radical-Liberal Party	14.6	24.0	8.7	7.4	7.4	10.3	7.7
3 Socialist Party	18.8	8.0	17.4	37.0	18.5	34.5	26.9
4 Independent National Party	6.3	16.0	8.7	–	–	–	–
5 Independent Popular Party	4.2	–	–	–	–	–	–
6 Communist Party	–	0.0	0.0	–	0.0	3.4	–
7 Independent Right Party	–	–	2.2	–	–	–	–
8 Left Party	–	–	4.3	–	–	–	–
9 Radical Socialists	–	–	10.9	–	7.4	–	–
10 Independents	–	–	–	3.7	3.7	0.0	–
11 List of Left Independents	–	–	–	7.4	–	–	–
12 Farmers and Middle Class Party	–	–	–	–	7.4	–	–
13 Progressive Democrats of the North	–	–	–	–	3.7	–	–
14 Independents of the East	–	–	–	–	–	10.3	–
15 Democratic List	–	–	–	–	–	–	7.7
16 Free List of Peasants, the Middle Class and Workers	–	–	–	–	–	–	3.8
17 Liberal Party	–	–	–	–	–	–	3.8
18 Peasants and Middle Class Party	–	–	–	–	–	–	0.0
Others	–	–	–	–	–	0.0	–

Table 14.7   LUXEMBOURG   Total Votes 1945—1968

	1945	1948[1]	1951[2]	1954	1959	1964	1968
Electorate	n.a.	84,724	92,110	183,590	188,286	191,788	192,601
Valid Votes	153,596	73,674	79,662	162,036	165,596	163,158	160,184
Invalid Votes	5,487	4,191	3,951	8,056	8,240	10,544	10,385
Total Votes	159,083	77,865	83,613	170,092	173,836	173,702	170,569
PARTY VOTES							
1 Christian Social Party	907,601	425,545	386,972	1,003,456	896,840	883,079	915,944
3 Socialist Party	569,025	372,177	481,155	831,836	848,523	999,843	837,555
6 Communist Party	295,701	25,662	195,956	211,121	220,425	330,909	402,610
19 Democratic Party	366,860	215,511	97,415	255,522	448,387	280,644	430,262
14 Independents of the East	13,977	–	–	–	–	–	–
17 Liberal Party	36,321	–	–	–	–	–	–
20 Middle Class Party	–	–	–	66,582	–	–	–
21 Popular Independent Movement	–	–	–	–	–	159,370	–
Others	2,015	–	–	–	15,821	–	10,355[3]

[1] Partial election in the South and East constituencies.
[2] Partial election in the North and Centre constituencies.
[3] Votes reported here cast for Solidarité Nationale.

Source: Annuaire statistique, 1969 : 170-171.

248

Table 14.8 LUXEMBOURG Percentage of Votes 1945–1968

	1945	1948	1951	1954	1959	1964	1968
Valid Votes	n.a.	87.0	86.5	88.3	87.9	85.1	83.2
Invalid Votes	n.a.	4.9	4.3	4.4	4.4	5.5	5.4
Total Votes	n.a.	91.9	90.8	92.6	92.3	90.6	88.6
Share Invalid	3.4	5.4	4.7	4.7	4.7	6.1	6.1
PARTY VOTES							
1 Christian Social Party	41.4	41.0	33.3	42.4	36.9	33.3	35.3
3 Socialist Party	26.0	35.8	41.4	35.1	34.9	37.7	32.3
6 Communist Party	13.5	2.5	16.9	8.9	9.1	12.5	15.5
19 Democratic Party	16.7	20.7	8.4	10.8	18.5	10.6	16.6
14 Independents of the East	0.6	–	–	–	–	–	–
17 Liberal Party	1.7	–	–	–	–	–	–
20 Middle Class Party	–	–	–	2.8	–	–	–
21 Popular Independent Movement	–	–	–	–	–	6.0	–
Others	0.1	–	–	–	0.7	–	0.4

Table 14.9 LUXEMBOURG Number of Seats Won in the Chambre des Deputés 1945–1968

	1945	1948[1]	1951[2]	1954	1959	1964	1968
1 Christian Social Party	25	12	9	26	21	22	21
3 Socialist Party	11	9	10	17	17	21	18
6 Communist Party	5	0	4	3	3	5	6
19 Democratic Party	9	5	3	6	11	6	11
14 Independents of the East	1	–	–	–	–	–	–
17 Liberal Party	0	–	–	–	–	–	–
20 Middle Class Party	–	–	–	0	–	–	–
21 Popular Independent Movement	–	–	–	–	–	2	–
Others	0	–	–	–	0	–	0
Total Seats	51	26	26	52	52	56	56

[1] Partial election in the South and East constituencies.
[2] Partial election in the North and Centre constituencies.

Source: Annuaire statistique, 1969 : 176-177

Table 14.10   LUXEMBOURG   Percentage of Seats Won in the Chambre des Deputés 1945–1968

	1945	1948	1951	1954	1959	1964	1968
1 Christian Social Party	49.0	46.2	34.6	50.0	40.4	39.3	37.5
3 Socialist Party	21.6	34.6	38.5	32.7	32.7	37.5	32.1
6 Communist Party	9.8	0.0	15.4	5.8	5.8	8.9	10.7
19 Democratic Party	17.6	19.2	11.5	11.5	21.2	10.7	19.6
14 Independents of the East	2.0	–	–	–	–	–	–
17 Liberal Party	0.0	–	–	–	–	–	–
20 Middle Class Party	–	–	–	0.0	–	–	–
21 Popular Independent Movement	–	–	–	–	–	3.6	–
Others	0.0	–	–	–	0.0	–	0.0

Chapter 15
MALTA

During the nineteenth century Malta was ruled by a British Governor, assisted by a Council of Government. After 1849 the Council included some elected members; in 1887 the elected members were given a majority of seats. Nationalist candidates committed to the defence of Italian, the language of the island's traditional social elite, were almost unfailingly elected. Conflict between the elected majority and the Governor over the language question led to the suspension of the Constitution. In 1903 a Council of Government was introduced in which elected members were in a minority. Nationalist members were regularly returned, often unopposed (Dobie, 1967 : 38-79).

In 1921 Malta was granted internal self-government. A bicameral legislature was established. The 32 members of the Legislative Assembly were elected by single transferable vote in multi-member constituencies. The ballot was secret. The vote was confined to literate men aged at least 21, who had an income from property of at least £5 a year or paid rent of at least £5 a year. Those who had received public assistance during the previous three years were disenfranchised. The Senate consisted of ten members elected by Legislative Assembly voters aged over 35 and ten chosen by different organizations: two each by the Archbishop of Malta, the Maltese nobility, university graduates, the Chamber of Commerce and the Trade Union Council.

The 1921 election was the first contested by well organised political parties. Two parties emerged as defenders of the Italian language—the Political Union and National Democratic Party. They were opposed by the pro-English language Constitutional Party and the Malta Labour Party. The Constitution was suspended in 1930 and restored in 1932. It was revoked in 1936 and replaced by a Council of Government of 20 members: eight ex-officio, two chosen by the governor and ten directly elected. In 1947 a single-chamber Legislative Assembly and universal adult suffrage were introduced. Following a political crisis over relations with the United Kingdom the Constitution was again suspended in 1958. In 1962 self-government was restored and in 1964 Malta became independent. The Independence Constitution made no changes in the franchise requirements or electoral system, but the Legislative Assembly was renamed the House of Representatives.

Sources:

Annual Abstract of Statistics (Valetta: Central Office of Statistics, 1970).
Colonial Office, Malta: Report of Constitutional Commissioner (London: Her Majesty's Stationery Office, 1947).

Dobie, E., *Malta's Road to Independence* (Norman: University of Oklahoma Press, 1967).

Foreign and Commonwealth Office, *A Yearbook of the Commonwealth* (London: Her Majesty's Stationery Office, 1972).

Table 15.1
POLITICAL PARTIES IN MALTA SINCE 1921

	Party Names	Elections contested	Number contested
1	Constitutional Party[1]	1921-1939; 1950-1953	8
2	Democratic Nationalist Party I	1921	1
3	Labour Party	1921ff	14
4	Maltese Political Union	1921	1
5	Nationalist Party[2]	1924-1939; 1947ff	12
6	Jones Party	1945-1947	2
7	Democratic Action Party	1947-1950	2
8	Gozo Party	1947	1
9	Malta Workers Party[3]	1950-1953	3
10	Progressive Constitutional Party[4]	1953ff	5
11	Christian Workers Party[5]	1962-1966	2
12	Democratic Nationalist Party II[6]	1962-1966	2

[1] The Constitutional Party did not contest the 1945 election because it was opposed to an election before self-government was restored. The party was dissolved in 1946 and revived in June 1950.

[2] A merger of the Democratic Nationalist Party and the Maltese Political Union in 1926. The Nationalist Party boycotted the 1945 election because it took place before the restoration of self-government.

[3] Formed in October 1949 by Dr. Paul Boffa, the former leader of the Labour Party.

[4] Formed in October 1953 by Miss Mabel Strickland, a former leader of the Constitutional Party.

[5] Former members of the Nationalist Party led by Dr. Herbert Ganado.

[6] Founded in 1961 by Anthony Pellegrini, formerly General Secretary of the Malta Labour Party.

Table 15.2
DATES OF ELECTIONS
TO THE LEGISLATIVE ASSEMBLY 1921–1971[1]

1.	18–19 October 1921	8.	2–4 September 1950
2.	9–10 June 1924	9.	5–7 May 1951
3.	7–9 August 1927	10.	12–14 December 1953
4.	11–13 June 1932	11.	26–28 February 1955
5.	22–24 July 1939	12.	17–19 February 1962
6.	10–12 November 1945	13.	26–28 March 1966
7.	25–27 October 1947	14.	12–14 June 1971

[1] In 1939 and 1945 elections to the Council of Government.
Since 1966 elections to the House of Representatives.

Source: The Electoral Registrar, Valetta.

Table 15.3   MALTA   Total Votes 1921—1939

	1921	1924	1927	1932	1939
Electorate	27,104	27,104	44,089	52,610	46,852
Valid Votes	20,475	24,069	34,444	47,305	35,139
Invalid Votes	159	179	277	1,353	378
Total Votes	20,634	24,248	34,721	48,658	35,517
PARTY VOTES					
1 Constitutional Party	5,183	8,128	14,130	13,513	19,156
3 Labour Party	4,742	4,891	4,773	4,221	3,100
2 Democratic Nationalist Party I	2,465	—	—	—	—
4 Maltese Political Union	7,999	—	—	—	—
5 Nationalist Party	—	10,777	15,079	28,906	11,618
Others	86	273	462	665	1,265

Source: *Annual Abstract of Statistics* : 74.

Table 15.4   MALTA   Percentage of Votes 1921–1939

	1921	1924	1927	1932	1939
Valid Votes	75.5	88.8	78.1	89.9	75.0
Invalid Votes	0.6	0.7	0.6	2.6	0.8
Total Votes	76.1	89.5	78.8	92.5	75.8
Share Invalid	0.8	0.7	0.8	2.8	1.1
PARTY VOTES					
1 Constitutional Party	25.3	33.8	41.0	28.6	54.5
3 Labour Party	23.2	20.3	13.9	8.9	8.8
2 Democratic Nationalist Party	12.0	–	–	–	–
4 Maltese Political Union	39.1	–	–	–	–
5 Nationalist Party	–	44.8	43.8	61.1	33.1
Others	0.4	1.1	1.3	1.4	3.6

Table 15.5 MALTA Number of Seats Won in the Legislative Assembly 1921–1939[1]

	1921	1924	1927	1932	1939[1]
1 Constitutional Party	7	9	14	10	6
3 Labour Party	7	8	3	1	1
2 Democratic Nationalist Party I	4	–	–	–	–
4 Maltese Political Union	14	–	–	–	–
5 Nationalist Party	–	15	15	21	3
Others	0	0	0	0	0
Total Seats	**32**	**32**	**32**	**32**	**10**

[1] In 1939 The Council of Government.

Source: *Annual Abstract of Statistics* : 76.

Table 15.6   MALTA   Percentage of Seats Won in the Legislative Assembly 1921–1939

		1921	1924	1927	1932	1939
1	Constitutional Party	21.9	28.1	43.8	31.3	60.0
3	Labour Party	21.9	25.0	9.4	3.1	10.0
2	Democratic Nationalist Party	12.5	–	–	–	–
4	Maltese Political Union	43.8	–	–	–	–
5	Nationalist Party	–	46.9	46.9	65.6	30.0
	Others	0.0	0.0	0.0	0.0	0.0

Table 15.7   MALTA   Total Votes 1945—1971

	1945	1947	1950	1951	1953	1955	1962	1966	1971
Electorate	61,206	140,703	140,516	151,977	148,478	149,380	166,936	161,490	181,768
Valid Votes	25,672	105,494	106,129	112,628	118,453	120,655	150,606	143,347	168,059
Invalid Votes	918[1]	647	691	738	880	588	927	1,526	854
Total Votes	26,590[1]	106,141	106,820	113,366	119,333	121,243	151,533	144,873	168,913
PARTY VOTES									
1 Constitutional Party	—	—	10,584	9,151	1,385	—	—	—	—
3 Labour Party	19,071	63,145	30,332	40,315	52,771	68,447	50,974	61,774	85,448
5 Nationalist Party	—	19,041	31,431	39,946	45,180	48,514	63,262	68,656	80,753
6 Jones Party	3,786	3,664	—	—	—	—	—	—	—
7 Democratic Action Party	—	14,010	6,361	—	—	—	—	—	—
8 Gozo Party	—	5,491	—	—	—	—	—	—	—
9 Malta Workers Party	—	—	24,616	21,053	14,000	—	—	—	—
10 Progressive Constitutional Party	—	—	—	—	5,117	3,649	7,290	2,086	1,756
11 Christian Workers Party	—	—	—	—	—	—	14,285	8,561	—
12 Democratic Nationalist Party II	—	—	—	—	—	—	13,968	1,878	—
Others	2,815	143	2,805	2,163	—	45	827	392	102

[1] Estimate based on percentage figures given in *Annual Abstract of Statistics* : 75.

Sources: *Annual Abstract of Statistics* : 75-77; and figures provided by the Central Office of Statistics and Electoral Office, Valetta.

Table 15.8 MALTA Percentage of Votes 1945–1971

	1945	1947	1950	1951	1953	1955	1962	1966	1971
Valid Votes	41.9	75.0	75.5	74.1	79.8	80.8	90.2	88.8	92.5
Invalid Votes	1.5	0.5	0.5	0.5	0.6	0.4	0.6	0.9	0.5
Total Votes	43.4	75.4	76.0	74.6	80.4	81.2	90.8	89.7	92.9
Share Invalid	3.5	0.6	0.6	0.7	0.7	0.5	0.6	1.1	0.5
PARTY VOTES									
1 Constitutional Party	–	–	10.0	8.1	1.2	–	–	–	–
3 Labour Party	74.3	59.9	28.6	35.8	44.6	56.7	33.8	43.1	50.8
5 Nationalist Party	–	18.0	29.6	35.5	38.1	40.2	42.0	47.9	48.1
6 Jones Party	14.7	3.5	–	–	–	–	–	–	–
7 Democratic Action Party	–	13.3	6.0	–	–	–	–	–	–
8 Gozo Party	–	5.2	–	–	–	–	–	–	–
9 Malta Workers Party	–	–	23.2	18.7	11.8	–	–	–	–
10 Progressive Constitutional Party	–	–	–	–	4.3	3.0	4.8	1.5	1.0
11 Christian Workers Party	–	–	–	–	–	–	9.5	6.0	–
12 Democratic Nationalist Party II	–	–	–	–	–	–	9.3	1.3	–
Others	11.0	0.1	2.6	1.9	–	0.0	0.5	0.3	0.1

Table 15.9 MALTA

Number of Seats Won in the Legislative Assembly 1945–1971[1]

	1945	1947	1950	1951	1953	1955	1962	1966	1971
1 Constitutional Party	–	–	4	4	0	–	–	–	–
3 Labour Party	9	24	11	14	19	23	16	22	28
5 Nationalist Party	7	7	12	15	18	17	25	28	27
6 Jones Party	1	2	–	–	–	–	–	–	–
7 Democratic Action Party	–	4	1	–	–	–	–	–	–
8 Gozo Party	–	3	–	–	–	–	–	–	–
9 Malta Workers Party	–	–	11	7	3	–	–	–	–
10 Progressive Constitutional Party	–	–	–	–	0	0	1	0	0
11 Christian Workers Party	–	–	–	–	–	–	4	0	–
12 Democratic Nationalist Party II	–	–	1[2]	0	–	0	4	0	–
Others	0	0			–		0	0	0
Total Seats	**10**	**40**	**40**	**40**	**40**	**40**	**50**	**50**	**55**

[1] In 1945 The Council of Government; since 1966 The House of Representatives.

[2] Independent.

Sources: *Annual Abstract of Statistics* : 76-77; and figures provided by the Central Office of Statistics and Electoral Office, Valetta.

Table 15.10   MALTA   Percentage of Seats Won in the Legislative Assembly 1945—1971

	1945	1947	1950	1951	1953	1955	1962	1966	1971
1 Constitutional Party	–	–	10.0	10.0	0.0	–	–	–	–
3 Labour Party	90.0	60.0	27.5	35.0	47.5	57.5	32.0	44.0	50.9
5 Nationalist Party	–	17.5	30.0	37.5	45.0	42.5	50.0	56.0	49.1
6 Jones Party	10.0	5.0	–	–	–	–	–	–	–
7 Democratic Action Party	–	10.0	2.5	–	–	–	–	–	–
8 Gozo Party	–	7.5	–	–	–	–	–	–	–
9 Malta Workers Party	–	–	27.5	17.5	7.5	–	–	–	0.0
10 Progressive Constitutional Party	–	–	–	–	0.0	0.0	2.0	0.0	–
11 Christian Workers Party	–	–	–	–	–	–	8.0	0.0	–
12 Democratic Nationalist Party II	–	–	–	–	–	–	8.0	0.0	–
Others	0.0	0.0	2.5	0.0	0.0	0.0	0.0	0.0	0.0

Chapter 16

THE NETHERLANDS

Representative government has a long history in the Netherlands. Responsible parliamentary government was introduced in 1848. The Dutch parliament, the States General, consists of two houses, the First Chamber (Eerste Kamer) and the Second Chamber (Tweede Kamer). The franchise was limited to males over 23 who paid a varying minimum of taxes on ownership of land, enterprise or visible signs of wealth. In 1850 11 per cent of the adult male population was entitled to vote. Until the 1880s the States General was dominated by Liberal, Conservative and Catholic groups. Party organization was virtually non-existent. It was not until the establishment of the Anti-Revolutionary Party in 1879 that a popularly based party system began to develop. The Conservatives quickly dwindled to a negligible political force; the Liberal and later, Catholic and Christian Historical groups began to establish their own party organizations.

In 1887 the franchise requirements were reduced, and the size of the electorate doubled. A new electoral system was introduced. Deputies were chosen in single-member constituencies except in the larger cities, which formed multi-member constituencies. If no candidate received a majority in the first ballot, a second ballot was held between the two leading candidates. In 1896 the qualifications for the suffrage were again reduced, but the minimum voting age was increased to 25. At the same time the multi-member constituencies were replaced by single-member ones.

In 1917 universal male suffrage and proportional representation, using the largest remainder system, was introduced. Voting was made compulsory. In 1919 women were given the vote. Since 1937 the highest average system using the d'Hondt method has been employed. In 1946 the voting age was reduced to 23. In October, 1956 there was a further reduction to 21 and since 1972 the voting age has been 18. In 1970 compulsory voting was abolished.

The country is divided into 18 constituencies for the establishment of electoral lists, but seats are allocated on a country-wide basis. In order to be represented in the Tweede Kamer a party has to obtain a minimum vote. This barrier clause has always been extremely low. As a proportion of the total valid vote it has varied between one-half of one per cent in 1918, three-quarters of one per cent from 1922 to 1933, one per cent from 1937 to 1952 and two-thirds of one per cent since 1956.

Sources:

Daalder, H., "Nationale politieke stelsels: Nederland." in L. van der Land (ed.) *Repertorium van de sociale vetenschappen:Politiek* (Amsterdam: Elsevier, 1958).

Ibid., "De kleine politieke partijen: een voorlopige poging tot inventarisatie." *Acta Politica* 1 : 1-4 (1966).

Ibid., "The Netherlands: opposition in a segmented society." in R.A. Dahl (ed.) *Political Opposition in Western Democracies* (New Haven: Yale University Press, 1966) pp. 188-236.

Geismann, G., *Politische Struktur und Regierungssystem in den Niederlanden* (Frankfurt am Main: Athenäum, 1964).

Lijphart, A., "The Netherlands." in R. Rose (ed.) *Electoral Behavior: a Comparative Handbook* (New York: Free Press, 1973).

Nohlen, D., "Niederlande." in D. Sternberger and B. Vogel (eds.) *Die Wahl der Parlamente. Band 1: Europa* (Berlin: de Gruyter, 1969) pp. 857-890.

Scholten, G.H. and Ringnalda, G., "Netherlands." in S. Rokkan and J. Meyriat (eds.) *International Guide to Electoral Statistics* Vol. 1 (Paris: Mouton, 1969) pp. 232-260.

Table 16.1
POLITICAL PARTIES IN THE NETHERLANDS SINCE 1888

	Party Names	Elections contested	Number contested
1	Anti-Revolutionary Party (Anti-Revolutionaire Partij—ARP)	1888ff	24
2	Catholic Party. From 1897 the Catholic Electoral League (Rooms-Katholieke Bond van Kiesverenigingen); from 1926 the Roman Catholic States Party (Rooms-Katholieke Staatspartij); since 1945 1945 the Catholic Peoples Party (Katholieke Volkspartij—KVP)	1888ff	24
3	Liberal Union (Liberale Unie)	1888-1918	9
4	Radicals (Radicalen); from 1901 the Liberal Democratic League (Vrijzinnig-Democratische Bond)	1888-1937	15
5	Social Democratic League (Sociaal-Democratische Bond)	1888-1891	2
6	Christian Historicals; various local lists until the establishment of the Christian Historical Union (Christelijk-Historische Unie—CHU) in 1908[1]	1894ff	22
7	Social Democratic Workers Party (Sociaal-Democratische Arbeiders Partij)[2]	1894-1937	13
8	Free Liberal League (Bond van Vrije Liberalen)[3]	1891-1918	9
9	Christian Democrats; various independent parties until the establishment of the Christian Democratic Union (Christen-Democratische Unie—CDU) in 1926	1918-1937	6
10	Communist Party. In 1918 the Social Democratic Party (Sociaal-Democratische Partij); then the Communistische Partij Holland—CPH; since 1936 the Communistische Partij Nederland—CPN	1918ff	15
11	Economic League (Economische Bond)	1918	1
12	Farmers League (Plattelandersbond); from 1933 the National Party of Farmers, Horticulturalists and Middle Class (Nationaal Boeren, Tuinders en Middenstandspartij)	1918-1937	6
13	Middle Class Party (Middenstandspartij)	1918	1
14	Political Reformed Party (Staatkundig Gereformeerde Partij—SGP)[4]	1918ff	15
15	Socialist Party (Socialistische Partij)	1918-1925	3
16	Liberal States Party "The Freedom League" (Liberale Staatspartij "De Vrijheidsbond")[5]	1922-1937	3
17	New Reformed State Party (Hervormd-Gereformeerde Staatspartij)[6]	1922-1937	6

18	Roman Catholic Peoples Party (Rooms-Katholieke Volkspartij)	1925-1933	3
19	Middle Party for City and Country (Middenpartij voor Stadt en Land)	1929	1
20	Revolutionary Socialist Party (Revolutionair Socialistische Partij)	1929-1933	2
21	League for National Renewal (Verbond voor Nationaal Herstel)	1933-1937	2
22	National Socialist Movement (Nationaal-Socialistische Beweging)	1937	1
23	Labour Party (Partij van der Arbeid—PvdA)[7]	1946ff	9
24	Liberal Party (Volkspartij voor Vrijheid en Democratie—VVD)[8]	1946ff	9
25	Catholic National Party (Katholieke Nationale Partij)[9]	1948-1952	2
26	Reformed Political Union (Gereformeerd Politiek Verbond)[10]	1952ff	7
27	Pacifist Socialist Party (Pacifistisch-Socialististische Partij)	1959ff	5
28	Farmers Party (Boerenpartij)	1963ff	4
29	Democrats '66 (Democraten '66—D'66)	1967ff	3
30	Democratic Socialists '70 (Democratische Socialisten '70—DS'70)[11]	1971ff	2
31	Netherlands Middle Class Party (Nederlands Middenstands Partij)	1971ff	2
32	Radical Political Party (Politieke Partij Radicalen)[12]	1971ff	2
33	Roman Catholic Party (Rooms-Katholieke Partij Nederland; in 1971 Nieuwe Roomse Partij)	1971ff	2

[1] Includes the Free Anti-Revolutionaries (Vrij Anti-Revolutionairen) who split from the ARP in 1894, the Christian Historical Electoral Union (Christelijk-Historische Kiezersbond) established in 1896 who united with the Free Anti-Revolutionaries to form the Christian Historical Party (Christelijk-Historische Partij) in 1903. The Friesian Christian Historical Party (Bond van Kiesverenigingen op Christelijk Historische Grondslag, literally League of Electoral Committees based on Christian Historical Principles) was established in 1898. It merged with the Christian Historical Party to form the Christian Historical Union in 1908.

[2] Includes the Free Socialists (Vrije Socialisten) from 1897 to 1905.

[3] Conservative deputies who left the Liberal Union in 1891, but did not form their own party until 1906.

[4] A fundamentalist Calvinist splinter from the Anti-Revolutionary Party in 1918.

[5] A merger of the Free Liberals, the Liberal Union, the Economic League and minor liberal groups.

[6] A splinter from the Christian Historical Union established in 1922.

[7] A merger of the Social Democratic Workers Party, the Radicals and some left-wing Catholics and Christian Historicals.

[8] In 1946 the Partij van de Vrijheid—successor to the Vrijheidsbond.

[9] A right-wing splinter from the Catholic Peoples Party which it rejoined in 1955.

[10] A splinter from the Anti-Revolutionary Party in 1948.

[11] Right-wing splinter from the Labour Party in 1970.

[12] Left-wing splinter from the Catholic Peoples Party in 1968.

Table 16.2
ELECTIONS TO THE TWEEDE KAMER 1888–1972[1]

1.	6 March 1888	13.	3 July 1929
2.	23 July 1891	14.	26 April 1933
3.	10 April 1894	15.	26 May 1937
4.	9 February 1897	16.	17 May 1946
5.	14 June 1901	17.	7 July 1948
6.	16 June 1905	18.	25 June 1952
7.	11 June 1909	19.	13 June 1956
8.	17 June 1913	20.	12 March 1959
9.	15 June 1917	21.	15 May 1963
10.	3 July 1918	22.	15 February 1967
11.	5 July 1922	23.	28 March 1971
12.	1 July 1925	24.	29 November 1972

[1] Dates for elections before 1918 refer to the first ballot.

Source: Netherlands Central Bureau of Statistics.

Table 16.3   NETHERLANDS   Total Votes 1888–1913[1]

	1888	1891	1894	1897	1901	1905	1909	1913
Electorate	292,613	293,888	299,073	576,598	609,634	752,692	843,487	960,595
Valid Votes	236,168	205,946	164,894	413,714	389,021	583,388	596,060	768,708
PARTY VOTES								
2 Catholic Party	48,922	41,579	33,454	83,826	61,160	76,605	76,087	111,081
1 Anti-Revolutionary Party	74,048	60,738	28,274	108,581	106,670	143,843	166,270	165,560
6 Christian Historicals	–	–	11,118	44,159	26,233	62,770	63,306	80,402
3 Liberal Union	96,157	86,888	82,099	126,199	107,249	164,376	106,086	128,706
8 Free Liberal League	–	–	–	–	–	–	33,464	50,541
4 Radicals	4,686	4,409	5,151	14,863	28,398	51,595	54,007	56,462
5 Social Democratic League	2,020	2,102	365	–	–	–	–	–
7 Social Democratic Workers	–	–	–	12,312[2]	36,981[2]	65,561[2]	82,855	142,185
Others	10,335	10,230	4,433	23,774	22,330	18,638	13,985	33,771

[1] The 1917 election is excluded. By prior agreement among the political parties the distribution of seats amongst the parties was to remain unchanged; 51 candidates were returned unopposed and only 21.4 per cent of the electorate voted.
[2] Includes Free Socialists (Vrije Socialisten).

Source: Figures provided by Jan Verhoef, University of Leiden.

Table 16.4 NETHERLANDS Percentage of Votes 1888–1913

	1888	1891	1894	1897	1901	1905	1909	1913
Valid Votes	80.7	70.1	55.1	71.8	63.8	77.5	70.7	80.0
PARTY VOTES								
2 Catholic Party	20.7	20.2	20.3	20.3	15.7	13.1	12.8	14.5
1 Anti-Revolutionary Party	31.4	29.5	17.1	26.2	27.4	24.7	27.9	21.5
6 Christian Historicals	–	–	6.7	10.7	6.7	10.8	10.6	10.5
3 Liberal Union	40.7	42.2	49.8	30.5	27.6	28.2	17.8	16.7
8 Free Liberal League	–	2.1	3.1	3.6	7.3	8.8	5.6	6.6
4 Radicals	2.0						9.1	7.3
5 Social Democratic League	0.9	1.0	0.2	–	–	–	–	–
7 Social Democratic Workers	–	–	2.7	3.0	9.5	11.2	13.9	18.5
Others	4.4	5.0	2.7	5.7	5.7	3.2	2.3	4.4

273

Table 16.5 NETHERLANDS Number of Seats Won in the Tweede Kamer 1888–1913

	1888[1]	1891[1]	1894[1]	1897[1]	1901	1905	1909	1913
2 Catholic Party	25	25	25	22	25	25	25	25
1 Anti-Revolutionary Party	27	21	15	17	22	15	25	11
6 Christian Historicals	–	–	0	6	10	8	10	10
3 Liberal Union	46	53	57	48	26	34	20	22
8 Free Liberal League	–	1	3	4	9	11	4	10
4 Radicals	0	1	3	4	9	11	9	7
5 Social Democratic League	1	0	–	–	–	–	–	–
7 Social Democratic Workers	–[2]	0	0	3	7	7	7	15
Others	1[2]	0	0	0	1[3]	0	0	0
Total Seats	100	100	100	100	100	100	100	100

[1] These figures vary slightly according to source.

[2] Conservative.

[3] Independent Anti-Revolutionary.

Sources: Geismann, 1964 : 131 and figures provided by the Central Bureau of Statistics, Amsterdam.

Table 16.6   NETHERLANDS   Percentage of Seats Won in the Tweede Kamer 1888—1913

	1888	1891	1894	1897	1901	1905	1909	1913
2 Catholic Party	25.0	25.0	25.0	22.0	25.0	25.0	25.0	25.0
1 Anti-Revolutionary Party	27.0	21.0	15.0	17.0	22.0	15.0	25.0	11.0
6 Christian Historicals	–	–	0.0	6.0	10.0	8.0	10.0	10.0
3 Liberal Union	46.0	53.0	57.0	48.0	26.0	34.0	20.0	22.0
8 Free Liberal League	–	–	–	–	–	–	4.0	10.0
4 Radicals	0.0	1.0	3.0	4.0	9.0	11.0	9.0	7.0
5 Social Democratic League	1.0	0.0	–	–	–	–	–	–
7 Social Democratic Workers	–	–	0.0	3.0	7.0	7.0	7.0	15.0
Others	1.0	0.0	0.0	0.0	1.0	0.0	0.0	0.0

275

Table 16.7   NETHERLANDS   Total Votes 1918—1937

	1918	1922	1925	1929	1933	1937
Electorate	1,517,380	3,299,672	3,543,058	3,821,612	4,126,490	4,462,859
Valid Votes	1,344,209	2,929,569	3,085,862	3,379,503	3,721,828	4,058,077
Invalid Votes	n.a.	n.a.	150,729	162,482	177,827	154,826
Total Votes	n.a.	n.a.	3,236,591	3,541,985	3,899,655	4,212,903
PARTY VOTES						
2 Catholic Party	402,908	874,745	883,333	1,001,589	1,037,343	1,170,431
18 Roman Catholic Peoples Party	–	–	36,571	23,804	40,894	–
1 Anti-Revolutionary Party	179,523	402,277	377,426	391,832	499,890	665,501
6 Christian Historical Union	87,983	318,669	305,587	354,548	339,808	302,829
9 Christian Democrats	27,221[1]	40,300[3]	13,944	12,780	38,459	85,004
14 Political Reformed Party	5,129	26,744	62,513	76,709	93,273	78,619
17 New Reformed State Party	–	20,431	30,258	35,931	33,988	24,543
7 Social Democratic Workers Party	296,145	567,769	706,689	804,714	798,632	890,661
15 Socialist Party	8,950	12,412	11,790	–	–	–
10 Communist Party	31,043	53,664	36,770	67,541[4]	118,236	136,026
20 Revolutionary Socialist Party	–	–	–	21,812	48,905	–
3 Liberal Union	83,173	–	–	–	–	–
8 Free Liberal League	51,195	–	–	–	–	–
4 Radicals	71,582	134,595	187,183	208,979	188,950	239,502
11 Economic League	42,042	–	–	–	–	–
12 Farmers League	9,068	45,816	62,639	34,805	47,653	6,891
13 Middle Class Party	12,663	–	–	–	–	–
16 Liberal States Party	–	271,358	269,564	249,105	258,732	160,260

19	Middle Party for City and Country	—	—	—	39,955	—
21	League for National Renewal	—	—	—	30,329	6,270
22	National Socialist Movement	—	160,789	—	—	171,137
	Others	35,584[2]	101,595	55,399	146,736	120,403

[1] Includes Christen-Democratische Partij, 10,653 votes; Christelijk Sociale Partij, 8,152 votes and Bond van Christen-Socialisten, 8,416 votes.
[2] Includes Neutrale Partij, 7,186 votes and the Verbond Democratisering Weermacht 6,830 votes.
[3] Includes Christen-Democratische Partij, 20,760 votes and Christelijk Sociale Partij, 19,540 votes.
[4] Includes Wijnkoop and de Wisser Communist parties with 29,863 and 37,678 votes respectively.

Source: Figures provided by Robbert van den Helm, University of Leiden.

Table 16.8   NETHERLANDS   Percentage of Votes 1918—1937

	1918	1922	1925	1929	1933	1937
Valid Votes	88.6	88.8	87.1	88.4	90.2	90.9
Invalid Votes	n.a.	n.a.	4.3	4.3	4.3	3.5
Total Votes	n.a.	n.a.	91.4	92.7	94.5	94.4
Share Invalid	n.a.	n.a.	4.7	4.6	4.6	3.7
PARTY VOTES						
2 Catholic Party	30.0	29.9	28.6	29.6	27.9	28.8
18 Roman Catholic Peoples Party	–	–	1.2	0.7	1.1	–
1 Anti-Revolutionary Party	13.4	13.7	12.2	11.6	13.4	16.4
6 Christian Historical Union	6.5	10.9	9.9	10.5	9.1	7.5
9 Christian Democrats	2.0	1.4	0.5	0.4	1.0	2.1
14 Political Reformed Party	0.4	0.9	2.0	2.3	2.5	1.9
17 New Reformed State Party	–	0.7	1.0	1.1	0.9	0.6
7 Social Democratic Workers	22.0	19.4	22.9	23.8	21.5	21.9
15 Socialist Party	0.7	0.4	0.4	–	–	–
10 Communist Party	2.3	1.8	1.2	2.0	3.2	3.4
20 Revolutionary Socialist Party	–	–	–	0.6	1.3	–
3 Liberal Union	6.2	–	–	–	–	–
8 Free Liberal League	3.8	–	–	–	–	–
4 Radicals	5.3	4.6	6.1	6.2	5.1	5.9
11 Economic League	3.1	–	–	–	–	–
12 Farmers League	0.7	1.6	2.0	1.0	1.3	0.2
13 Middle Class Party	0.9	–	–	–	–	–
16 Liberal States Party	–	9.3	8.7	7.4	7.0	3.9

	19 Middle Party for City and Country	21 League for National Renewal	22 National Socialist Movement	Others
	–	–	–	2.6
	–	–	–	5.5
	–	–	–	3.3
	1.2	–	–	1.6
	–	0.8	–	3.9
	–	0.2	4.2	3.0

Table 16.9   NETHERLANDS   Number of Seats Won in the Tweede Kamer 1918–1937

		1918	1922	1925	1929	1933	1937
2	Catholic Party	30	32	30	30	28	31
18	Roman Catholic Peoples Party	–	–	1	0	1	–
1	Anti-Revolutionary Party	13	16	13	12	14	17
6	Christian Historical Union	7	11	11	11	10	8
9	Christian Democrats	3[1]	0	0	0	1	2
14	Political Reformed Party	0	1	2	3	3	2
17	New Reformed State Party	–	0	1	1	1	0
7	Social Democratic Workers Party	22	20	24	24	22	23
15	Socialist Party	1	0	0	–	–	–
10	Communist Party	2	2	1	2[2]	4	3
20	Revolutionary Socialist Party	–	–	–	0	1	–
3	Liberal Union	6	–	–	–	–	–
8	Free Liberal League	4	–	–	–	–	–
4	Radicals	5	5	7	7	6	6
11	Economic League	3	–	1	1	1	–
12	Farmers League	1	2	1	1	–	0
13	Middle Class Party	1	–	–	–	–	–
16	Liberal States Party	–	10	9	8	7	4

19 Middle Party for City and Country	–	–	–	1	–	–
21 League for National Renewal	–	–	–	–	1	0
22 National Socialist Movement	2²	1³	–	–	–	4
Others			0	0	0	0
Total Seats	**100**	**100**	**100**	**100**	**100**	**100**

[1] Christen-Democratische Party, one; Christelijk Sociale Partij, one and Bond van Christen-Socialisten, one.
[2] Neutrale Partij, one and Verbond Democratisering Weermacht, one.
[3] Liberale Partij.
[4] Wijnkoop Communist Party, one; De Wisser Communist Party, one.

Source: Figures provided by Robbert P. van den Helm, University of Leiden.

Table 16.10   NETHERLANDS   Percentage of Seats Won in the Tweede Kamer 1918–1937

		1918	1922	1925	1929	1933	1937
2	Catholic Party	30.0	32.0	30.0	30.0	28.0	31.0
18	Roman Catholic Peoples Party	–	–	1.0	0.0	1.0	0.0
1	Anti-Revolutionary Party	13.0	16.0	13.0	12.0	14.0	17.0
6	Christian Historical Union	7.0	11.0	11.0	11.0	10.0	8.0
9	Christian Democrats	3.0	0.0	0.0	0.0	1.0	2.0
14	Political Reformed Party	0.0	1.0	2.0	3.0	3.0	2.0
17	New Reformed State Party	–	0.0	1.0	1.0	1.0	0.0
7	Social Democratic Workers Party	22.0	20.0	24.0	24.0	22.0	23.0
15	Socialist Party	1.0	0.0	0.0	–	–	–
10	Communist Party	2.0	2.0	1.0	2.0	4.0	3.0
20	Revolutionary Socialist Party	–	–	–	0.0	1.0	–
3	Liberal Union	6.0	–	–	–	–	–
8	Free Liberal League	4.0	–	–	–	–	–
4	Radicals	3.0	5.0	7.0	7.0	6.0	6.0
11	Economic League	3.0	–	–	–	–	–
12	Farmers League	1.0	2.0	1.0	1.0	1.0	0.0
13	Middle Class Party	1.0	–	–	–	–	–
16	Liberal States Party	–	10.0	9.0	8.0	7.0	4.0

	C1	C2	C3	C4	C5	C6
19 Middle Party for City and Country	—	—	—	1.0	—	—
21 League for National Renewal	—	—	—	—	1.0	0.0
22 National Socialist Movement	—	—	—	—	—	4.0
Others	2.0	1.0	0.0	0.0	0.0	0.0

283

Table 16.11   NETHERLANDS   Total Votes 1946—1972

	1946	1948	1952	1956	1959	1963	1967	1971	1972
Electorate	5,275,888	5,433,633	5,792,679	6,125,210	6,427,864	6,748,611	7,452,776	8,048,726	8,915,359
Valid Votes	4,760,711	4,932,959	5,335,747	5,727,742	5,999,531	6,258,521	6,878,030	6,318,152	7,394,045
Invalid Votes	152,304	156,623	165,981	121,910	143,878	161,443	198,298	46,567	51,242
Total Votes	4,913,015	5,089,582	5,501,726	5,849,652	6,143,409	6,419,964	7,076,328	6,364,719	7,445,287
PARTY VOTES									
2 Catholic Peoples Party	1,466,582	1,531,154	1,529,508	1,815,310	1,895,914	1,995,352	1,822,904	1,379,672	1,305,401
25 Catholic National Party	–	62,376	144,520	–	–	–	–	–	–
32 Radical Political Party	–	–	–	–	–	–	–	116,049	354,829
33 Roman Catholic Party	–	–	–	–	–	–	–	23,047	67,658
1 Anti-Revolutionary Party	614,201	651,612	603,329	567,535	563,091	545,836	681,060	542,742	653,609
6 Christian Historical Union	373,217	453,226	476,195	482,918	486,429	536,801	560,033	399,106	354,463
14 Political Reformed Party	101,759	116,937	129,081	129,517	129,678	143,818	138,069	148,192	163,114
26 Reformed Political Union	–	–	35,497	37,206	39,972	46,324	59,156	101,790	131,236
23 Labour Party	1,347,940	1,263,058	1,545,867	1,872,209	1,821,285	1,753,084	1,620,112	1,554,280	2,021,454
10 Communist Party	502,963	382,001	328,621	272,054	144,542	173,325	248,318	246,569	330,398
27 Pacifist Socialist Party	–	–	–	–	110,499	189,373	197,206	90,738	111,262
30 Democratic Socialists '70	–	–	–	–	–	–	–	336,714	304,714
24 Liberal Party	305,287	391,923	471,040	502,530	732,658	643,839	738,202	653,370	1,068,375
28 Farmers Party	–	–	–	–	–	133,231	327,953	69,656	143,239
29 Democrats '66	–	–	–	–	–	–	307,810	428,067	307,048
31 Middle Class Party	–	–	–	–	–	–	–	95,706	32,970
Others	48,762	80,670	72,087	48,463	75,463	97,538	177,207	132,449	44,275

Sources: Scholten and Ringnalda, 1969 : 258-260 and figures provided by the Central Bureau of Statistics, Amsterdam.

Table 16.12   NETHERLANDS   Percentage of Votes 1946—1972

	1946	1948	1952	1956	1959	1963	1967	1971	1972
Valid Votes	90.2	90.8	92.1	93.5	93.3	92.7	92.3	78.5	82.9
Invalid Votes	2.9	2.9	2.9	2.0	2.2	2.4	2.7	0.6	0.6
Total Votes	93.1	93.7	95.0	95.5	95.6	95.1	94.9	79.1	83.5
Share Invalid	3.1	3.1	3.0	2.1	2.3	2.5	2.8	0.7	0.7
PARTY VOTES									
2 Catholic Peoples Party	30.8	31.0	28.7	31.7	31.6	31.9	26.5	21.8	17.7
25 Catholic National Party	–	1.3	2.7	–	–	–	–	–	–
32 Radical Political Party	–	–	–	–	–	–	–	1.8	4.8
33 Roman Catholic Party	–	–	–	–	–	–	–	0.4	0.9
1 Anti-Revolutionary Party	12.9	13.2	11.3	9.9	9.4	8.7	9.9	8.6	8.8
6 Christian Historical Union	7.8	9.2	8.9	8.4	8.1	8.6	8.1	6.3	4.8
14 Political Reformed Party	2.1	2.4	2.4	2.3	2.2	2.3	2.0	2.3	2.2
26 Reformed Political Union	–	–	0.7	0.6	0.7	0.7	0.9	1.6	1.8
23 Labour Party	28.3	25.6	29.0	32.7	30.4	28.0	23.6	24.6	27.3
10 Communist Party	10.6	7.7	6.2	4.7	2.4	2.8	3.6	3.9	4.5
27 Pacifist Socialist Party	–	–	–	–	1.8	3.0	2.9	1.4	1.5
30 Democratic Socialists '70	–	–	–	–	–	–	–	5.3	4.1
24 Liberal Party	6.4	7.9	8.8	8.8	12.2	10.3	10.7	10.3	14.4
28 Farmers Party	–	–	–	–	–	2.1	4.8	1.1	1.9
29 Democrats '66	–	–	–	–	–	–	4.5	6.8	4.2
31 Middle Class Party	–	–	–	–	–	–	–	1.5	0.4
Others	1.0	1.6	1.4	0.8	1.3	1.6	2.6	2.1	0.6

Table 16.13   NETHERLANDS   Number of Seats Won in the Tweede Kamer 1946—1972

	1946	1948	1952	1956	1959	1963	1967	1971	1972
2 Catholic Peoples Party	32	32	30	49	49	50	42[1]	35	27
25 Catholic National Party	—	1	2	—	—	—	—	—	—
32 Radical Political Party	—	—	—	—	—	—	—	2	7
33 Roman Catholic Party	—	—	—	—	—	—	—	0	1
1 Anti-Revolutionary Party	13	13	12	15	14	13	15	13	14
6 Christian Historical Union	8	9	9	13	12	13	12	10	7
14 Political Reformed Party	2	2	2	3	3	3	3	3	3
26 Reformed Political Union	—	—	0	0	0	1	1	2	2
23 Labour Party	29	27	30	50	48	43	37[2]	39	43
10 Communist Party	10	8	6	7	3	4	5	6	7
27 Pacifist Socialist Party	—	—	—	—	2	4	4	2	2
30 Democratic Socialists '70	—	—	—	—	—	—	—	8	6
24 Liberal Party	6	8	9	13	19	16	17	16	22
28 Farmers Party	—	—	—	—	—	3	7	1	3
29 Democrats '66	—	—	—	—	—	—	7	11	6
31 Middle Class Party	—	—	—	—	—	—	—	2	0
Others	0	0	0	0	0	0	0	0	0
Total Seats	**100**	**100**	**100**	**150**	**150**	**150**	**150**	**150**	**150**

[1] In 1968 one Catholic Peoples Party member left the party, one resigned from the Chamber and three sat as the Groep-Aarden which later became the Radical Political Party.

[2] In 1968 one Labour Party member left the party to form the Groep-Goedhart. He was later joined by two other members. They later formed the Democratic Socialists '70.

Sources: Scholten and Ringnalda, 1969 : 258-260 and figures provided by the Central Bureau of Statistics, Amsterdam.

Table 16.14 NETHERLANDS   Percentage of Seats Won in the Tweede Kamer 1946–1972

	1946	1948	1952	1956	1959	1963	1967	1971	1972
2 Catholic Peoples Party	32.0	32.0	30.0	32.7	32.7	33.3	28.0	23.3	18.0
25 Catholic National Party	–	1.0	2.0	–	–	–	–	–	–
32 Radical Political Party	–	–	–	–	–	–	–	1.3	4.7
33 Roman Catholic Party	–	–	–	–	–	–	–	0.0	0.7
1 Anti-Revolutionary Party	13.0	13.0	12.0	10.0	9.3	8.7	10.0	8.7	9.3
6 Christian Historical Union	8.0	9.0	9.0	8.7	8.0	8.7	8.0	6.7	4.7
14 Political Reformed Party	2.0	2.0	2.0	2.0	2.0	2.0	2.0	2.0	2.0
26 Reformed Political Union	–	–	0.0	0.0	0.0	0.7	0.7	1.3	1.3
23 Labour Party	29.0	27.0	30.0	33.3	32.0	28.7	24.7	26.0	28.7
10 Communist Party	10.0	8.0	6.0	4.7	2.0	2.7	3.3	4.0	4.7
27 Pacifist Socialist Party	–	–	–	–	1.3	2.7	2.7	1.3	1.3
30 Democratic Socialists '70	–	–	–	–	–	–	–	5.3	4.0
24 Liberal Party	6.0	8.0	9.0	8.7	12.7	10.7	11.3	10.7	14.7
28 Farmers Party	–	–	–	–	–	2.0	4.7	0.7	2.0
29 Democrats '66	–	–	–	–	–	–	4.7	7.3	4.0
31 Middle Class Party	–	–	–	–	–	–	–	1.3	0.0
Others	0.0	0.0	0.0	0.0	0.0	0.0	0.0	0.0	0.0

Chapter 17

NEW ZEALAND

Representative institutions were first established in New Zealand in 1852, when a bi-cameral parliament, consisting of a nominated Legislative Council and an elected House of Representatives was created. Organized political parties did not develop until the 1890s. The initial electoral success of the Liberal Party was followed by the gradual disintegration of the Conservative opposition. For a period the parliamentary 'Opposition' consisted of a number of individuals rather than a coherent party. By 1911 the 'Opposition' had coalesced as the Reform Party. Labour candidates began to stand independently of the Liberal Party at the end of the nineteenth century. But no unified organisation was created until the establishment of the Labour Party in 1916. The growing strength of the Labour Party led to the formation of an electoral alliance between the Liberal and Reform parties and to their eventual merger as the National Party in 1936. (Milne, 1966: 28ff).

Members of the House of Representatives are elected by plurality in single-member constituencies. The franchise was originally limited to European men aged over 21 who possessed a minimum property qualification. In 1867 voting rights were extended to the indigenous Maori population. Because Maori land was held in common it was not possible to impose a property test. Maori voters elect four representatives in single-member constituencies. In 1879 manhood suffrage was extended to the Europeans but plural voting continued until the end of the nineteenth century. The secret ballot was introduced in 1871. Women were given the vote in 1893. For the 1908 and 1911 elections only, a two-ballot system was used. In the event of no candidate receiving an absolute majority, a run-off election was held between the two leading candidates. The Legislative Council was abolished in 1950. In 1969 the voting age was reduced to 20.

Sources:

General Election, 1957 ff. Parliamentary Paper H33; in 1972 E9. (Wellington: Government Printer, 1957ff.)

Lipson, L., *The Politics of Equality* (Chicago: Chicago University Press, 1948).

Milne, R.S., *Political Parties in New Zealand* (Oxford: the Clarendon Press, 1966)

New Zealand Parliament, House of Representatives, *Appendices to the Journals: 1890ff.*

Wilson, J.D., *New Zealand Parliamentary Record 1840–1949. Supplement 1950–1969.* (Wellington: A.R. Shearer, Government Printer, 1969).

Table 17.1
POLITICAL PARTIES IN NEW ZEALAND SINCE 1890

	Party Names	Elections contested	Number contested
1	Conservative Party	1890-1899	4
2	Liberal Party[1]	1890-1935	15
3	Labour Party	1902ff	23
4	Opposition	1902-1908	3
5	Reform Party	1911-1935	8
6	Democrat Party	1935	1
7	National Party[2]	1938ff	12
8	Democratic Soldier Labour	1943	1
9	Communist Party	1946-1969	9
10	Social Credit Political League	1954ff	7
11	Values Party	1972	1

[1] Known as the Liberal Labour Party in the 1922 election, and the National Party in the 1925 election; re-named the United Party in 1927.

[2] A merger of the Reform and United parties in 1936. The two parties formed a coalition government in 1931 and electoral alliances in the elections of 1931 and 1935.

Table 17.2
DATES OF ELECTIONS
TO THE HOUSE OF REPRESENTATIVES 1890–1972[1]

1.	5 December 1890	15.	27 November 1935
2.	28 November 1893	16.	15 October 1938
3.	4 December 1896	17.	23 September 1943
4.	6 December 1899	18.	27 November 1946
5.	25 November 1902	19.	30 November 1949
6.	6 December 1905	20.	1 September 1951
7.	17 and 24 November 1908[2]	21.	13 November 1954
8.	7 and 14 December 1911[2]	22.	30 November 1957
9.	10 December 1914	23.	26 November 1960
10.	17 December 1919	24.	30 November 1963
11.	7 December 1922	25.	26 November 1966
12.	4 November 1925	26.	29 November 1969
13.	14 November 1928	27.	25 November 1972
14.	2 December 1931		

[1] Until 1951 European and Maori constituencies voted on different days. The dates refer to the European polling day.

[2] In 1908 and 1911 the two dates given are for the first and second ballots.

Sources: *New Zealand Parliamentary Record,* 1969: 25 and the Chief Electoral Officer.

Table 17.3 NEW ZEALAND   Total Votes 1890—1914[1]

	1890	1893	1896	1899	1902	1905	1908[2]	1911[2]	1914
Electorate	183,171	302,997	339,230	373,744	415,789	476,473	537,003	590,042	616,043
Valid Votes	136,337	304,176	359,404	387,629	416,962	391,189	424,052	488,769	515,907
Invalid Votes	n.a.	n.a.	n.a.	n.a.	n.a.	5,468	4,596	4,143	5,618
Total Votes	73,332	220,082	258,254	279,330	318,859	396,657	428,648	492,912	521,525
PARTY VOTES									
1 Conservative Party	39,338	74,482	134,397	141,758	–	–	–	–	–
2 Liberal Party	76,548	175,814	165,259	204,331	215,845	209,731	242,261	191,323	222,299
3 Labour Party	–	–	–	–	10,501	3,623	17,492	40,759	49,482
4 Opposition	–	–	–	–	85,769	117,118	114,245	–	–
5 Reform Party	–	–	–	–	–	–	–	164,627	243,122
Others	20,451	53,880	59,748	41,540	104,847	60,717	36,508	68,859	1,004

[1] The figures for the electorate refer to the number of names on the electoral roll. Total votes figures indicate the number of persons voting. Because of plural voting by some individuals the number of valid votes cast exceeds the number of persons voting from 1890-1902. The four Maori constituencies are excluded.

[2] Two-ballot elections. Lipson's totals are calculated from the first round figures where this was decisive and from the second ballot when it was not.

Sources: Lipson, 1948 : 187-188; *Appendices to the Journals, 1890—1914.*

Table 17.4   NEW ZEALAND   Percentage of Votes 1890—1914

	1890	1893	1896	1899	1902	1905	1908	1911	1914
Valid Votes	n.a.	n.a.	n.a.	n.a.	n.a.	82.1	79.0	82.8	83.7
Invalid Votes	n.a.	n.a.	n.a.	n.a.	n.a.	1.1	0.9	0.7	0.9
Total Votes	40.0	72.6	71.9	72.1	76.5	83.2	79.8	83.5	84.7
Share Invalid	n.a.	n.a.	n.a.	n.a.	n.a.	1.4	1.1	0.8	1.1
PARTY VOTES									
1 Conservative Party	28.9	24.5	37.4	36.6	–	–	–	–	–
2 Liberal Party	56.1	57.8	46.0	52.7	51.8	53.6	59.0	41.1	43.1
3 Labour Party	–	–	–	–	2.5	0.9	4.3	8.8	9.6
4 Opposition	–	–	–	–	20.6	29.9	27.8	–	–
5 Reform Party	–	–	–	–	–	–	–	35.4	47.1
Others	15.0	17.7	16.6	10.7	25.1	15.5	8.9	14.8	0.2

Table 17.5 NEW ZEALAND   Number of Seats Won in the House of Representatives 1890–1914[1]

	1890	1893	1896	1899	1902	1905	1908	1911	1914
1 Conservative Party	25	13	25	19	–	–	–	–	–
2 Liberal Party	38	51	39	49	47	55	47	30	31
3 Labour Party	–	–	–	–	0	0	1	4	6
4 Opposition	–	–	–	–	19	15	25	–	–
5 Reform Party	–	–	–	–	–	–	–	36	39
Others	7	6	6	2	10	6	3	6	0
Total Seats	**70**	**70**	**70**	**70**	**76**	**76**	**76**	**76**	**76**
Unopposed Returns	6	3	0	3	0	0	0	1	0

[1] The four Maori seats are excluded.

Source: Lipson, 1948: 187-188.

Table 17.6 NEW ZEALAND Percentage of Seats Won in the House of Representatives 1890–1914

	1890	1893	1896	1899	1902	1905	1908	1911	1914
1 Conservative Party	35.7	18.6	35.7	27.1	–	–	–	–	–
2 Liberal Party	54.3	72.9	55.7	70.0	61.8	72.4	61.8	39.5	40.8
3 Labour Party	–	–	–	–	0.0	0.0	1.3	5.3	7.9
4 Opposition	–	–	–	–	25.0	19.7	32.9	–	–
5 Reform Party	–	–	–	–	–	–	–	47.4	51.3
Others	10.0	8.6	8.6	2.9	13.2	7.9	3.9	7.9	0.0
Unopposed Returns	8.6	4.3	0.0	4.3	0.0	0.0	0.0	1.3	0.0

Table 17.7   NEW ZEALAND   Total Votes 1919–1943[1]

	1919	1922	1925	1928	1931	1935	1938	1943
Electorate	683,420	700,111	754,113	844,633	838,344	919,798	995,173	1,000,197
Valid Votes	542,740	614,070	671,971	735,391	693,072	827,795	917,684	911,370
Invalid Votes	7,587	6,580	6,906	8,300	4,955	6,887	6,373	9,957
Total Votes	550,327	620,650	678,877	743,691	698,027	834,682	924,057	921,327

PARTY VOTES

	1919	1922	1925	1928	1931	1935	1938	1943
2 Liberal/United Party	155,708	162,149	135,419	219,648	304,750[2]	258,270[2]	368,809	390,343
7 National Party	–	–	–	–			368,809	390,343
5 Reform Party	193,676	245,281	312,932	256,014	304,750[2]	258,270[2]	–	–
3 Labour Party	131,402	150,448	184,616	197,759	242,301	392,321	513,397	439,207
6 Democrat Party	–	–	–	–	–	65,217	–	–
8 Democratic Soldier Labour	–	–	–	–	–	–	–	40,423
Others	61,954	56,192	39,004	61,970	146,021	111,987	35,478	41,397

[1] The four Maori seats are excluded.
[2] An electoral alliance of the United and Reform Parties.

Sources: Lipson, 1948 : 187-188; Appendices to the Journals, 1919–1943.

Table 17.8 NEW ZEALAND Percentage of Votes 1919–1943

	1919	1922	1925	1928	1931	1935	1938	1943
Valid Votes	79.4	87.7	89.1	87.1	82.7	90.0	92.2	91.1
Invalid Votes	1.1	0.9	0.9	1.0	0.6	0.7	0.6	1.0
Total Votes	80.5	88.7	90.0	88.0	83.3	90.7	92.9	92.1
Share Invalid	1.4	1.1	1.0	1.1	0.7	0.8	0.7	1.1
PARTY VOTES								
2 Liberal/United Party	28.7	26.4	20.2	29.9	–	–	–	–
7 National Party	–	–	–		44.0	31.2	40.2	42.8
5 Reform Party	35.7	39.9	46.6	34.8	–	–	–	–
3 Labour Party	24.2	24.5	27.5	26.9	35.0	47.4	55.9	48.2
6 Democrat Party	–	–	–	–	–	7.9	–	–
8 Democratic Soldier Labour	–	–	–	–	–	–	–	4.4
Others	11.4	9.2	5.8	8.4	21.1	13.5	3.9	4.5

297

Table 17.9   NEW ZEALAND   Number of Seats Won in the House of Representatives 1919–1943[1]

		1919	1922	1925	1928	1931	1935	1938	1943
2	Liberal/United Party	17	21	9	25 ⎱	–	–	–	–
7	National Party	–	–	–	– ⎰	42	17	24	34
5	Reform Party	43	35	51	25	–	–	–	–
3	Labour Party	8	17	12	19	24	53	50	41
6	Democrat Party	–	–	–	–	–	0	–	–
8	Democratic Soldier Labour	–	–	–	–	–	–	–	0
	Others	8	3	4	7	10	6	2	1
	Total Seats	76	76	76	76	76	76	76	76
	Unopposed Returns	0	1	1	0	4	0	0	2

[1] Excluding the four Maori seats.

Source: Lipson, 1948 : 187-188.

Table 17.10   NEW ZEALAND   Percentage of Seats Won in the House of Representatives 1919–1943

	1919	1922	1925	1928	1931	1935	1938	1943
2 Liberal/United Party	22.4	27.6	11.8	32.9	–	–	–	–
7 National Party	–	–	–	–	55.3	22.4	31.6	44.7
5 Reform Party	56.6	46.1	67.1	32.9	–	–	–	–
3 Labour Party	10.5	22.4	15.8	25.0	31.6	69.7	65.8	53.9
6 Democrat Party	–	–	–	–	–	0.0	–	–
8 Democratic Soldier Labour	–	–	–	–	–	–	–	0.0
Others	10.5	3.9	5.3	9.2	13.2	7.9	2.6	1.3
Unopposed Returns	0.0	1.3	1.3	0.0	5.3	0.0	0.0	2.6

Table 17.11   NEW ZEALAND   Total Votes 1946–1972[1]

	1946	1949	1951	1954	1957	1960	1963	1966	1969	1972
Electorate	1,081,898	1,148,748	1,205,772	1,209,670	1,244,748	1,303,955	1,332,371	1,399,720	1,519,889	1,569,937
Valid Votes	1,047,205	1,073,181	1,069,791	1,096,893	1,157,365	1,170,503	1,198,045	1,205,095	1,340,168	1,400,924
Invalid Votes	7,999	6,724	3,632	8,716	5,696	6,460	7,277	7,032	11,645	10,377
Total Votes	1,055,204	1,079,905	1,073,423	1,105,609	1,163,061	1,176,963	1,205,322	1,212,127	1,351,813	1,411,301
PARTY VOTES										
3 Labour Party	536,994	506,100	490,143	484,082	559,096	508,179	524,066	499,392	592,055	677,475
7 National Party	507,139	556,805	577,630	485,630	511,699	557,046	563,875	525,945	605,960	581,422
9 Communist Party	1,181	3,499	528	1,134	706	2,423	3,167	1,060	368	–
10 Social Credit	–	–	–	122,068	83,498	100,905	95,176	174,515	121,576	93,197
11 Values Party	–	–	–	–	–	–	–	–	–	27,467
Others	1,891	6,777	1,490	3,979	2,366	1,950	11,761	4,183	20,209	21,363

[1] Including the four Maori constituencies.

Sources' Lipson, 1948 : 187-188; *Appendices to the Journals, 1946ff*; *General Election, 1957ff*.

Table 17.12   NEW ZEALAND   Percentage of Votes 1946–1972

	1946	1949	1951	1954	1957	1960	1963	1966	1969	1972
Valid Votes	96.8	93.4	88.7	90.7	93.0	89.8	89.9	86.1	88.2	89.2
Invalid Votes	0.7	0.6	0.3	0.7	0.5	0.5	0.5	0.5	0.8	0.7
Total Votes	97.5	94.0	89.0	91.4	93.4	90.3	90.5	86.6	88.9	89.9
Share Invalid	0.8	0.6	0.3	0.8	0.5	0.5	0.6	0.6	0.9	0.7
PARTY VOTES										
3 Labour Party	51.3	47.2	45.8	44.1	48.3	43.4	43.7	41.4	44.2	48.4
7 National Party	48.4	51.9	54.0	44.3	44.2	47.6	47.1	43.6	45.2	41.5
9 Communist Party	0.1	0.3	0.0	0.1	0.1	0.2	0.3	0.1	0.0	–
10 Social Credit	–	–	–	11.1	7.2	8.6	7.9	14.5	9.1	6.7
11 Values Party	–	–	–	–	–	–	–	–	–	2.0
Others	0.2	0.6	0.1	0.4	0.2	0.2	1.0	0.3	1.5	1.5

Table 17.13   NEW ZEALAND   Number of Seats Won in the House of Representatives 1946—1972[1]

	1946	1949	1951	1954	1957	1960	1963	1966	1969	1972
3 Labour Party	42	34	30	35	41	34	35	35	39	55
7 National Party	38	46	50	45	39	46	45	44	45	32
9 Communist Party	0	0	0	0	0	0	0	0	0	–
10 Social Credit	–	–	–	0	0	0	0	1	0	0
11 Values Party	–	–	–	–	–	–	–	–	–	0
Others	0	0	0	0	0	0	0	0	0	0
Total Seats	80	80	80	80	80	80	80	80	84	87

[1] Including the four Maori constituencies.

Sources: Lipson, 1948 : 187-188; *General Election, 1957 ff.*

Table 17.14   NEW ZEALAND   Percentage of Seats Won in the House of Representatives 1946—1972

		1946	1949	1951	1954	1957	1960	1963	1966	1969	1972
3	Labour Party	52.5	42.5	37.5	43.8	51.2	42.5	43.8	43.8	46.4	63.2
7	National Party	47.5	57.5	62.5	56.3	48.7	57.5	56.3	55.0	53.6	36.8
9	Communist Party	0.0	0.0	0.0	0.0	0.0	0.0	0.0	0.0	0.0	0.0
10	Social Credit	–	–	–	0.0	0.0	0.0	0.0	1.2	0.0	0.0
11	Values Party	–	–	–	–	–	–	–	–	–	0.0
	Others	0.0	0.0	0.0	0.0	0.0	0.0	0.0	0.0	0.0	0.0

Chapter 18

NORWAY

The 1882 election to the Storting was the first expressly partisan contest in Norwegian history (Rokkan, 1967 : 376). The initial political division between the Left, an alliance of urban radicals and the peasantry, and the Right, which supported the Royal Prerogative, remained the basic political cleavage until the emergence of the Labour Party as a major competitor for working-class votes.

The Norwegian parliament, the Storting is elected as a single unit. One-quarter of its members are then elected by the whole house to serve as members of the upper house, the Lagting. The remainder form the lower house, the Odelsting. Until 1905 elections were indirect. In each constituency the voters elected members of an electoral college, who then chose the representatives on a plurality basis. The voters consisted of King's officials, freehold and leasehold farmers, owners of urban property, citizens licensed as merchants and artisans (Rokkan, 1969 : 262). In 1884 citizens paying more than a minimum amount of income tax were also enfranchised and the secret ballot was introduced. In 1898 all men aged over 25 except bankrupts and men receiving public assistance, were given the vote. In 1905 direct elections in single member constituencies replaced the indirect system. An absolute majority was required on the first ballot and a plurality on the second. Voting rights were granted to bankrupts in 1914 and those in receipt of public assistance in 1919. Women were enfranchised in 1907, but only if their own or their husband's income was above a minimum figure. In 1913 they were granted equal voting rights.

In 1919 proportional representation in multi-member constituencies using the d'Hondt system was introduced and the minimum voting age reduced to 23. It was further reduced to 21 in 1946. In 1953 the Saint-Laguë system of proportional representation (with an initial divisor of 1.4) replaced the d'Hondt system.

Sources:

Central Bureau of Statistics, *Historical Statistics, 1968* (Oslo, 1969).
Norges Officielle Statistik sub-series *Stortingsvalget* (Oslo: various publishers, 1906ff).
Rokkan, S., "Geography, religion and social class: crosscutting cleavages in Norwegian politics" in S.M. Lipset and S. Rokkan (eds.) *Party Systems and Voter Alignments* (New York: Free Press, 1967) pp. 367-444.
Rokkan, S., "Norway" in S. Rokkan and J. Meyriat (eds.) *International Guide to Electoral Statistics,* (Paris: Mouton, 1969) pp. 261-280.

Table 18.1
POLITICAL PARTIES IN NORWAY SINCE 1882

	Party Names	Elections contested	Number contested
1	Liberals (Venstre—literally Left)	1882ff	26
2	Conservatives (Høyre—literally Right); known as the Unionist Party (Samlingspartiet) from 1903 to 1913	1882ff	26
3	Moderates (Moderate Venstre—literally, Moderate Left)	1888-1903	6
4	Labour Party (Norske Arbeiderparti)	1894ff	22
5	National Liberals. In 1903 the Liberal Left (Liberale Venstre). From 1909 the Freethinking Left (Frisinnede Venstre). From 1931 the Free-thinking Peoples Party (Frisinnede Folkeparti)	1903; 1909-1936	11
6	Worker Democrats (Arbeiderdemokratene)	1906-1918	5
7	Agrarian League (Landmandsforbundet); from 1921 the Farmers Party (Bondepartiet); re-named the Centre Party (Senterpartiet) in 1959	1915ff	15
8	Radical Peoples Party (Radikale Folkeparti)	1921-1936	6
9	Social Democratic Workers Party (Norges Socialdemokratiske Arbeiderparti)[1]	1921-1924	2
10	Communist Party (Norges Kommunistiske Parti)	1924ff	12
11	Christian Peoples Party (Kristelig Folkeparti)	1933ff	9
12	Commonwealth Party (Samfunnspartiet)[2]	1933-1949	4
13	National Socialists (Nasjonal Samling—literally National Unity)	1933-1936	2
14	Joint Non-Socialist Lists[3]	1949ff	6
15	Socialist Peoples Party (Sosialistisk Folkeparti)	1961ff	3

[1] The Social Democrats left the Labour Party in 1919 when the latter decided to join the Third International. The two parties were reunited in 1927.

[2] The party contested the 1945 election under the name Nytt Norge (New Norway).

[3] Local electoral alliances formed by the Conservative, Liberal, Agrarian (Centre) and Christian Peoples parties.

Table 18.2
DATES OF ELECTIONS
TO THE STORTING 1882–1969

1.	1882[1]	14.	24 October 1921
2.	1885[1]	15.	21 October 1924
3.	8 July–15 November 1888	16.	17 October 1927
4.	8 June–18 November 1891	17.	20 October 1930
5.	11 August–13 November 1894	18.	16 October 1933
6.	14 August–15 November 1897	19.	19 October 1936
7.	13 August–10 September 1900	20.	8 October 1945
8.	5 August–7 September 1903	21.	10 October 1949
9.	5 August–28 August 1906	22.	12 October 1953
10.	2 October–25 October 1909	23.	7 October 1957
11.	21 October 1912	24.	11 September 1961
12.	11 October 1915	25.	12 September 1965
13.	21 October 1918	26.	7 September 1969

[1] The dates of elections were fixed by the individual communes.

Source: Central Bureau of Statistics, Oslo.

Table 18.3   NORWAY   Total Votes 1882—1903

	1882	1885	1888	1891	1894	1897	1900	1903
Electorate	99,501	122,952	128,368	139,690	184,124	195,956	426,593	433,448
Vaild Votes	71,304	90,967	89,629	101,839	165,147	166,177	235,410	236,641
PARTY VOTES								
1 Liberals	44,803	57,683	37,320	51,780	83,165	87,548	127,142	101,142
3 Moderates	–	–	17,745	50,059	81,462	77,682	96,092	106,042
2 Conservatives	26,501	33,284	34,564					
5 National Liberals	–	–	–	–	–	–	–	–
4 Labour Party	–	–	–	–	520	947	7,013	22,948
Others	–	–	–	–	–	–	5,163	6,509

Sources: Rokkan, 1969, pp.275-276; *Historical Statistics*, p. 631;

Table 18.4 NORWAY   Percentage of Votes 1882—1903

	1882	1885	1888	1891	1894	1897	1900	1903
Valid Votes	71.7	74.0	69.8	72.9	89.7	84.8	55.2	54.6
PARTY VOTES								
1 Liberals	62.8	63.4	41.6	50.8	50.4	52.7	54.0	42.7
3 Moderates	–	–	19.8	–	–	–	40.8	44.8
2 Conservatives	37.2	36.6	38.6	49.2	49.3	46.7	–	
5 National Liberals	–	–	–	–	–	–		
4 Labour Party	–	–	–	–	0.3	0.6	3.0	9.7
Others	–	–	–	–	–	–	2.2	2.8

Table 18.5   NORWAY   Number of Seats Won in the Storting 1882–1903

	1882	1885	1888	1891	1894	1897	1900	1903
1 Liberals	83	84	39	63	59	79	77	50
3 Moderates	–	–	24	16	15	10	6	11
2 Conservatives	31	30	51	35	40	25	31	47
5 National Liberals	–	–	–	–	–	–	–	5
4 Labour Party	–	–	–	–	0	0	0	4
Others	–	–	–	–	–	–	0	0
Total Seats	114	114	114	114	114	114	114	117

Sources: Rokkan, 1969, pp.276-276 and figures provided by the Central Bureau of Statistics, Oslo.

Table 18.6   NORWAY   Percentage of Seats Won in the Storting 1882–1903

	1882	1885	1888	1891	1894	1897	1900	1903
1 Liberals	72.8	73.7	34.2	55.3	51.8	69.3	67.5	42.7
3 Moderates	–	–	21.1	14.0	13.2	8.8	5.3	9.4
2 Conservatives	27.2	26.3	44.7	30.7	35.1	21.9	27.2	40.2
5 National Liberals	–	–	–	–	–	–	–	4.3
4 Labour Party	–	–	–	–	0.0	0.0	0.0	3.4
Others	–	–	–	–	–	–	0.0	0.0

Table 18.7   NORWAY   Total Votes 1906—1918[1]

	1906	1909	1912	1915	1918
Electorate	446,705	760,277	809,582	1,086,557	1,186,602
Valid Votes	269,281	422,684	488,903	617,670	662,521
PARTY VOTES					
1 Liberals	121,562	128,367	195,526	204,243	187,657
6 Worker Democrats	12,819	15,550		25,658	21,980
2 Conservatives	88,323	175,388	162,074	179,028	201,325
5 National Liberals	–				
4 Labour Party	43,134	91,268	128,455	198,111	209,560
7 Agrarian League	–	–	–	6,351	30,925
Others	3,443	12,111	2,848	4,279	11,074

[1] Two ballot elections. Party votes are for the first ballot.

Sources: Rokkan, 1969, pp.278-279; *Historical Statistics*, p.631; *Stortingsvalget, 1906—1918.*

Table 18.8   NORWAY   Percentage of Votes 1906—1918

	1906	1909	1912	1915	1918
Valid Votes	60.3	55.6	60.4	56.8	55.8
PARTY VOTES					
1 Liberals	45.1	30.4 ⎫	40.0	33.1	28.3
6 Worker Democrats	4.8	3.7 ⎬		4.2	3.3
2 Conservatives	32.8 ⎫	41.5	33.2	29.0	30.4
5 National Liberals	– ⎬				
4 Labour Party	16.0	21.6	26.3	32.1	31.6
7 Agrarian League	–	–	–	1.0	4.7
Others		2.9	0.6	0.7	1.7

Table 18.9   NORWAY   Number of Seats Won in the Storting 1906—1918

		1906	1909	1912	1915	1918
1	Liberals	73	46	70	74	51
6	Worker Democrats	4	2	6	6	3
2	Conservatives	36	41	20	20	40
5	National Liberals	–	23	4	1	10
4	Labour Party	10	11	23	19	18
7	Agrarian League	–	–	–	1	3
	Others	0	0	0	2	1
	Total Seats	123	123	123	123	126

Sources: Rokkan, 1969, p.277.

Table 18.10   NORWAY   Percentage of Seats Won in the Storting 1906—1918

	1906	1909	1912	1915	1918
1 Liberals	59.3	37.4	56.9	60.2	40.5
6 Worker Democrats	3.3	1.6	4.9	4.9	2.4
2 Conservatives	29.3	38.3	16.3	16.3	31.7
5 National Liberals	–	18.7	3.3	0.8	1.9
4 Labour Party	8.1	8.9	18.7	15.4	14.3
7 Agrarian League	–	–	–	0.8	2.4
Others	0.0	0.0	0.0	1.6	0.8

Table 18.11   NORWAY   Number of Candidates 1906—1918[1]

	1906	1909	1912	1915	1918
1 Liberals	189 ⎫	163	156	154	168[3]
6 Worker Democrats	13 ⎭			23	14
2 Conservatives	138	158	126	107	110
5 National Liberals	–				
4 Labour Party	75	99	107	114	124
7 Agrarian League	–	–	–	n.a.	3
Others	19	331	7	18[2]	7
Total	434	453	396	416	426

[1] In many constituencies there was more than one candidate of the same party.

[2] Includes Agrarian League candidates.

[3] Includes four joint candidates with the Worker Democrats.

Source: Central Bureau of Statistics, Oslo.

Table 18.12   NORWAY   Percentage of Seats Contested 1906—1918

	1906	1909	1912	1915	1918
1 Liberals	98.4	100.0	100.0	97.6	96.8
6 Worker Democrats	10.6			18.7	11.1
2 Conservatives	74.8	95.1	91.9	83.7	83.3
5 National Liberals	–				
4 Labour Party	60.2	78.0	84.6	92.7	98.4
7 Agrarian League	–	–	–	n.a.	2.4

317

Table 18.13   NORWAY   Total Votes 1921–1936

	1921	1924	1927	1930	1933	1936
Electorate	1,351,183	1,412,441	1,484,409	1,550,077	1,643,498	1,741,905
Valid Votes	904,699	973,941	999,297	1,194,755	1,248,686	1,455,238
Invalid Votes	13,037	13,244	11,328	7,346	6,352	8,230
Total Votes	917,736	987,185	1,010,625	1,202,101	1,255,038	1,463,468
PARTY VOTES						
1 Liberals	181,989	180,979	172,568	241,355	213,153	232,784
2 Conservatives	301,372	316,846	240,091	327,731	252,506	310,324
5 National Liberals			14,439	31,003	20,184	19,236
4 Labour Party	192,616	179,567	368,106	374,854	500,526	618,616
7 Farmers Party	118,657	131,706	149,026	190,220	173,634	168,038
8 Radical Peoples Party	22,970	17,144	13,459	9,228	6,858	6,407
9 Social Democratic Workers Party	83,629	85,743	–		–	–
10 Communist Party	–	59,401	40,075	20,351	22,773	4,376
11 Christian Peoples Party	–	–	–	–	10,272	19,612
12 Commonwealth Party	–	–	–	–	18,786	45,109
13 National Socialists	–	–	–	13	27,850	26,577
Others	3,466	2,555	1,533		2,144	4,159

Source: *Stortingsvalget*, 1921–1936.

Table 18.14 NORWAY Percentage of Votes 1921–1936

	1921	1924	1927	1930	1933	1936
Valid Votes	67.0	69.0	67.3	77.1	76.0	83.5
Invalid Votes	1.0	0.9	0.8	0.5	0.4	0.5
Total Votes	67.9	69.9	68.1	77.6	76.4	84.0
Share Invalid	1.4	1.3	1.1	0.6	0.5	0.6
PARTY VOTES						
1 Liberals	20.1	18.6	17.3	20.2	17.1	16.0
2 Conservatives	33.3	32.5	24.0	27.4	20.2	21.3
5 National Liberals	21.3	18.4	1.4	2.6	1.6	1.3
4 Labour Party	21.3	18.4	36.8	31.4	40.1	42.5
7 Farmers Party	13.1	13.5	14.9	15.9	13.9	11.5
8 Radical Peoples Party	2.5	1.8	1.3	0.8	0.5	0.4
9 Social Democratic Workers Party	9.2	8.8	–	–	–	–
10 Communist Party	–	6.1	4.0	1.7	1.8	0.3
11 Christian Peoples Party	–	–	–	–	0.8	1.3
12 Commonwealth Party	–	–	–	–	1.5	3.1
13 National Socialists	–	–	–	–	2.2	1.8
Others	0.4	0.3	0.2	0.0	0.2	0.3

Table 18.15 NORWAY   Number of Seats Won in the Storting 1921–1936

	1921	1924	1927	1930	1933	1936
1 Liberals	37	34	30	33	24	23
2 Conservatives	42	43	30	41	30	36
5 National Liberals	15	11	1	3	1	0
4 Labour Party	29	24	59	47	69	70
7 Farmers Party	17	22	26	25	23	18
8 Radical Peoples Party	2	2	1	1	1	0
9 Social Democratic Workers Party	8	8	–	–	–	–
10 Communist Party	–	6	3	0	0	0
11 Christian Peoples Party	–	–	–	–	1	2
12 Commonwealth Party	–	–	–	–	1	1
13 National Socialists	–	–	–	–	0	0
Others	0	0	0	0	0	0
Total Seats	**150**	**150**	**150**	**150**	**150**	**150**

Source: *Stortingsvalget, 1921–1936.*

320

Table 18.16　NORWAY　Percentage of Seats Won in the Storting 1921—1936

	1921	1924	1927	1930	1933	1936
1 Liberals	24.7	22.7	20.0	22.0	16.0	15.3
2 Conservatives	28.0	28.7	20.0	27.3	20.0	24.0
5 National Liberals	10.0	7.3	0.7	2.0	0.7	0.0
4 Labour Party	19.3	16.0	39.3	31.3	46.0	46.7
7 Farmers Party	11.3	14.7	17.3	16.7	15.3	12.0
8 Radical Peoples Party	1.3	1.3	0.7	0.7	0.7	0.0
9 Social Democratic Workers Party	5.3	5.3	–	–	–	–
10 Communist Party	–	4.0	2.0	0.0	0.0	0.0
11 Christian Peoples Party	–	–	–	–	0.7	1.3
12 Commonwealth Party	–	–	–	–	0.7	0.7
13 National Socialists	–	–	–	–	0.0	0.0
Others	0.0	0.0	0.0	0.0	0.0	0.0

Table 18.17 NORWAY   Total Votes 1945–1969

	1945	1949	1953	1957	1961	1965	1969
Electorate	1,961,977	2,159,005	2,256,799	2,298,376	2,340,495	2,406,866	2,579,566
Valid Votes	1,485,225	1,758,366	1,779,831	1,791,128	1,840,225	2,047,394	2,158,712
Invalid Votes	12,969	12,531	10,500	9,027	10,323	8,697	3,884
Total Votes	1,498,194	1,770,897	1,790,331	1,800,155	1,850,548	2,056,091	2,162,596

PARTY VOTES

	1945	1949	1953	1957	1961	1965	1969
1 Liberals	204,852	218,866	177,662	171,407	132,429	207,834	202,553
2 Conservatives	252,608	279,790	327,971	301,395	354,369	415,292	406,209
4 Labour Party	609,348	803,471	830,448	865,675	860,526	883,319	1,004,348
7 Farmers Party/Centre Party	119,362	85,418	157,018	154,761	125,643	192,022	194,128
10 Communist Party	176,535	102,722	90,422	60,060	53,678	27,996	21,517
11 Christian Peoples Party	117,813	147,068	186,627	183,243	171,451	160,332	169,303
12 Commonwealth Party	1,845	13,088	–	–	–	–	–
14 Joint Non-Socialist Lists	–	107,913	9,661	51,360	95,231	37,513	83,073
15 Socialist Peoples Party	–	–	–	–	43,996	122,721	73,284
Others	2,862	30	22	3,227	2,902	365	4,297[1]

[1] Includes 3,203 votes cast for a joint Socialist Peoples Party-Communist Party List in Bergen.

Source: *Stortingsvalget, 1945–1969.*

Table 18.18   NORWAY   Percentage of Votes 1945—1969

	1945	1949	1953	1957	1961	1965	1969
Valid Votes	75.7	81.4	78.9	77.9	78.6	85.1	83.7
Invalid Votes	0.7	0.6	0.5	0.4	0.4	0.4	0.2
Total Votes	76.4	82.0	79.3	78.3	79.1	85.4	83.8
Share Invalid	0.9	0.7	0.6	0.5	0.6	0.4	0.2
PARTY VOTES							
1 Liberals	13.8	12.4	10.0	9.6	7.2	10.2	9.4
2 Copservatives	17.0	15.9	18.4	16.8	19.3	20.3	18.8
4 Labour Party	41.0	45.7	46.7	48.3	46.8	43.1	46.5
7 Farmers Party/Centre Party	8.0	4.9	8.8	8.6	6.8	9.4	9.0
10 Communist Party	11.9	5.8	5.1	3.4	2.9	1.4	1.0
11 Christian Peoples Party	7.9	8.4	10.5	10.2	9.3	7.8	7.8
12 Commonwealth Party	0.1	0.7	–	–	–	–	–
14 Joint Non-Socialist Lists	–	6.1	0.5	2.9	5.2	1.8	3.8
15 Socialist Peoples Party	–	–	–	–	2.4	6.0	3.4
Others	0.2	0.0	0.0	0.2	0.2	0.0	0.2

Table 18.19   NORWAY   Number of Seats Won in the Storting 1945—1969

	1945	1949	1953	1957	1961	1965	1969
1 Liberals	20	21	15	15	14	18	13
2 Conservatives	25	23	27	29	29	31	13
4 Labour Party	76	85	77	78	74	68	74
7 Farmers Party/Centre Party	10	12	14	15	16	18	20
10 Communist Party	11	0	3	1	0	0	0
11 Christian Peoples Party	8	9	14	12	15	13	14
12 Commonwealth Party	0	0	–	–	–	–	–
15 Socialist Peoples Party	–	–	–	–	2	2	0
Others	0	0	0	0	0	0	0
Total Seats	150	150	150	150	150	150	150

Source: *Stortingsvalget, 1945—1969*.

Table 18.20   NORWAY   Percentage of Seats Won in the Storting 1945—1969

		1945	1949	1953	1957	1961	1965	1969
1	Liberals	13.3	14.0	10.0	10.0	9.3	12.0	8.7
2	Conservatives	16.7	15.3	18.0	19.3	19.3	20.7	8.7
4	Labour Party	50.7	56.7	51.3	52.0	49.3	45.3	49.3
7	Farmers Party/Centre Party	6.7	8.0	9.3	10.0	10.7	12.0	13.3
10	Communist Party	7.3	0.0	2.0	0.7	0.0	0.0	0.0
11	Christian Peoples Party	5.3	6.0	9.3	8.0	10.0	8.7	9.3
12	Commonwealth Party	0.0	0.0	–	–	–	–	–
15	Socialist Peoples Party	–	–	–	–	1.3	1.3	0.0
	Others	0.0	0.0	0.0	0.0	0.0	0.0	0.0

Chapter 19

REPUBLIC OF SOUTH AFRICA

During the nineteenth century the territory which was later to become the Republic of South Africa was divided amongst two British colonies, Cape Colony and Natal, and two independent Afrikaner republics, the Orange Free State and the South African Republic (the Transvaal). Representative government was introduced in the Cape in 1853 and in Natal in 1856. In the Cape the franchise was limited, irrespective of race, to men aged over 21, who had an income of at least £50 per year or occupied property worth at least £25. By 1893 the property qualification had been increased to £75 and a literacy test introduced in order to check the increase in the number of non-white voters. In Natal a similar property-based franchise was introduced in 1856. In 1865 the granting of the vote to Africans was limited to the personal discretion of the Governor. In 1896 the members of the Indian community were effectively disenfranchised by a law which denied the vote to persons or descendants of persons born in countries which did not have elective representative institutions. In the Orange Free State and the South African Republic the vote was limited to adult white males.

In 1899 war broke out between the Afrikaner republics and Britain. The British forces were victorious and the republics were annexed in 1902. Self-government was granted to the Transvaal in 1906 and the Orange Free State in 1907. In 1910 the four colonies were united as the Union of South Africa. In 1919 South Africa was given a League of Nations mandate over the former German territory of South West Africa. The territory has since been administered by South Africa and her white population has sent six representatives to the House of Assembly since 1950. In 1961, following a referendum of the previous year, South Africa became a republic.

Political parties did not develop in the Transvaal and the Orange Free State until after their annexation by Britain. In Natal there were no organized political parties until after the formation of the Union. In the Cape the Afrikaner Bond was the only organized political party until the establishment of the pro-British Progressive Party in the 1890s. The growth of Afrikaner parties in the former republics, Oranjie Unie in the Orange Free State and Het Volk in the Transvaal, was matched by parties defending the interests of the English-speaking population: in the Orange Free State, the Constitutional Party, and in the Transvaal, the Progressive Association and the National Association. After the merger of the four colonies Het Volk, Oranjie Unie and the South African Party (formerly the Afrikaner Bond) united as the South African Party. The Progressive Association, the Constitutional Party and the Progressive Party came together as the Unionist Party (Worrall, 1971: 188).

In the 1910 election the South African Party won 66 seats in the House of Assembly, the Unionist Party 38 seats, the newly-formed Labour Party four seats and Independents 13 seats (Standard Encyclopaedia, 1972:272). The constitution of the Republic of South Africa provides for a parliament consisting of a partly elected and partly nominated Senate and a House of Assembly. Members of the House of Assembly are directly elected by plurality in single-member constituencies. The ballot is secret.

Racial discrimination in the franchise originally varied from province to province because each retained its own franchise laws. In the Orange Free State and the Transvaal the vote continued to be limited to adult white males. In the Cape whites formed 85 per cent of the electorate, although they were only 23 per cent of the population. In Natal the white eight per cent of the population comprised 99 per cent of the electorate (Wilson and Thompson, Vo. II, 1971:388). In every case the minimum voting age was 21; this was reduced to 18 in 1958.

Racial composition of the electorate in Cape Colony and Natal in 1909

Racial Group	Cape Colony	Natal
White	121,367	23,480
Coloured	14,388	50
African	6,633	6
Asian	—	150
Total	142,367	23,686

Source: *Standard Encyclopaedia,* 1972.

In 1930 the Union government gave white women the vote on the same basis as men and in the following year provincial income, property and literacy requirements were abolished for Europeans only. In 1936 African voters in the Cape Province were placed on a separate voters roll, electing three white representatives to the Assembly. In 1956 Coloured voters were also placed on a separate roll. They were to elect four white representatives.

In pursuance of the government's policy of apartheid, or separate development, African representation in the Assembly was abolished in 1961 and Coloured representation in 1968. All adult Coloureds may now vote for a Coloured Persons Representative Council consisting of 40 elected and 20 nominated members; it has limited legislative authority. Very limited powers of self-government have been granted to some of the African tribal homelands.

As a result of the policy of apartheid South Africa's House of Assembly now represents only the white community, which forms less than 20 per cent of the total population

Racial Distribution of the Population of South Africa, 1970

		per cent
White	3,751,328	17.5
African	15,057,952	70.2
Coloured	2,018,453	9.4
Asian	620,000	2.9
Total	21,448,172	100.0

Source: *Statesmans Year Book,* 1972 : 1294.

Sources:

Carter, G.M., *The Politics of Inequality* (New York: Praeger, 1958).

Farquharson, R.R., "South Africa, 1958" in D.E. Butler (ed.) *Elections Abroad* (London: Macmillan, 1959).

The Standard Encyclopaedia of Southern Africa (East London: Nasionale Boekhandel, 1972).

Verkiesings 1910 tot 1970 (Johannesburg: Vootrekkerpers, 1970).

Wilson, M. and Thompson, L., (eds.), *The Oxford History of South Africa* (Oxford: Clarendon Press, 1971).

Worrall, D., (ed.), *South Africa: Government and Politics* (Pretoria: van Schaik, 1971).

Table 19.1

POLITICAL PARTIES IN SOUTH AFRICA SINCE 1910

	Party Names	Elections contested	Number contested
1	South African Party/Suid Afrikaanse Party	1910-1933	7
2	Unionist Party/Unionistese Party[1]	1910-1920	3
3	Labour Party/Arbeidersparty	1910-1953	11
4	National Party I/Nasionale Party[2]	1915-1933	6
5	Natal Home Rule Party	1933	1
6	Roos Party/Roosiet or Sentrale Party	1933	1
7	Dominion Party; renamed the South African Party in 1946	1938-1948	3
8	United Party/Verenigde Party[3]	1938ff	8
9	Purified National Party/Herenigde Nasionale Party[4]	1938-1948	3
10	Afrikaner Party[5]	1943-1948	2
11	Central Group	1948	1
12	Communist Party/Kommunisties Party[6]	1948	1
13	National Party II/Nasionale Party[7]	1953ff	5
14	Conservative Workers Party/Konserwatiewe Werkersparty	1961	1
15	National Union/Nasionale Unie	1961	1
16	Progressive Party/Progressiewe Party[8]	1961ff	3
17	Reconstituted National Party/Herstigte Nasionale Party[9]	1970	1

[1] Merged with the South African Party in 1920.

[2] Formed by ex-members of the South African Party led by General Hertzog in 1914.

[3] A merger of the South African and National Parties in 1934.

[4] Former Nationalists, led by Daniel Malan, who left the United Party in 1934.

[5] In 1939 the United Party split on South African involvement in the Second World War. A section of the party led by General Hertzog joined the Nationalist Party. Disagreement within the Nationalist ranks led some of Hertzog's supporters to establish the Afrikaner Party in 1941. This party formed an electoral alliance with the Nationalists in 1948 and the two parties merged in 1951.

[6] The Communist Party was declared illegal in 1950.

[7] Merger of the National Party and the Afrikaner Party.

[8] Established by former United Party members in 1959.

[9] A right-wing splinter from the Nationalist Party.

Table 19.2
DATES OF ELECTIONS
TO THE HOUSE OF ASSEMBLY 1910–1970

1.	15 September 1910	9.	7 July 1943
2.	20 October 1915	10.	26 May 1948
3.	10 March 1920	11.	15 April 1953
4.	8 February 1921	12.	16 April 1958
5.	17 June 1924	13.	18 October 1961
6.	17 June 1929	14.	30 March 1966
7.	17 May 1933	15.	22 April 1970
8.	18 May 1938		

Source: *Standard Encyclopaedia,* 1972 : 272-273.

Table 19.3 SOUTH AFRICA Total Votes 1915–1943

	1915	1920	1921	1924	1929	1933	1938	1943
Electorate	365,307	421,790	449,531	413,136	461,820	957,820	1,052,652	1,114,110
Valid Votes	257,103	277,494	275,313	316,242	343,897	320,011	828,897	876,263
Invalid Votes	4,330	4,867	2,429	2,805	4,027	3,406	6,481	9,360
Total Votes	261,433	282,361	277,742	319,047	347,924	323,417	835,378	885,623
PARTY VOTES								
3 Labour Party	24,755	40,639	29,406	45,380	33,919	20,276	48,641	38,206
2 Unionist Party	49,917	38,946	–	–	–	–	–	–
1 South African Party	94,285	90,512	137,389	148,769	159,896	71,486	–	–
8 United Party	–	–	–	–	–	–	446,032	435,297
4 National Party I	75,623	101,227	105,039	111,483	141,579	101,159	259,543	321,601
9 Purified National Party	–	–	–	–	–	12,328	–	–
5 Natal Home Rule Party	–	–	–	–	–	27,441	–	–
6 Roos Party	–	–	–	–	–	–	–	–
7 Dominion Party	–	–	–	–	–	–	52,356	29,023
10 Afrikaner Party	–	–	–	–	–	–	–	15,601
Others	12,523	6,170	3,479	10,610	8,503	87,321	22,325	36,535

Source: *Standard Encyclopaedia*, 1972 : 272-273

Table 19.4   SOUTH AFRICA   Percentage of Votes 1915—1943

	1915	1920	1921	1924	1929	1933	1938	1943
Valid Votes	70.4	65.8	61.2	76.5	74.5	33.4	78.7	78.7
Invalid Votes	1.2	1.2	0.5	0.7	0.9	0.4	0.6	0.8
Total Votes	71.6	66.9	61.8	77.2	75.3	33.8	79.4	79.5
Share Invalid	1.7	1.7	0.9	0.9	1.2	1.1	0.8	1.1
PARTY VOTES								
3 Labour Party	9.6	14.6	10.7	14.3	9.9	6.3	5.9	4.4
2 Unionist Party	19.4	14.0	–	–	–	–	–	–
1 South Africa Party	36.7	32.6	49.9	47.0	46.5	22.3	–	–
8 United Party	–	–	–	–	–	–	53.8	49.7
4 National Party I	29.4	36.5	38.2	35.3	41.2	31.6	–	–
9 Purified National Party	–	–	–	–	–	–	31.3	36.7
5 Home Rule Party	–	–	–	–	–	3.9	–	–
6 Roos Party	–	–	–	–	–	8.6	–	–
7 Dominion Party	–	–	–	–	–	–	6.3	3.3
10 Afrikaner Party	–	–	–	–	–	–	–	1.8
Others	4.9	2.2	1.3	3.4	2.5	27.3	2.7	4.2

Table 19.5   SOUTH AFRICA   Number of Seats Won in the House of Assembly 1915—1943[4]

		1915	1920	1921	1924	1929	1933	1938	1943
3	Labour Party	3	21	10	17	8	4	3	9
2	Unionist Party	40	25	–	–	–	–	–	–
1	South Africa Party	54	41	77	54	61	61	–	–
8	United Party	–	–	–	–	–	–	111	89
4	National Party I	27	43	44	63	77	75	–	–
9	Purified National Party	–	–	–	–	–	–	27	43
5	Home Rule Party	–	–	–	–	–	2	–	–
6	Roos Party	–	–	–	–	–	2	–	–
7	Dominion Party	–	–	–	–	–	–	8	7
10	Afrikaner Party	–	–	–	–	–	–	–	0
	Others	6	3	1	1	1	6	1	2
	Total Seats	**130**	**134[1]**	**134[2]**	**135**	**148[3]**	**150**	**150**	**150**
	Unopposed Returns	8	3	12	0	9	78	4	18

[1] Including one vacancy.
[2] Including two vacancies.
[3] Including one vacancy.
[4] In 1938 and 1943 excludes the three white members elected by African voters on a separate roll.

Source: *Standard Encyclopedia*, 1972 : 272-273.

Table 19.6 SOUTH AFRICA   Percentage of Seats Won in the House of Assembly 1915—1943

		1915	1920	1921	1924	1929	1933	1938	1943
3	Labour Party	2.3	15.8	7.6	12.6	5.4	2.7	2.0	6.0
2	Unionist Party	30.8	18.8	–	–	–	–	–	–
1	South Africa Party	41.5	30.8	58.3	40.0	41.5	40.7	–	–
8	United Party	–	–	–	–	–	–	74.0	59.3
4	National Party I	20.8	32.3	33.3	46.7	52.4	50.0	–	–
9	Purified National Party	–	–	–	–	–	–	18.0	28.7
5	Home Rule Party	–	–	–	–	–	1.3	–	–
6	Roos Party	–	–	–	–	–	1.3	–	–
7	Dominion Party	–	–	–	–	–	–	5.3	4.7
10	Afrikaner Party	–	–	–	–	–	–	–	0.0
	Others	4.6	2.3	0.8	0.7	0.7	4.0	0.7	1.3
	Unopposed Returns	6.2	2.2	9.0	0.0	6.1	52.0	2.7	12.0

Table 19.7   SOUTH AFRICA   Total Votes 1948—1970

	1948	1953	1958	1961	1966	1970
Electorate	1,337,543	1,385,591	1,563,426	1,811,160	1,901,479	2,161,234
Valid Votes	1,065,971	1,209,922	1,155,003	797,561	1,302,151	1,497,652
Invalid Votes	7,393	8,709	7,573	4,518	7,494	9,982
Total Votes	1,073,364	1,218,631	1,162,576	802,079	1,309,645	1,507,634
PARTY VOTES						
3 Labour Party	27,360	34,730	2,670	2,461	–	–
8 United Party	524,230	576,474	492,080	281,361	476,815	553,280
9 Purified National Party	401,834	–	–	–	–	–
13 National Party II	–	598,718	642,006	370,395	759,331	822,034
10 Afrikaner Party	41,885	–	–	–	–	–
7 South African Party	11,894	–	–	–	–	–
11 Central Group	15,460	–	–	–	–	–
12 Communist Party	1,783	–	–	–	–	–
14 Conservative Workers	–	–	–	8,554	–	–
15 National Union	–	–	–	50,279	–	–
16 Progressive Party	–	–	–	69,045	39,717	51,742
17 Reconstituted National Party	–	–	–	–	–	53,735
Others	41,525	–	19,247	15,466	26,288	16,861

Source: *Standard Encyclopaedia*, 1972 : 273.

336

Table 19.8   SOUTH AFRICA   Percentage of Votes 1948–1970

	1948	1953	1958	1961	1966	1970
Valid Votes	79.7	87.3	73.9	44.0	68.5	69.3
Invalid Votes	0.6	0.6	0.5	0.2	0.4	0.5
Total Votes	80.2	88.0	74.4	44.3	68.9	69.8
Share Invalid	0.7	0.7	0.7	0.6	0.6	0.7
PARTY VOTES						
3 Labour Party	2.6	2.9	0.2	0.3	–	–
8 United Party	49.2	47.6	42.6	35.3	36.6	36.9
9 Purified National Party	37.7	–	–	–	–	–
13 National Party II	–	49.5	55.5	46.4	58.3	54.9
10 Afrikaner Party	3.9	–	–	–	–	–
7 South African Party	1.1	–	–	–	–	–
11 Central Group	1.5	–	–	–	–	–
12 Communist Party	0.2	–	–	–	–	–
14 Conservative Workers Party	–	–	–	1.1	–	–
15 National Union	–	–	–	6.3	–	–
16 Progressive Party	–	–	–	8.7	3.1	3.5
17 Reconstituted National Party	–	–	–	–	–	3.6
Others	3.9	–	1.7	1.9	2.0	1.1

Table 19.9   SOUTH AFRICA   Number of Seats Won in the House of Assembly 1948—1970[1]

		1948	1953	1958	1961	1966	1970
3	Labour Party	6	5	0	0	—	—
8	United Party	65	57	53	49	39	47
9	Purified National Party	70	—	—	—	—	—
13	National Party II	—	94	103	105	126	117
10	Afrikaner Party	9	—	—	—	—	—
7	South African Party	0	—	—	—	—	—
11	Central Group	0	—	—	—	—	—
12	Communist Party	0	—	—	—	—	—
14	Conservative Workers Party	—	—	—	0	—	—
15	National Union	—	—	—	1	—	—
16	Progressive Party	—	—	—	1	1	1
17	Reconstituted National Party	—	—	—	—	—	0
	Others	0	—	0	0	0	0
	Total Seats	150	156	156	156	166	166[2]
	Unopposed Returns	12	22	24	70	19	11

[1] Excludes white members elected by the Coloured and African voters on separate rolls.
[2] Including one vacancy. This seat was won by the National Party as a subsequent by-election.

Source: *Standard Encyclopaedia,* 1972 : 273.

Table 19.10   SOUTH AFRICA   Percentage of Seats Won in the House of Assembly 1948–1970

		1948	1953	1958	1961	1966	1970
3	Labour Party	4.0	3.2	0.0	0.0	–	–
8	United Party	43.3	36.5	34.0	31.4	23.5	28.5
9	Purified National Party	46.7	–	–	–	–	–
13	National Party II	–	60.3	66.0	67.3	75.9	70.9
10	Afrikaner Party	6.0	–	–	–	–	–
7	South African Party	0.0	–	–	–	–	–
11	Central Group	0.0	–	–	–	–	–
12	Communist Party	0.0	–	–	0.0	–	–
14	Conservative Workers Party	–	–	–	0.0	–	–
15	National Union Party	–	–	–	0.6	–	–
16	Progressive Party	–	–	–	0.6	0.6	0.6
17	Reconstituted National Party	–	–	–	–	–	0.0
	Others	0.0	–	0.0	0.0	0.0	0.0
	Unopposed Returns	8.0	14.1	15.4	44.9	11.4	6.6

Chapter 20

SWEDEN

The modern Swedish party system dates from the controversy over the tariff reform question in the 1880's. The first election contested by nationally organized political parties was held in 1887 (Stjernquist, 1966 : 120).

Elections were held under the electoral law of 1866, which replaced the traditional form of representation by estates with a two chamber parliament, the Riksdag, consisting of an upper house — the First Chamber (Första Kammaren) and a lower house — the Second Chamber (Andra Kammaren). The franchise for elections to the Second Chamber was limited to men over 21 years of age who met minimum property requirements: an income of 800 riksdalers a year, freehold property at 1,000 riksdalers or leasehold property assessed at a minimum of 6,000 riksdalers. Deputies were chosen by a plurality system. Single-member constituencies were used, except for the five largest towns, which each formed a multi-member constituency. In the larger towns elections were direct. In other constituencies elections could be either direct or indirect, according to the wishes of the locality. The number of constituencies where indirect elections were held declined steadily from 139 in 1866 to 39 in 1890 and one in 1908 (Lewin et al., 1972 : 31). The ballot was secret.

The 1907 election reform abolished the property requirement for the franchise, raised the minimum voting age to 24 and introduced direct proportional representation in multi-member constituencies using the d'Hondt system. In 1921 universal adult suffrage was introduced and the voting age reduced to 23. In 1945 the voting age was again reduced to 21. In 1952 the Saint-Laguë system (with an initial divisor of 1.4) replaced the d'Hondt system.

In 1970 a major reform of the constitution involved further changes in the electoral system. Of the 350 deputies in the new single-chamber Riksdag, 310 are elected directly in multi-member constituencies as previously. The remaining 40 seats are allocated to under-represented parties with the aim of ensuring that the total allocation of seats in the Riksdag reflects as closely as possible the nationwide distribution of the vote. However, a barrier clause denies parliamentary representation to any party which does not win at least four per cent of the total vote, with the proviso that any party which won at least 12 per cent of the vote in a particular constituency would still be allowed to compete for seats in that constituency. The minimum voting age was again reduced, so that all Swedish citizens now become entitled to vote in the year following their nineteenth birthday.

Sources:

Carlsson, S. and Rosen, J., *Svensk historia, II* (Stockholm; Scandinavian University Books, 1961).

Central Bureau of Statistics, *Historisk statistik för Sverige: statistiska oversikts-tabeller* (Stockholm, 1960).

Central Bureau of Statistics, *Sveriges officiella statistik,* sub-series *Almänna val* (Stockholm, 1914ff.).

Central Bureau of Statistics, *Statistisk arsbok*, 1971 (Stockholm, 1971).

Lewin, L. Jansson, B. and Sorböm, D., *The Swedish Electorate, 1887–1968* (Stockholm: Almqvist and Wicksell, 1972).

Stjernquist, N., "Sweden: stability or deadlock?" in R.A. Dahl (ed.) *Political Oppositions in Western Democracies* (New Haven: Yale University Press, 1966) pp. 116-146.

Verney, D.V., *Parliamentary Reform in Sweden, 1866–1921* (Oxford: Clarendon Press, 1957).

Table 20.1
POLITICAL PARTIES IN SWEDEN SINCE 1887

	Party Names	Elections contested	Number contested
1	Protectionists (Protektionistiska Högermän; literally Protectionist Right)	1887-1896	5
2	Free Traders (Frihandelssinade)	1887-1890	3
3	Liberals (Liberaler)[1]	1893-1921	13
4	Moderate Free Traders (Frihandelssinade Högerman; literally Free Trade Right)	1893-1896	2
5	Social Democrats (Sveriges Socialdemokratistiska Arbetarparti)	1890ff	27
6	Conservatives (Högerpartiet; literally the Right Party). In 1969 renamed the Moderate Unity Party (Moderate Samlingspartiet)	1899ff	23
7	Agrarian Party (Bondeförbundet). In 1957 renamed the Centre Party (Centerpartiet)	1917ff	17
8	Farmers Union (Jordbrukarnas Riksförbund)	1917-1921	2
9	Left Socialists (Vänstersocialister)[2]	1917-1921	3
10	Communist Party (Sveriges Kommunistiska Parti). In 1967 renamed the Left Party Communists (Vänsterpartiet Kommunisterna)	1921ff	15
11	Höglund Communists (Höglundkommunister)	1924	1
12	Kilbom Communists (Kilbomskommunister)	1932	1
13	Socialists (Socialister)[3]	1936-1944	3
14	Prohibitionist Liberals (Frisinnade Folkpartiet)	1924-1932	3
15	Swedish Liberal Party (Sveriges Liberale Parti)	1924-1932	3
16	Peoples Party (Folkpartiet)	1936ff	11
17	Christian Democrats (Kristen Demokratisk Samling)	1964ff	3
18	Citizens Coalition (Medborgerlig Samling)[4]	1964-1968	2
19	Middle Parties (Mittenpartierna)[5]	1964-1968	2

[1] In 1923 the Liberals split on the prohibition question, forming two separate parties, the Frisinnade Folkpartiet and the Sveriges Liberale Parti. They were reunited as the Peoples Party in 1934.

[2] In 1921 the majority of the Left Socialists joined the Communist International and formed the Swedish Communist Party. A minority, however, decided to remain independent and contested the 1921 election under the old party label.

[3] A party created by the merger of the Kilbom Communists with ex-Social Democrats.

[4] An electoral alliance in the Four Cities constituency (Malmö, Helsinborg, Lund and Landskrona) of the Conservative, Centre and Peoples parties. In 1968 an alliance of the Conservative and Peoples parties only, known as Coalition 68 (Samling-68).

An electoral alliance of the Centre and Peoples parties in the Gotland constituency. Known as the Intermediate Parties (Mellanpartierna) in 1964.

Table 20.2
DATES OF ELECTIONS
TO THE ANDRA KAMMAREN 1887–1970[1]

1	29 March–30 April 1887	16	19–21 September 1924
2	9 August–29 September 1887	17	15–21 September 1928
3	14 July–29 September 1890	18	17–18 September 1932
4	2 July–30 September 1893	19	20 September 1936
5	28 June–29 September 1896	20	15 September 1940
6	16 July–30 September 1899	21	17 September 1944
7	7–13 September 1902	22	19 September 1948
8	10–16 September 1905	23	21 September 1952
9	6–12 September 1908	24	26 September 1956
10	9–24 September 1911	25	1 June 1958
11	29 March–7 April 1914	26	18 September 1960
12	5–13 September 1914	27	20 September 1964
13	1–16 September 1917	28	15 September 1968
14	4–17 September 1920	29	20 September 1970
15	10–26 September 1921		

[1] In 1970 the Riksdag.

Source: Swedish Central Bureau of Statistics.

Table 20.3 SWEDEN   Total Votes 1887–1908

	1887	1887	1890	1893	1896	1899	1902	1905	1908
Electorate	274,733	278,039	288,096	298,810	309,889	339,876	382,075	432,099	503,128
Valid Votes	129,717	95,874	105,807	126,617	140,588	136,945	180,527	217,323	308,389
PARTY VOTES									
1 Protectionists	53,692	44,915	45,149	48,963	54,282	–	–	–	–
2 Free Traders	76,025	50,959	60,658[1]	–	–	–	–	–	–
5 Social Democrats	–	–	–	–	–	–	6,321	20,677	45,155
3 Liberals	–	–	–	44,618[1]	53,388[1]	64,145[1]	92,503	98,287	144,426
4 Moderate Free Traders	–	–	–	33,036	32,918	–	–	–	–
6 Conservatives	–	–	–	–	–	72,800	81,703	98,359	118,808

[1] Includes a few votes cast for joint lists with the Social Democrats.

Sources: *Historisk statistisk*, 1960 : 270; Lewin, 1973 : 120.

Table 20.4   SWEDEN   Percentage of Votes 1887–1908

	1887	1887	1890	1893	1896	1899	1902	1905	1908
Valid Votes	47.2	34.5	36.7	42.4	45.4	40.3	47.2	50.3	61.3
Party PARTY VOTES									
1 Protectionists	41.4	46.8	42.7	38.7	38.6	–	–	–	–
2 Free Traders	58.6	53.2	57.3	–	–	–	–	–	–
5 Social Democrats	–	–	–	–	–	–	3.5	9.5	14.6
3 Liberals	–	–	–	35.2	38.0	46.8	51.2	45.2	46.8
4 Moderate Free Traders	–	–	–	26.1	23.4	–	–	–	–
6 Conservatives	–	–	–	–	–	53.2	45.3	45.3	38.5

Table 20.5   SWEDEN   Number of Seats Won in the Andra Kammaren 1887–1908

	1887	1887	1890	1893	1896	1899	1902	1905	1908
1 Protectionists	112	85	88	86	98	–	–	–	–
2 Free Traders	102	136	140	–	–	–	–	–	–
5 Social Democrats	–	–	0	0	1	1	4	13	34
3 Liberals	–	–	–	76	73	92	107	109	105
4 Moderate Free Traders	–	–	–	66	58	–	–	–	–
6 Conservatives	–	–	–	–	–	137	119	108	91
Total Seats	214	221	228	228	230	230	230	230	230

Source: Carlsson, 1961 : 595.

348

Table 20.6   SWEDEN   Percentage of Seats Won in the Andra Kammaren 1887–1908

	1887	1887	1890	1893	1896	1899	1902	1905	1908
1 Protectionists	52.3	38.5	38.6	37.7	42.6	–	–	–	–
2 Free Traders	47.7	61.5	61.4	–	–	–	–	–	–
5 Social Democrats	–	–	0.0	0.0	0.4	0.4	1.7	5.7	14.8
3 Liberals	–	–	–	33.3	31.7	40.0	46.5	47.4	45.7
4 Moderate Free Traders	–	–	–	28.9	25.2	–	–	–	–
6 Conservatives	–	–	–	–	–	59.6	51.7	47.0	39.6

Table 20.7   SWEDEN   Total Votes 1911–1921

	1911	1914 (March)	1914 (Sept.)	1917	1920	1921
Electorate	1,066,200	1,092,454	1,111,767	1,123,969	1,192,922	3,222,917
Valid Votes	603,974	760,194	731,361	735,984	657,583	1,741,952
Invalid Votes	3,513	3,229	4,124	3,069	2,610	5,601
Total Votes	607,487	763,423	735,485	739,053	660,193	1,747,553
PARTY VOTES						
5 Social Democrats	172,196	228,712	266,133	228,777	195,121	630,855
3 Liberals	242,795	245,107	196,493	202,936	143,355	325,608
6 Conservatives	188,691	286,250	267,124	182,070	183,019	449,302
7 Agrarian Party	–	–	1,507	39,262	52,318	192,269
8 Farmers Union	–	–	–	22,659	40,623	–
9 Left Socialists	–	–	–	59,243	42,056	56,241
10 Communists	–	–	–	–	–	80,355
Others	292	125	104	1,037	1,091	7,322

Sources: 1911, *Historisk statistisk*, 1960 : 218-269; 1914–1921, *Almänna val.*

Table 20.8   SWEDEN   Percentage of Votes 1911—1921

	1911	1914 (March)	1914 (Sept.)	1917	1920	1921
Valid Votes	56.6	69.6	65.8	65.5	55.1	54.0
Invalid Votes	0.3	0.3	0.4	0.3	0.2	0.2
Total Votes	57.0	69.9	66.2	65.8	55.3	54.2
Share Invalid	0.6	0.4	0.6	0.4	0.4	0.3
PARTY VOTES						
5 Social Democrats	28.5	30.1	36.4	31.1	29.7	36.2
3 Liberals	40.2	32.2	26.9	27.6	21.8	18.7
6 Conservatives	31.2	37.7	36.5	24.7	27.8	25.8
7 Agrarian Party	–	–	0.2	5.3	8.0	11.0
8 Farmers Union	–	–	–	3.1	6.2	–
9 Left Socialists	–	–	–	8.0	6.4	3.2
10 Communists	–	–	–	–	–	4.6
Others	0.0	0.0	0.0	0.1	0.2	0.4

Table 20.9   SWEDEN   Number of Seats Won in the Andra Kammaren 1911–1921

	1911	1914 (March)	1914 (Sept.)	1917	1920	1921
5 Social Democrats	64	73	87	86	75	93
3 Liberals	101	71	57	62	47	41
6 Conservatives	65	86	86	59	70	62
7 Agrarian Party	–	–	0	9	19	21
8 Farmers Union	–	–	–	3	10	–
9 Left Socialists	–	–	–	11	7	6
10 Communists	–	–	–	–	–	7
Others	0	0	0	0	2	0
Total Seats	230	230	230	230	230	230

Sources: 1911, *Historisk statistik*, 1960 : 269; 1914–1921 : *Almänna val.*

Table 20.10   SWEDEN   Percentage of Seats Won in the Andra Kammaren 1911—1921

	1911	1914 (March)	1914 (Sept.)	1917	1920	1921
5 Social Democrats	27.8	31.7	37.8	37.4	32.6	40.4
3 Liberals	43.9	30.9	24.8	27.0	20.4	17.8
6 Conservatives	28.3	37.4	37.4	25.7	30.4	27.0
7 Agrarian Party	–	–	0.0	3.9	8.3	9.1
8 Farmers Union	–	–	–	1.3	4.3	–
9 Left Socialists	–	–	–	4.8	3.0	2.6
10 Communists	–	–	–	–	–	3.0
Others	0.0	0.0	0.0	0.0	0.9	0.0

Table 20.11 SWEDEN   Total Votes 1924—1944

	1924	1928	1932	1936	1940	1944
Electorate	3,338,892	3,505,672	3,698,935	3,924,598	4,110,720	4,310,241
Valid Votes	1,765,586	2,358,811	2,495,106	2,917,753	2,874,417	3,086,304
Invalid Votes	5,021	4,357	5,663	7,502	14,720	12,799
Total Votes	1,770,607	2,363,168	2,500,769	2,925,255	2,889,137	3,099,103
PARTY VOTES						
5 Social Democrats	725,407	873,931	1,040,689	1,338,120	1,546,804	1,436,571
14 Prohibitionist Liberals	228,913	303,995	244,577	376,161	–	–
16 Peoples Party	–	–	–		344,113	398,293
15 Swedish Liberal Party	69,627	70,820	48,722		–	–
6 Conservatives	461,257	692,434	585,248	512,781	518,346	488,921
7 Agrarian Party	190,396	263,501	351,215	418,840	344,345	421,094
10 Communists	63,601	151,567	74,245	96,519	101,424	318,466
11 Höglund Communists	26,301	–	–	–	–	–
12 Kilbom Communists	–	–	132,564	–	–	–
13 Socialists	–	–	–	127,832	18,430	5,279
Others	84	2,563	17,846	47,500	955	17,680

Source: Almänna val.

354

Table 20.12   SWEDEN

Percentage of Votes 1924–1944

	1924	1928	1932	1936	1940	1944
Valid Votes	52.9	67.3	67.5	74.3	69.9	71.6
Invalid Votes	02	0.1	0.2	0.2	0.4	0.3
Total Votes	53.0	67.4	67.6	74.5	70.3	71.9
Share Invalid	0.3	0.2	0.2	0.3	0.5	0.4
PARTY VOTES						
5 Social Democrats	41.1	37.0	41.7	45.9	53.8	46.5
14 Prohibitionist Liberals	13.0	12.9	9.8	–	–	–
16 Peoples Party	–	–	–	12.9	12.0	12.9
15 Swedish Liberal Party	3.9	3.0	2.0	–	–	–
6 Conservatives	26.1	29.4	23.5	17.6	18.0	15.8
7 Agrarian Party	10.8	11.2	14.1	14.4	12.0	13.6
10 Communists	3.6	6.4	3.0	3.3	3.5	10.3
11 Höglund Communists	1.5	–	–	–	–	–
12 Kilbom Communists	–	–	5.3	–	–	–
13 Socialists	–	–	–	4.4	0.6	0.2
Others	0.0	0.1	0.7	1.6	0.0	0.6

Table 20.13   SWEDEN   Number of Seats Won in the Andra Kammaren 1924—1944

	1924	1928	1932	1936	1940	1944
5 Social Democrats	104	90	104	112	134	115
14 Prohibitionist Liberals	28	28	20	–	–	–
16 Peoples Party	–	–	–	27	23	26
15 Swedish Liberal Party	5	4	4	–	–	–
6 Conservatives	65	73	58	44	42	39
7 Agrarian Party	23	27	36	36	28	35
10 Communists	4	8	2	5	3	15
11 Höglund Communists	1	–	–	–	–	–
12 Kilbom Communists	–	–	6	–	–	–
13 Socialists	–	–	–	6	–	0
Others	0	0	0	0	0	0
Total Seats	230	230	230	230	230	230

Source: *Almänna Val.*

356

Table 20.14   SWEDEN   Percentage of Seats Won in the Andra Kammaren 1924—1944

	1924	1928	1932	1936	1940	1944
5 Social Democrats	45.2	39.1	45.2	48.7	58.3	50.0
14 Prohibitionist Liberals	12.2	12.2	8.7	–	–	–
16 Peoples Party	–	–	–	11.7	10.0	11.3
15 Swedish Liberal Party	2.2	1.7	1.7	–	–	–
6 Conservatives	28.3	31.7	25.2	19.1	18.3	17.0
7 Agrarian Party	10.0	11.7	15.7	15.7	12.2	15.2
10 Communists	1.7	3.5	0.9	2.2	1.3	6.5
11 Höglund Communists	0.4	–	–	–	–	–
12 Kilbom Communists	–	–	2.6	–	–	–
13 Socialists	–	–	–	2.6	0.0	0.0
Others	0.0	0.0	0.0	0.0	0.0	0.0

Table 20.15   SWEDEN   Total Votes 1948—1970

	1948	1952	1956	1958	1960	1964	1968	1970
Electorate	4,707,783	4,805,216	4,902,114	4,992,421	4,972,177	5,095,850	5,445,333	5,645,804
Valid Votes	3,878,991	3,783,707	3,879,330	3,844,252	4,254,114	4,245,780	4,829,379	4,976,196
Invalid Votes	16,170	17,577	22,784	20,711	17,496	27,815	32,522	8,011
Total Votes	3,895,161	3,801,284	3,902,114	3,864,963	4,271,610	4,273,595	4,861,901	4,984,207
PARTY VOTES								
5 Social Democrats	1,789,459	1,742,284	1,729,463	1,776,667	2,033,016	2,006,923	2,420,277	2,256,369
6 Conservatives	478,786	543,825	663,693	750,332	704,365	582,609	621,031	573,812
7 Agrarian/Centre Party	480,421	406,183	366,612	486,760	579,007	559,632	757,215	991,208
16 Peoples Party	882,437	924,819	923,564	700,019	744,142	720,733	688,456	806,667
10 Communists	244,826	164,194	194,016	129,319	190,560	221,746	145,172	236,659
17 Christian Democrats	–	–	–	–	–	75,389	72,377	88,770
18 Citizens Coalition	–	–	–	–	–	64,807	82,082	–
19 Middle Parties	–	–	–	–	–	13,557	41,307	–
Others	3,062	2,402	1,982	1,155	3,024	384	1,462	22,711

Sources: 1948—1964 : *Almänna val;* 1968—1970, *Statistisk årsbok,* 1971 : 393-394.

Table 20.16   SWEDEN   Percentage of Votes 1948–1970

		1948	1952	1956	1958	1960	1964	1968	1970
	Valid Votes	82.4	78.7	79.1	77.0	85.6	83.3	88.7	88.1
	Invalid Votes	0.3	0.4	0.5	0.4	0.4	0.5	0.6	0.1
	Total Votes	82.7	79.1	79.6	77.4	85.9	83.9	89.3	88.3
	Share Invalid	0.4	0.5	0.6	0.5	0.4	0.7	0.7	0.2
	PARTY VOTES								
5	Social Democrats	46.1	46.0	44.6	46.2	47.8	47.3	50.1	45.3
6	Conservatives	12.3	14.4	17.1	19.5	16.6	13.7	12.9	11.5
7	Agrarian/Centre Party	12.4	10.7	9.5	12.7	13.6	13.2	15.7	19.9
16	Peoples Party	22.7	24.4	23.8	18.2	17.5	17.0	14.3	16.2
10	Communists	6.3	4.3	5.0	3.4	4.5	5.2	3.0	4.8
17	Christian Democrats	–	–	–	–	–	1.8	1.5	1.8
18	Citizens Coalition	–	–	–	–	–	1.5	1.7	–
19	Middle Parties	–	–	–	–	–	0.3	0.9	–
	Others	0.1	0.1	0.1	0.0	0.1	0.0	0.0	0.5

Table 20.17   SWEDEN   Number of Seats Won in the Andra Kammaren 1948—1970[1]

	1948	1952	1956	1958	1960	1964	1968	1970
5 Social Democrats	112	110	106	111	114	113	125	163
6 Conservatives	23	31	42	45	39	32	29	41
7 Agrarian/Centre Party	30	26	19	32	34	33	37	71
16 Peoples Party	57	58	58	38	40	42	32	58
10 Communists	8	5	6	5	5	8	3	17
17 Christian Democrats	–	–	–	–	–	0	0	0
18 Citizens Coalition	–	–	–	–	–	3[2]	4[3]	–
19 Middle Parties	–	–	–	–	–	2[2]	3[3]	–
Others	0	0	0	0	0	0	0	0
Total Seats	230	230	231	231	232	233	233	350

[1] Since 1970 the Riksdag.

[2] In 1964 the two representatives of the Middle Parties joined the Centre Party parliamentary group. Of the three Citizens Coalition representatives one joined the Peoples Party and one the Conservatives. The third representative was not accepted by the Peoples Party. This gave the Peoples Party 43 seats (18.5%); the Conservatives 33 seats (14.2%); and the Centre Party 35 seats (15.0%).

[3] In 1968 two of the three representatives of the Middle Parties joined the Centre Party and one the Peoples Party. Of the four Citizens Coalition representatives, three joined the Conservatives and one the Peoples Party. This results in Peoples Party 34 seats (14.6%), Conservatives 32 seats (13.1%), Centre Party 39 seats (16.7%).

Sources: 1948—1964, Almänna val; 1968—1970, Statistisk årsbok, 1971 : 393-394.

Table 20.18   SWEDEN   Percentage of Seats Won in the Andra Kammaren 1948–1970

	1948	1952	1956	1958	1960	1964	1968	1970
5 Social Democrats	48.7	47.8	45.9	48.1	49.1	48.5	53.6	46.6
6 Conservatives	10.0	13.5	18.2	19.5	16.8	13.7	12.4	11.7
7 Agrarian/Centre Party	13.0	11.3	8.2	13.9	14.7	14.2	15.9	20.3
16 Peoples Party	24.8	25.2	25.1	16.5	17.2	18.0	13.7	16.6
10 Communists	3.5	2.2	2.6	2.2	2.2	3.4	1.3	4.9
17 Christian Democrats	–	–	–	–	–	0.0	0.0	0.0
18 Citizens Coalition	–	–	–	–	–	1.3	1.7	–
19 Middle Parties	–	–	–	–	–	0.9	1.3	–
Others	0.0	0.0	0.0	0.0	0.0	0.0	0.0	0.0

Chapter 21

SWITZERLAND

Until the end of the nineteenth century Swiss party organisation was almost entirely cantonal. Three broad political *tendances* have been identified (Grüner and Frei, 1966: 82–83) The Protestant Left, which favoured a strong federal government, dominated the Assembly until 1919. The Right defended the autonomy of the Catholic cantons. The Centre was a conservative offshoot of the Left.

The Swiss Federal Assembly (in German, Bundesversammlung; in French, Assemblée Nationale) consists of the Council of States (Standerat/Conseil des Etats) and the National Council (Nationalrat/Conseil National). Since 1848 all Swiss males aged over 20 and resident in the country have been entitled to vote in elections to the National Council.

During the nineteenth and early twentieth century a multiple-ballot system was employed, usually in multi-member constituencies. At the first ballot an absolute majority was required for election. In the event of insufficient candidates obtaining a majority, a second ballot was held. At this stage an absolute majority was still required. If any seats were still unfilled, a third ballot was held at which a plurality sufficed for election. After 1900 the third ballot was abandoned and a plurality at the second ballot secured election. In 1872 federal legislation established a secret ballot.

The present-day party system began to emerge in the 1890s. In 1894 the historic Left formed the Radical Democratic Party. In the same year the Right came together as the Popular Catholic Party. The Centre had formed the Liberal Democratic group in the National Council in 1893 but without creating a national party organization. The Social Democratic Party, formed in 1888, won its first seat in the National Council in 1893. Until 1911 the Social Democrats formed part of the Social Political Group in the Nationalrat, an alliance of several small cantonal parties which later became the Democrats. By the 1920s the growth of support for the Social Democrats and the emergence of the Farmers Traders and Citizens Party, created by ex-Radicals in 1919, had established the broad framework of the present Swiss party system.

In 1919 proportional representation using the Hagenbach-Bischoff system was introduced. Representation in the National Council is proportional to population with the proviso that every canton or half-canton is entitled to at least one representative. Four very small cantons—Uri, Obwald, Nidwald and Appenzell Innerrhoden—benefit from this exception. In these single-member constitiencies election is by plurality. In Schaffhausen, St. Gallen,

Aargau and Thurgau voting is compulsory. It was not until 1971 that a referendum approved the extension of the franchise to women.

The federal structure of the Swiss state limits the significance of nationwide political organization. Most parties do not contest elections throughout the country. Electoral support for the smaller parties is confined to a few cantons only. In some of the smallest cantons unopposed returns are frequent (Girod, 1964: 154—61). The importance of cantonal politics is such that parties give it priority in choosing party labels and alliances. Hence there are inconsistencies in the labels applied to political groups at the cantonal level, in federal elections and in groups within the Nationalrat.

Sources:

Federal Office of Statistics, *Statistik der Nationalratswahlen/Statistique des elections au Conseil national, 1919, 1922, 1925, 1918* Bern: A. Franke, 1929). Volumes in the same series have been published for each subsequent election except 1939 (for which figures are included in the volume covering the 1943 election).

Girod, R., "Geography of the Swiss party system". in E. Allardt and Y. Littunen (eds.) *Cleavages, Ideologies and Party Systems* (Helsinki: Westermarck Society, 1964) pp. 132—161.

Grüner, E. and Frei, K., *Die Schweizerische Bundesversammlung 1848—1920* (Bern: A. Francke, 1966).

Table 21.1
POLITICAL PARTIES IN SWITZERLAND SINCE 1896

	Party Names	Elections contested	Number contested
1	Catholic Conservatives. Until 1957 the Conservative Peoples Party (Schweizerische Konservative Volkspartei/Parti populaire conservateur suisse). In 1957 renamed the Conservative Christian Social Party (Konservativ-Christlich Soziale Partei/Parti conservateur chrétien social) and in 1971 the Christian Democratic Peoples Party (Christlich Demokratische Volkspartei/Parti démocrate chrétien suisse)[1]	1896ff	23
2	Democrats (Demokraten/Groupe des démocrates)[2]	1896-1967	22
3	Liberal Conservatives (Liberale-konservative Partei/Parti liberal conservateur)[3]	1896ff	23
4	Radical Democrats (Freisinnige-demokratische Partei/Parti radical-démocratique)[4]	1896ff	23
5	Social Democrats (Sozialdemokratische Partei der Schweiz/Parti socialiste suisse)	1896ff	23
6	Farmers Traders and Citizens Party (Schweizerische Bauern, Gewerbe und Bürger Partei — BGB/Parti suisse des paysans, artisans et bourgeois)[5]	1919ff	15
7	Grutli Union (Grütliverein/Association des Grutléens)	1919-1925	3
8	Protestant Peoples Party (Evangelische Volkspartei/Parti populaire evangélique)	1919ff	15
9	Communist Party (Kommunistische Partei der Schweiz/Parti communiste suisse. Banned in 1940 the party was reformed in 1944 as the Labour Party (Partei der Arbeit der Schweiz/Parti suisse du travail)	1922-1939; 1947ff	13
10	Free Market Party (Freiwirtschafter/Parti de l'economie franche)	1922-1925; 1935-1955	8
11	Front Party (Fronten/Parti des fronts)	1935	1
12	Independents Party (Landesring der Unabhängigen/Alliance des indépendants)	1935ff	10
13	Young Peasants Party (Jungbauern/Jeunes paysans)	1935-1947	4
14	National Action against Foreign Domination (National Aktion gegen die Überfremdung von Volk und Heimat/Action nationale contre l'emprise et la surpopulation etrangère)	1967ff	2
15	Republican Movement (Schweizerische Republikanische Bewegung/Mouvement Nationale d'Action Republicaine et Sociale)	1971	1

[1] Often known as the Catholic Conservatives (Katholisch-konservative Partei/ Parti conservateur-catholique) the name of the party's parliamentary group.

[2] In German Freethinking Democratic Party and in French Radical Democratic Party. From 1919 to 1935 and since 1971 includes the Democratic Party of Zurich.

[3] Often known as the Liberal Democrats (Liberaldemokratische Partei/Parti libéral-démocratique) the name of the party's parliamentary group.

[4] The Democrats were not a national party, but a group of cantonal parties who formed the core of the Social-Political Group in the Assembly from 1896 until 1931 and who subsequently formed the Democratic Group (Demokraten/Groupe des démocrates). For details of the changing party composition of this group see Federal Bureau of Statistics, 1929 : 29-30 and Ibid. 1968 : 142.

[5] In 1971 the party changed its name to the Swiss Peoples Party (Schweizer- ische Volkspartei/Union démocratique du centre). In the same year it merged with the Democratic parties of Glarus and Grisons.

Table 21.2
DATES OF ELECTIONS
TO THE NATIONALRAT 1896–1971

1.	25 October 1896	13.	25 October 1931
2.	29 October 1899	14.	27 October 1935
3.	26 October 1902	15.	29 October 1939
4.	29 October 1905	16.	31 October 1943
5.	25 October 1908	17.	26 October 1947
6.	29 October 1911	18.	28 October 1951
7.	25 October 1914	19.	30 October 1955
8.	28 October 1917	20.	25 October 1959
9.	26 October 1919	21.	27 October 1963
10.	29 October 1922	22.	29 October 1967
11.	25 October 1925	23.	31 October 1971
12.	28 October 1928		

Elections to the Nationalrat take place on the last Sunday in October. For elections before 1919 the dates refer to the first ballot.

Source: The Secretariat of the Federal Assembly, Bern.

Table 21.3 SWITZERLAND Total Votes 1897—1917

	1896	1899	1902	1905	1908	1911	1914	1917
Electorate	713,367	737,696	760,252	779,835	809,508	830,102	855,142	916,642
Valid Votes	371,133	368,735	407,322	411,493	398,224	400,870	340,250	515,022
PARTY VOTES								
1 Catholic Conservatives	85,229	76,845	94,031	92,600	81,733	76,726	71,668	84,784
2 Democrats	19,946	18,003	15,053	18,028	14,414	12,610	9,069	16,818
3 Liberal Conservatives	55,832	51,764	34,928	27,643	23,597	27,062	25,142	25,188
4 Radical Democrats	179,113	183,216	205,235	202,664	202,732	198,300	191,054	210,323
5 Social Democrats	25,263	35,488	51,338	60,323	70,003	80,050	34,204	158,450
Others[1]	—	—	4,481	6,584	3,982	3,608	6,805	18,025

[1] Estimates based on percentage figures.

Source: figures provided by Professor Erich Grüner, University of Bern.

Table 21.4   SWITZERLAND   Percentage of Votes 1896—1917

	1896	1899	1902	1905	1908	1911	1914	1917
Valid Votes	52.0	50.0	53.6	52.8	49.2	48.3	39.8	56.2
PARTY VOTES								
1 Catholic Conservatives	23.3	20.9	23.2	22.7	20.6	19.3	21.2	16.5
2 Democrats	5.5	4.9	3.7	4.4	3.6	3.2	2.7	3.3
3 Liberal Conservatives	15.3	14.2	8.6	6.8	6.0	6.8	7.4	4.9
4 Radical Democrats	49.0	50.2	50.7	49.7	51.1	49.8	56.5	41.0
5 Social Democrats	6.9	9.7	12.7	14.8	17.7	20.1	10.1	30.9
Others	—	—	1.1	1.6	1.0	0.9	2.0	3.5

Table 21.5   SWITZERLAND   Number of Seats Won in the Nationalrat 1896—1917

	1896	1899	1902	1905	1908	1911	1914	1917
1 Catholic Conservatives	30	32	34	34	34	38	38	42
2 Democrats	9	6	3	5	4	5	3	4
3 Liberal Conservatives	22	19	19	18	16	13	14	12
4 Radical Democrats	83	83	99	104	104	114	111	105
5 Social Democrats	2	4	7	2	7	17	19	22
Others	1	3	5	4	2	2	4	4
Total Seats	147	147	167	167	167	189	189	189

Source: Grüner and Frei, 1966 : 84.

370

Table 21.6 SWITZERLAND   Percentage of Seats Won in the Nationalrat 1896—1917

	1896	1899	1902	1905	1908	1911	1914	1917
1 Catholic Conservatives	20.4	21.8	20.4	20.4	20.4	20.1	20.1	22.2
2 Democrats	6.1	4.1	1.8	3.0	2.4	2.6	1.6	2.1
3 Liberal Conservatives	15.0	12.9	11.3	10.8	9.6	6.9	7.4	6.3
4 Radical Democrats	56.5	56.5	59.3	62.3	62.3	60.3	58.7	55.6
5 Social Democrats	1.4	2.7	4.2	1.2	4.2	9.1	10.1	11.6
Others	0.7	2.0	3.0	2.4	1.2	1.1	2.1	2.1

Table 21.7 SWITZERLAND Total Votes 1919—1943

	1919	1922	1925	1928	1931	1935	1939	1943
Electorate	959,971	983,238	1,018,191	1,066,500	1,118,841	1,194,910	1,232,643	1,310,445
Valid Votes	749,954	737,423	747,138	807,472	866,575	917,575	623,740	887,676
Invalid Votes	10,646	13,436	17,456	14,917	15,361	18,181	16,125	20,570
Total Votes	760,600	750,859	764,594	822,389	881,936	935,756	639,865	908,246

PARTY VOTES

	1919	1922	1925	1928	1931	1935	1939	1943
1 Catholic Conservatives	156,702	153,836	155,467	172,516	184,602	185,052	105,018	182,916
2 Democrats	14,677	19,287	16,362	15,116	10,726	10,665	16,891	29,627
3 Liberal Conservatives	28,497	29,041	30,523	23,752	24,573	30,476	10,241	28,434
4 Radical Democrats	215,566	208,144	206,485	220,135	232,562	216,664	128,163	197,746
5 Social Democrats	175,292	170,974	192,208	220,141	247,946	255,843	160,377	251,576
6 Farmers, Traders and Citizens	114,537	118,382	113,512	126,961	131,809	100,300	91,182	101,998
7 Grutli Union	20,559	9,313	427	–	–	–	–	–
8 Protestant Peoples Party	6,031	6,306	6,888	5,618	8,454	6,780	5,726	3,627
9 Communist Party	–	13,441	14,837	14,818	12,778	12,569	15,962	–
10 Free Market Party	–	1,106	1,602	–	–	11,078	10,865	9,031
11 Front Party	–	–	–	–	–	13,740	–	–
12 Independents Party	–	–	–	–	–	37,861	43,735	41,565
13 Young Peasants Party	–	–	–	–	–	28,161	27,708	18,310
Others	15,342	4,574	5,368	5,550	9,841	4,334	7,872	14,930

Source: *Nationalratswahlen*, 1967 : 120-144.

Table 21.8　　SWITZERLAND　　Percentage of Votes 1919—1943

	1919	1922	1925	1928	1931	1935	1939	1943
Valid Votes	78.1	75.0	73.4	75.7	77.5	76.8	50.6	67.7
Invalid Votes	1.1	1.4	1.7	1.4	1.4	1.5	1.3	1.6
Total Votes	79.2	76.4	75.1	77.1	78.8	78.3	51.9	69.3
Share Invalid	1.4	1.8	2.3	1.8	1.7	1.9	2.5	2.3
PARTY VOTES								
1 Catholic Conservatives	21.0	20.9	20.9	21.4	21.4	20.3	16.8	20.8
2 Democrats	2.0	2.6	2.2	1.9	1.2	1.2	2.7	3.4
3 Liberal Conservatives	3.8	4.0	4.1	3.0	2.8	3.3	1.6	3.2
4 Radical Democrats	28.8	28.3	27.8	27.4	26.9	23.7	20.5	22.5
5 Social Democrats	23.5	23.3	25.8	27.4	28.7	28.0	25.7	28.6
6 Farmers, Traders and Citizens	15.3	16.1	15.3	15.8	15.3	11.0	14.6	11.6
7 Grutli Union	2.8	1.3	0.1	–	–	–	–	–
8 Protestant Peoples Party	0.8	0.9	0.9	0.7	1.0	0.7	0.9	0.4
9 Communist Party	–	1.8	2.0	1.8	1.5	1.4	2.6	–
10 Free Market Party	–	0.2	0.2	–	–	1.2	1.7	1.0
11 Front Party	–	–	–	–	–	1.5	–	–
12 Independents Party	–	–	–	–	–	4.1	7.0	4.7
13 Young Peasants Party	–	–	–	–	–	3.1	4.4	2.1
Others	2.1	0.6	0.7	0.7	1.1	0.5	1.3	1.7

Table 21.9   SWITZERLAND   Number of Seats Won in the Nationalrat 1919–1943

	1919	1922	1925	1928	1931	1935	1939	1943
1 Catholic Conservatives	41	44	42	46	44	42	43	43
2 Democrats	4	4	5	3	2	3	7	5
3 Liberal Conservatives	9	10	7	6	6	6	6	8
4 Radical Democrats	60	60	60	58	52	48	47	47
5 Social Democrats	41	43	49	50	49	50	45	56
6 Farmers, Traders and Citizens	30	34	30	31	30	21	22	22
7 Grutli Union	2	0	0	–	–	–	–	–
8 Protestant Peoples Party	1	1	1	1	1	1	0	1
9 Communist Party	–	2	3	2	2	2	4	–
10 Free Market Party	–	0	0	–	–	0	1	0
11 Front Party	–	–	–	–	–	1	–	–
12 Independents Party	–	–	–	–	–	7	9	7
13 Young Peasants Party	–	–	–	–	–	4	3	3
Others	1	0	1	1	1	2	0	2
Total Seats	189	198	198	198	187	187	187	194

Source: *Nationalratswahlen, 1967* : 150-151.

Table 21.10 SWITZERLAND   Percentage of Seats Won in the Nationalrat 1919–1943

	1919	1922	1925	1928	1931	1935	1939	1943
1 Catholic Conservatives	21.7	22.2	21.2	23.2	23.5	22.5	23.0	22.2
2 Democrats	2.1	2.0	2.5	1.5	1.1	1.6	3.7	2.6
3 Liberal Conservatives	4.8	5.1	3.5	3.0	3.2	3.2	3.2	4.1
4 Radical Democrats	31.7	30.3	30.3	29.3	27.8	25.7	25.1	24.2
5 Social Democrats	21.7	21.7	24.7	25.3	26.2	26.7	24.1	28.9
6 Farmers, Traders and Citizens	15.9	17.2	15.2	15.7	16.0	11.2	11.8	11.3
7 Grutli Union	1.1	0.0	0.0	–	–	–	–	–
8 Protestant Peoples Party	0.5	0.5	0.5	–	0.5	0.5	0.0	0.5
9 Communist Party	–	1.0	1.5	1.0	1.1	1.1	2.1	–
10 Free Market Party	–	0.0	0.0	–	–	0.0	0.5	0.0
11 Front Party	–	–	–	–	–	0.5	–	–
12 Independents Party	–	–	–	–	–	3.7	4.8	3.6
13 Young Peasants Party	–	–	–	–	–	2.1	1.6	1.5
Others	0.5	0.0	0.5	0.5	0.5	1.1	0.0	1.0

Table 21.11   SWITZERLAND   Total Votes 1947–1971

	1947	1951	1955	1959	1963	1967	1971
Electorate	1,374,740	1,414,308	1,453,807	1,473,155	1,531,164	1,599,479	3,551,008
Valid Votes	966,680	967,989	982,020	989,005	969,037	1,001,863	1,992,422
Invalid Votes	18,819	18,948	16,861	19,558	17,960	18,044	25,700
Total Votes	985,499	986,937	998,881	1,008,563	986,997	1,019,907	2,018,122
PARTY VOTES							
1 Catholic Conservatives	203,202	216,616	226,122	229,088	225,160	219,184	402,528
2 Democrats	28,096	21,606	21,003	21,170	16,978	14,270	–
3 Liberal Conservatives	30,492	24,813	21,688	22,934	21,501	23,208	43,338
4 Radical Democrats	220,486	230,687	227,370	232,557	230,200	230,095	431,364
5 Social Democrats	251,625	249,857	263,664	259,139	256,063	233,873	452,194
6 Farmers, Traders and Citizens	115,976	120,819	117,847	113,611	109,202	109,621	217,907
8 Protestant Peoples Party	9,072	9,559	10,581	14,038	15,690	15,728	42,298
9 Communist Party	49,353	25,659	25,060	26,346	21,088	28,723	50,834
10 Free Market Party	4,626	8,194	3,471	–	–	–	–
12 Independents Party	42,428	49,100	53,450	54,049	48,224	89,950	150,684
14 National Action	–	–	–	–	–	6,275	62,749
15 Republican Movement	–	–	–	–	–	–	88,327
Others	4,931	4,588	5,639	9,438	17,643	22,921	33,370

Source: Nationalratswahlen, 1967 : 120-144 and figures provided by the Secretariat of the Federal Assembly, Bern.

376

Table 21.12   SWITZERLAND   Percentage of Votes 1947–1971

	1947	1951	1955	1959	1963	1967	1971
Valid Votes	70.3	68.4	67.5	67.1	63.3	62.6	56.1
Invalid Votes	1.4	1.3	1.2	1.3	1.2	1.1	0.7
Total Votes	71.7	69.8	68.7	68.5	64.5	63.8	56.8
Share Invalid	1.9	1.9	1.7	1.9	1.8	1.8	1.3
PARTY VOTES							
1 Catholic Conservatives	21.2	22.5	23.2	23.3	23.4	22.1	20.4
2 Democrats	2.9	2.2	2.2	2.2	1.8	1.4	–
3 Liberal Conservatives	3.2	2.6	2.2	2.3	2.2	2.3	2.2
4 Radical Democrats	23.0	24.0	23.3	23.7	23.9	23.2	21.8
5 Social Democrats	26.2	26.0	27.0	26.4	26.6	23.5	22.9
6 Farmers, Traders and Citizens	12.1	12.6	12.1	11.6	11.4	11.0	11.0
8 Protestant Peoples Party	0.9	1.0	1.1	1.4	1.6	1.6	2.1
9 Communist Party	5.1	2.7	2.6	2.7	2.2	2.9	2.6
10 Free Market Party	0.5	0.9	0.4	–	–	–	–
12 Independents Party	4.4	5.1	5.5	5.5	5.0	9.1	7.6
14 National Action	–	–	–	–	–	0.6	3.2
15 Republican Movement	–	–	–	–	–	–	4.5
Others	0.5	0.5	0.6	1.0	1.8	2.3	1.7

377

Table 21.13 SWITZERLAND Number of Seats Won in the Nationalrat 1947–1971

	1947	1951	1955	1959	1963	1967	1971
1 Catholic Conservatives	44	48	47	47	48	45	44
2 Democrats	5	4	4	4	4	3	–
3 Liberal Conservatives	7	5	5	5	6	6	6
4 Radical Democrats	52	51	50	51	51	49	49
5 Social Democrats	48	49	53	51	53	51	46
6 Farmers, Traders and Citizens	21	23	22	23	22	21	23
8 Protestant Peoples Party	1	1	1	2	2	3	3
9 Communist Party	7	5	4	3	4	5	5
10 Free Market Party	1	0	0	–	–	–	–
12 Independents Party	8	10	10	10	10	16	13
14 National Action	–	–	–	–	–	1	4
15 Republican Movement	–	–	–	–	–	–	7
Others	0	0	0	0	0	0	0
Total Seats	194	196	196	196	200	200	200

Sources: *Nationalratswahlen, 1967* : 150-151 and figures provided by the Secretariat of the Federal Assembly, Bern.

Table 21.14   SWITZERLAND   Percentage of Seats Won in the Nationalrat 1947–1971

	1947	1951	1955	1959	1963	1967	1971
1 Catholic Conservatives	22.7	24.5	24.0	24.0	24.0	22.5	22.0
2 Democrats	2.6	2.0	2.0	2.0	2.0	1.5	–
3 Liberal Conservatives	3.6	2.6	2.6	2.6	3.0	3.0	3.0
4 Radical Democrats	26.8	26.0	25.5	26.0	25.5	24.5	24.5
5 Social Democrats	24.7	25.0	27.0	26.0	26.5	25.5	23.0
6 Farmers, Traders and Citizens	10.8	11.7	11.2	11.7	11.0	10.5	11.5
8 Protestant Peoples Party	0.5	0.5	0.5	1.0	1.0	1.5	1.5
9 Communist Party	3.6	2.6	2.0	1.5	2.0	2.5	2.5
10 Free Market Party	0.5	0.0	0.0	–	–	–	–
12 Independents Party	4.1	5.1	5.1	5.1	5.0	8.0	6.5
14 National Action	–	–	–	–	–	0.5	2.0
15 Republican Movement	–	–	–	–	–	–	3.5
Others	0.0	0.0	0.0	0.0	0.0	0.0	0.0

Chapter 22

UNITED KINGDOM

The origins of the United Kingdom parliament can be traced directly to the English parliament of the Middle Ages. Since the thirteenth century parliament has consisted of a House of Lords of hereditary peers and *ex-officio* leaders of law and church and a directly elected House of Commons. The tradition of election by plurality dates back to the Middle Ages. Since the Act of Union of 1707 Scotland has been represented in the House of Commons and MPs from Ireland were included after the abolition of the Irish parliament in 1800. Franchise laws in England and Wales varied enormously from constituency to constituency. Scottish and Irish laws and procedures were strikingly different from those of England. An excellent chronological list of statutes concerning elections since 1696 can be found in Gwyn, 1962: 255—256.

The Reform Act of 1832 led to a small increase in the electorate, from 2.1 per cent of the total population to 3.3 per cent. It also began a century-long process of rationalization of the electorate, abolishing the grossest anomalies in population between constituencies and establishing uniform franchise requirements (Seymour, 1915). In 1867 the introduction of household suffrage (subject to the payment of rates) in the English and Scottish boroughs and minor extensions of the franchise requirements elsewhere increased the electorate to 7.9 per cent of the total population. The secret ballot was introduced in 1872.

The present British party system has its origins in this period (Hanham, 1959), but more than half the constituencies were usually uncontested (Butler and Cornford, 1969: 336). Because even the most reliable published election results contain numerous innacuracies (McCalmont, 1915) only the composition of the House of Commons can be determined with any degree of accuracy. Moreover, party labels were not rigidly defined throughout the United Kingdom during the period 1868 to 1884. The following table gives a general picture of election outcomes.

	1868	1874	1880
Conservatives	279	352	238
Liberals	379	242	349
Irish Nationalists	—	58	65
Total	658	652	652
Unopposed returns	212	188	109

Source: Butler and Cornford, 1969: 336, Lloyd, 1965: 262

The 1884 Reform Act introduced a uniform franchise for the United Kingdom. The majority of adult males (15.6 per cent of the population) were now entitled to vote. The main exceptions were domestic servants resident with their employers, and persons in receipt of poor relief. By 1911 these groups amounted to only 12 per cent of the adult male population. Stringent residence requirements and registration procedures combined to reduce the proportion actually on the register to 59 per cent of adult men (Blewett, 1965: 31—34). Until 1884 most MPs were elected in two-member constituencies in which each elector had two votes. Most of these were now replaced by single-member constituencies. The number of unopposed returns between 1885 and 1910 varied from 43 in 1885 to 243 in 1900. The average was 139, 20.7 per cent of the seats in the House of Commons.

In 1918 adult male suffrage based for the first time on a simple residence requirement was introduced. Women over 30 were given the vote if they or their husbands were householders; in 1928 women were enfranchised on the same basis as men. Limited plural voting continued. University graduates elected 12 MPs by single transferable vote. In 1922 there were 72,000 university voters in the United Kingdom, 0.3 per cent of the electorate (Butler, 1953: 148—153). Occupiers of business premises worth over £10 a year were allowed to vote in the constituency where their business was located as well as from their residence. In 1922 there were 209,000 business voters in England and Wales, or 1.1 per cent of the electorate (Butler, 1953: 146-148). In 1948 the university and the remaining two-member constituencies were abolished. The voting age was reduced from 21 to 18 in 1969.

Divisions within the Liberal Party and the development of Labour representation sometimes make for difficulties in the presentation of voting figures and election outcomes. The Liberal Unionists seceded from the Liberal Party in 1886 in opposition to Irish Home Rule, contesting elections as allies of the Conservatives. Before the 1918 election the Liberal Party was again divided. The Lloyd George Liberals fought the election as part of an electoral alliance with the Conservatives, with whom they had shared government during the war. The Asquith Liberals were opposed to the continuation of the coalition. In the 1931 election the Liberals were again split. The followers of Lloyd George stood as independent Liberals in opposition to the Liberal Party's endorsement of the National Government. The Liberal National organisation also presented their own candidates.

The first working class candidates elected to parliament were trade unionists, elected on a Liberal ticket as Lib-Labs i.e. Liberal Labour. An independent labour candidate was first elected in 1892. In 1900 trades union leaders and the Independent Labour Party established the Labour Representation Committee to nominate labour candidates independent of the Liberal Party. After the 1906 election, the successful LRC candidates became known as the Labour Party.

The boundary of the United Kingdom was altered in 1921 when 26 counties of Southern Ireland became self-governing as the Irish Free State. Northern Ireland remained part of the United Kingdom with its own parliament at Stormont as well as 12 seats in the United Kingdom Parliament. The

Northern Ireland House of Commons was initially chosen by a single transferable vote; this was replaced by the plurality system in 1929. (See Elliott 1973). The Stormont Parliament was suspended in 1972 and replaced in 1973 by a unicameral legislative assembly elected by single transferable vote. Northern Ireland parties are organizationally separate from parties in Great Britain but votes gained and seats won by the Conservative, Labour and Liberal parties are included here with British parties.

Sources:

Blewett, N., "The franchise in the United Kingdom, 1885—1918." *Past and Present* 45:27—56 (1965).

Butler, D.E., *The Electoral System of Britain since 1918* (Oxford: Clarendon Press, 1953).

Butler, D.E. and Cornford, J., "United Kingdom" in S. Rokkan and J. Meyriat (eds) *International Guide to Electoral Statistics* (Paris: Mouton, 1969) pp. 330—351.

Carbery, T.F., *The Consumer in Politics: a history and general review of the Co-operative Party* (Manchester: University Press, 1969).

Craig, F.W.S., *British Parliamentary Election Results, 1918—1949* (Glasgow: Political Reference Publications, 1969).

Ibid., British Parliamentary Election Results 1950—1970 (Chichester: 1971). Political Reference Publications, 1971).

Ibid., British Parliamentary Election Statistics, 1918—1970 (Chichester: Political Reference Publications, 1971).

Ibid., British Parliamentary Election Results, 1885—1918 (London: Macmillan, 1974).

Elliott, S., *Northern Ireland Parliamentary Election Results 1921—1972* (Chichester: Political Reference Publications, 1973).

Gwyn, W.B., *Democracy and the Cost of Politics in Britain* (London: The Athlone Press, 1962).

Hanham, H.J., *Elections and Party Management: Politics in the Age of Disraeli and Gladstone* (London: Longman, Green & Co., 1959).

Lloyd, T., "Uncontested seats in British General Elections, 1852—1910." *Historical Journal* 8: 260—265 (1965).

McCalmont, F.H., *Parliamentary Poll book: British Election Results 1832—1918* 7th Edition, 1915. Reprinted with additional material by J. Vincent and M. Stenton by the Harvester Press, Brighton, 1971).

Seymour, C., *Electoral Reform in England and Wales: the Development and Operation of the Parliamentary Franchise, 1832—1885* (New Haven: Yale University Press, 1915. Reprinted by David and Charles, Newton Abbot, 1970).

Table 22.1
POLITICAL PARTIES IN THE UNITED KINGDOM SINCE 1885

	Party Names	Elections contested	Number contested
1	Conservative Party[1]	1885ff	23
2	Liberal Unionists[2]	1886-1910	7
3	Liberal Party	1885ff	23
4	Irish Nationalist Party[3]	1885-1918	9
5	Independent Labour Party — ILP[4]	1895-1945	13
6	Labour Party[5]	1900ff	19
7	Irish Republicans[6]	1918ff	15
8	Lloyd George Liberals[7]	1918-1922; 1931	3
9	National Democratic Party	1918-1922	2
10	Communist Party	1922ff	14
11	Scottish National Party — SNP	1929ff	12
12	Welsh Nationalists (Plaid Cymru)	1929ff	12
13	National Labour	1931-1935	2
14	National Liberal Party[8]	1931-1945	3

[1] Also known as the Unionist Party in Scotland and (Northern) Ireland.

[2] The Liberal Unionists, led by Joseph Chamberlain, broke away from the Liberal Party in June 1886 because they were opposed to the granting of Home Rule to Ireland. They contested elections in alliance with the Conservatives. The two parties were amalgamated on May 9, 1912.

[3] Known in Ireland as the Irish Parliamentary Party.

[4] The ILP participated in the establishment of the Labour Representation Committee in 1900. Until 1932 it was affiliated to the Labour Party. A few ILP candidates have stood at every election since 1945, except for 1964, but have never won more than 4,000 votes at any of these elections.

[5] Since 1918 the Labour Party vote includes that for the Co-operative Party candidates. The party constitution allows for the affiliation of trades unions and co-operative societies who may sponsor their own candidates (Carbery, 1969).

[6] In 1918 Sinn Féin and in subsequent elections those classified as Irish Nationalist or Republican in Craig, *British Parliamentary Election Statistics 1918–1970,* 1971 : 63.

[7] In 1918 the followers of Lloyd George who contested the election as supporters of the Coalition government with the Conservatives. They were reunited with the Liberal Party in November 1923. In 1931 they stood independently in opposition to the Liberal Party's support of the National Government.

[8] The Liberal National Organization broke away from the Liberal Party in 1931. It contested elections in alliance with the Conservatives.

Table 22.2
DATES OF ELECTIONS
TO THE HOUSE OF COMMONS 1885–1970[1]

1.	24 November – 9 December 1885	13.	30 May 1939
2.	1 July – 17 July 1886	14.	27 October 1931
3.	4 – 19 July 1892	15.	14 November 1935
4.	13 – 29 July 1895	16.	5 July 1945
5.	1 – 15 October 1900	17.	23 February 1950
6.	12 – 29 January 1906	18.	25 October 1951
7.	15 – 31 January 1910	19.	26 May 1955
8.	3 – 19 December 1910	20.	8 October 1959
9.	14 December 1918	21.	15 October 1964
10.	15 November 1922	22.	31 March 1966
11.	6 December 1923	23.	18 June 1970
12.	29 October 1924		

[1] Until 1918 the day of polling for individual constituencies was spaced over several weeks. The dates of the first and last polls noted above exclude the University constituencies and until 1931 Orkney and Shetland. In University constituencies the poll remained open for five days. Voting was either in person or by post. Until 1918 Orkney and Shetland voted a week after the rest of the United Kingdom and from 1918 to 1929 the poll was open for two days. In 1945 the poll was delayed for one week in 22 constituencies and a fortnight in one constituency because 5 July fell during the local holiday week.

Source: Political Reference Publications

Table 22.3 UNITED KINGDOM   Total Votes 1885—1910

	1885	1886	1892	1895	1900	1906	1910 (Jan.)	1910 (Dec.)
Electorate	5,708,030	5,708,030	6,160,541	6,330,519	6,730,935	7,264,608	7,694,741	7,709,981
Valid Votes[1]	4,407,507	2,771,287	4,343,252	3,606,666	3,282,711	5,278,637	6,253,495	4,902,797
PARTY VOTES[2]								
1 Conservative Party	2,020,927	1,520,886	2,159,150	1,894,772	1,767,958	2,422,071	3,104,407	2,420,169
2 Liberal Unionists	–							
3 Liberal Party	2,199,998	1,353,581	2,088,019	1,765,266	1,572,323	2,751,057	2,866,157	2,293,869
4 Irish Nationalist Party	310,608	97,905	311,509	152,959	91,055	35,031	126,647	131,720
5 Independent Labour Party	–	–	–	44,325	–	–	–	–
6 Labour Party	–	–	–	–	62,698	321,663	505,657	371,802
Others	106,702	1,791	39,641	3,730	29,448	96,269	64,532	17,678

[1] Total number of electors casting valid votes.
[2] The sum of party votes is larger than the number of valid votes because of plural voting.

Source: Information provided by Political Reference Publications.

Table 22.4   UNITED KINGDOM   Percentage of Votes 1885–1910

	1885	1886	1892	1895	1900	1906	1910 (Jan.)	1910 (Dec.)
Valid Votes	77.2	48.6	70.5	57.0	48.8	72.7	81.3	63.6
PARTY VOTES[1]								
1 Conservative Party	43.6	51.4	47.0	49.1	50.3	43.4	46.8	46.6
2 Liberal Unionists	–							
3 Liberal Party	47.4	45.0	45.1	45.7	45.0	49.4	43.5	44.2
4 Irish Nationalist Party	6.9	3.5	7.0	4.0	2.6	0.7	1.9	2.5
5 Independent Labour Party	–	–	–	1.0	–	–	–	–
6 Labour Party	–	–	–	–	1.3	4.8	7.0	6.4
Others	2.2	0.1	0.9	0.2	0.8	1.7	0.8	0.3

[1] Percentages have been adjusted to allow for two-member seats which lasted until 1950. In calculating the percentage of votes, each vote in a two-member seat has been counted as half a vote.

387

Table 22.5 UNITED KINGDOM Number of Seats Won in the House of Commons 1885–1910

	1885	1886	1892	1895	1900	1906	1910 (Jan.)	1910 (Dec.)
1 Conservative Party	249	317	268	340	334	131	230[2]	224[2]
2 Liberal Unionists	–	77	46	71	68	26[2]	43	49
3 Liberal Party	335[1]	191	272[2]	177	184	400[2]	275[2]	271
4 Irish Nationalist Party	86	85	81	82	82	83	82	84
5 Independent Labour Party	–	–	–	0	–	–	–	–
6 Labour Party	–	–	–	–	2	29	40	42
Others	0	0	3[3]	0	0	1[4]	0	0
Total Seats	670	670	670	670	670	670	670	670
Unopposed Returns	43	224	63	189	243	114	75	163

[1] Includes 11 Independents, one Independent Liberal and four Independent Liberal/Crofters.
[2] Includes one Independent.
[3] Independent labour MPs elected with varying degrees of Liberal support. One, Keir Hardie, joined the ILP when it was founded in 1893.
[4] Joined the Parliamentary Labour Party immediately upon election.

Source: Information provided by Political Reference Publications.

388

Table 22.6   UNITED KINGDOM   Percentage of Seats Won in the House of Commons 1885—1910

	1885	1886	1892	1895	1900	1906	1910 (Jan.)	1910 (Dec.)
1 Conservative Party	37.2	47.3	40.0	50.7	49.9	19.6	34.3	33.4
2 Liberal Unionists	–	11.5	6.9	10.6	10.1	3.9	6.4	7.3
3 Liberal Party	50.0	28.5	40.6	26.4	27.5	59.7	41.0	40.4
4 Irish Nationalist Party	12.8	12.7	12.1	12.2	12.2	12.4	12.2	12.5
5 Independent Labour Party	–	–	–	0.0	–	–	–	–
6 Labour Party	–	–	–	–	0.3	4.3	6.0	6.3
Others	0.0	0.0	0.4	0.0	0.0	0.1	0.0	0.0
Unopposed Returns	6.4	33.4	9.4	28.2	36.3	17.0	11.2	24.3

Table 22.7 UNITED KINGDOM   Number of Candidates 1885—1910

	1885	1886	1892	1895	1900	1906	1910 (Jan.)	1910 (Dec.)
1 Conservative Party	602 ⎱	563	606	588	569	556	594	548
2 Liberal Unionists	– ⎰							
3 Liberal Party	572	449	532	447	402	536	511	467
4 Irish Nationalist Party	94	100	134	105	101	87	105	106
5 Independent Labour Party	–	–	–	28	–	–	–	–
6 Labour Party[1]	–	–	–	–	15	50	78	56
Others	70	3	31	12	15	44	27	14
Total	**1,338**	**1,115**	**1,303**	**1,180**	**1,102**	**1,273**	**1,315**	**1,191**

[1] Includes ILP candidates endorsed by the Labour Party.

Source: Information provided by Political Reference Publications.

Table 22.8 UNITED KINGDOM Percentage of Seats Contested 1885—1910

	1885	1886	1892	1895	1900	1906	1910 (Jan.)	1910 (Dec.)
1 Conservative Party	89.9 ⎫	84.0	90.4	87.8	84.9	83.0	88.7	81.8
2 Liberal Unionists	– ⎰							
3 Liberal Party	85.4	67.0	79.4	66.7	60.0	80.0	76.3	69.7
4 Irish Nationalist Party	14.0	14.9	20.0	15.7	15.1	13.0	15.7	15.8
5 Independent Labour Party	–	–	–	4.2	–	–	–	–
6 Labour Party	–	–	–	–	2.2	7.5	11.6	8.4

391

Table 22.9　UNITED KINGDOM　Total Votes 1918–1945

	1918	1922	1923	1924	1929	1931	1935	1945
Electorate	21,392,220	20,874,456	21,283,085	21,730,988	28,854,748	29,952,361	31,374,449	33,240,391
Valid Votes[1]	10,478,983	13,809,720	13,960,590	15,906,127	21,755,397	21,716,039	21,016,676	24,117,191
PARTY VOTES[2]								
1　Conservative Party	4,144,192[3]	5,502,298	5,514,541	7,854,523	8,656,225	11,978,745[6]	10,549,489[6]	9,234,278[7]
14　National Liberal Party	–	–	–	–	–	809,302[6]	866,354[6]	737,732[8]
13　National Labour	–	–	–	–	–	341,370[6]	339,811[6]	–
9　National Democratic Party	181,331[3]	52,233	–	–	–	–	–	–
8　Lloyd George Liberals	1,396,590[3]	1,412,772	–	–	–	103,528	–	–
2　Liberal Party	1,388,784	2,668,143	4,301,481	3,035,257[4]	5,308,738	1,403,102[6]	1,443,093	2,252,430
6　Labour Party	2,357,524[3]	4,237,349	4,439,780	5,489,087	8,370,417	6,324,737	8,325,491	11,967,746
3　Irish Nationalist Party	238,197	–	–	–	–	–	–	–
7　Irish Republicans	497,107	102,667	97,993	46,457	24,177	123,053	158,327	148,078
10　Communist Party		33,637	39,448	55,346	50,634	74,824	27,117	102,780
11　Scottish National Party		–	–	–	3,313	20,954	29,517	30,595
12　Welsh Nationalists		–	–	–	609	2,050	2,534	16,017
5　Independent Labour Party		–	–	–	–	317,354	139,577	46,769
Others	583,093[3]	383,231	154,452	159,609[5]	234,262	157,354	115,744	658,870

[1] Total number of electors casting votes.

[2] The sum of party votes is larger than the number of valid votes because of plural voting.

[3] Coalition candidates include all the Lloyd George Liberals; Conservatives with 3,472,738 votes; Labour candidates with 53,962 votes; National Democratic with 156,834 votes and one Independent with 9,274 votes.

[4] Includes votes cast for six Constitutional candidates included in the list of official Liberal candidates (Craig, Statistics, 1971 : 6). Votes calculated from Craig, 1969.

[5] Includes votes cast for six Constitutional candidates. Votes calculated from Craig, 1969.

[6] Parties supporting the National Government; Conservative includes National.

[7] Includes National.

[8] Fought the election in alliance with the Conservative Party.

Table 22.10   UNITED KINGDOM   Percentage of Votes 1918–1945

	1918	1922	1923	1924	1929	1931	1935	1945
Valid Votes	49.0	66.2	65.6	73.2	75.4	72.5	67.0	72.6
PARTY VOTES¹								
1 Conservative Party	39.6	38.5	38.0	46.8	38.1	55.3	48.1	36.8
14 National Liberal Party	–	–	–	–	–	3.7	3.7	2.8
13 National Labour	–	–	–	–	–	1.5	1.5	–
9 National Democratic Party	1.7	0.4	–	–	–	–	–	–
8 Lloyd George Liberals	12.6	9.4	–	–	–	0.5	–	–
2 Liberal Party	13.0	18.9	29.7	18.4	23.6	6.7	6.8	9.0
6 Labour Party	21.4	29.7	30.7	33.3	37.1	29.3	38.1	48.0
3 Irish Nationalist Party	2.2	–	–	–	–	–	–	–
7 Irish Republicans	4.6	0.4	0.4	0.2	0.1	0.4	0.4	0.4
10 Communist Party	–	0.2	0.2	0.3	0.2	0.3	0.1	0.4
11 Scottish National Party	–	–	–	–	0.0	0.1	0.1	0.1
12 Welsh Nationalists	–	–	–	–	0.0	0.0	0.0	0.1
5 Independent Labour Party	–	–	–	–	–	1.5	0.6	0.2
Others	4.9	2.5	1.0	1.0	0.9	0.7	0.6	2.2

¹Percentages have been adjusted to allow for two-member seats which lasted until 1950. In calculating the percentage of votes, each vote in a two-member seat has been counted as half a vote.

Source: Craig, *British Parliamentary Election Statistics 1918–1970*, 1971 : 1-13, 46-47 and figures provided by Political Reference Publications.

Table 22.11 UNITED KINGDOM   Number of Seats Won in the House of Commons 1918–1945

		1918	1922	1923	1924	1929	1931	1935	1945
1	Conservative Party	382	344	258	415	260	473	388	199
14	National Liberal Party	–	–	–	–	–	35	33	11
13	National Labour	–	–	–	–	–	13	8	–
9	National Democratic Party	9	0	–	–	–	–	–	–
8	Lloyd George Liberals	127	53	—	–	–	4	–	–
2	Liberal Party	36	62	158	44	59	33	21	12
6	Labour Party	62	142	191	151	287	46	154	393
3	Irish Nationalist Party	7	–	–	–	–	–	–	–
7	Irish Republicans	73[1]	3	3	1	3	2	2	2
10	Communist Party	–	1	0	1	0	0	1	2
11	Scottish National Party	–	–	–	–	0	0	0	0
12	Welsh Nationalists	–	–	–	–	0	0	0	0
5	Independent Labour Party	–	–	–	–	–	6	4	3
	Others	11	10	5	3	6	3	4	18
	Total Seats	707	615	615	615	615	615	615	640
	Unopposed Returns	107	57	50	32	7	67	40	3

[1] The 73 Sinn Féin MPs refused to take their seats in the House of Commons.

Source: Craig, *British Parliamentary Election Statistics 1918–1970*, 1971 : 1-13.

Table 22.12   UNITED KINGDOM   Percentage of Seats Won in the House of Commons 1918–1945

		1918	1922	1923	1924	1929	1931	1935	1945
1	Conservative Party	54.0	55.9	42.0	67.5	42.3	76.9	63.1	31.1
14	National Liberal Party	–	–	–	–	–	5.7	5.4	1.7
13	National Labour	–	–	–	–	–	2.1	1.3	–
9	National Democratic Party	1.3	0.0	–	–	–	–	–	–
8	Lloyd George Liberals	18.0	8.6	–	–	–	0.7	–	–
2	Liberal Party	5.1	10.1	25.7	7.2	9.6	5.4	3.4	1.9
6	Labour Party	8.8	23.1	31.1	24.6	46.7	7.5	25.0	61.4
3	Irish Nationalist Party	1.0	–	–	–	–	–	–	–
7	Irish Republicans	10.3	0.5	0.5	0.2	0.5	0.3	0.3	0.3
10	Communist Party	–	0.2	0.0	0.2	0.0	0.0	0.2	0.3
11	Scottish National Party	–	–	–	–	0.0	0.0	0.0	0.0
12	Welsh Nationalists	–	–	–	–	0.0	0.0	0.0	0.0
5	Independent Labour Party	–	–	–	–	–	1.0	0.7	0.5
	Others	1.6	1.6	0.8	0.5	1.0	0.5	0.7	2.8
	Unopposed Returns	15.1	9.3	8.1	5.2	1.1	10.9	6.6	0.9

Table 22.13   UNITED KINGDOM   Number of Candidates 1918—1945

	1918	1922	1923	1924	1929	1931	1935	1945
1 Conservative Party	445	482	536	540	590	522[2]	519[2]	569[2]
14 National Liberal Party	–	–	–	–	–	41	44	49
13 National Labour	–	–	–	–	–	20	20	–
9 National Democratic Party	26	7	–	–	–	–	–	–
8 Lloyd George Liberals	145	144	–	–	–	–	–	–
2 Liberal Party	276	333	457	345	513	112	161	306
6 Labour Party[1]	376	414	427	514	569	491	552	603
3 Irish Nationalist Party	60	–	–	–	–	–	–	–
7 Irish Republicans	102	4	4	9	4	3	5	3
10 Communist Party	–	5	4	8	25	26	2	21
11 Scottish National Party	–	–	–	–	2	5	8	8
12 Welsh Nationalists	–	–	–	–	1	2	1	7
5 Independent Labour Party	–	–	–	–	–	24	17	5
Others	193	52	18	12	26	40	19	110
Total	1,623	1,441	1,446	1,428	1,730	1,292	1,348	1,683

[1] From 1918 to 1929 includes ILP candidates endorsed by the Labour Party.
[2] Including National.

Source: Craig, British Parliamentary Election Statistics 1918–1970, 1971 : 1-13.

Table 22.14   UNITED KINGDOM   Percentage of Seats Contested 1918—1945

	1918	1922	1923	1924	1929	1931	1935	1945
1 Conservative Party	62.9	78.4	87.2	87.8	95.9	84.9	84.4	88.9
14 National Liberal Party	–	–	–	–	–	6.7	7.2	7.7
13 National Labour	–	–	–	–	–	3.3	3.3	–
9 National Democratic Party	3.7	1.1	–	–	–	–	–	–
8 Lloyd George Liberals	20.5	23.4	–	–	–	1.0	–	–
2 Liberal Party	39.0	54.1	74.3	56.1	83.4	18.2	26.2	47.8
6 Labour Party	53.2	67.3	69.4	83.6	92.5	79.8	89.8	94.2
3 Irish Nationalist Party	8.5	–	–	–	–	–	–	–
7 Irish Republicans	14.4	0.7	0.7	1.5	0.7	0.5	0.8	0.5
10 Communist Party	–	0.8	0.7	1.3	4.1	4.2	0.3	3.3
11 Scottish National Party	–	–	–	–	0.3	0.8	1.3	1.2
12 Welsh Nationalists	–	–	–	–	0.2	0.3	0.2	1.1
5 Independent Labour Party	–	–	–	–	–	3.9	2.8	·0.8

Table 22.15   UNITED KINGDOM   Total Votes 1950—1970

	1950	1951	1955	1959	1964	1966	1970
Electorate	34,412,255	34,919,331	34,852,179	35,397,304	35,894,054	35,957,245	39,342,013
Valid Votes	28,771,124	28,596,594	26,759,729	27,862,652	27,657,148	27,264,747	28,344,798
Invalid Votes[1]	n.a.	n.a.	n.a.	n.a.	41,073	49,899	41,347
Total Votes[1]	n.a.	n.a.	n.a.	n.a.	27,698,221	27,314,646	28,386,145

PARTY VOTES

	1950	1951	1955	1959	1964	1966	1970
1 Conservative Party	12,492,404	13,718,199	13,310,891	13,750,875	12,002,642	11,418,455	13,145,123
2 Liberal Party	2,621,487	730,546	722,402	1,640,760	3,099,283	2,327,457	2,117,035
5 Labour Party	13,266,176	13,948,883	12,405,254	12,216,172	12,205,808	13,096,629	12,208,758
7 Irish Republicans	88,573	92,787	152,310	63,415	116,306	125,886	190,462
10 Communist Party	91,765	21,640	33,144	30,896	46,442	62,092	37,970
11 Scottish National Party	9,708	7,299	12,112	21,738	64,044	128,474	306,802
12 Welsh Nationalists	17,580	10,920	45,119	77,571	69,507	61,071	175,016
Others	183,431	66,320	78,497	61,225	53,116	44,683	163,632

[1] Figures centrally reported only since 1964.

Source: Craig, *British Parliamentary Election Statistics 1918–1970, 1971* : 14-20.

398

Table 22.16 UNITED KINGDOM   Percentage of Votes 1950—1970

	1950	1951	1955	1959	1964	1966	1970
Valid Votes	83.6	81.9	76.8	78.7	77.1	75.8	72.0
Invalid Votes	n.a.	n.a.	n.a.	n.a.	0.1	0.1	0.1
Total Votes	n.a.	n.a.	n.a.	n.a.	77.2	76.0	72.2
Share Invalid	n.a.	n.a.	n.a.	n.a.	0.1	0.2	0.1
PARTY VOTES							
1 Conservative Party	43.4	48.0	49.7	49.4	43.4	41.9	46.4
2 Liberal Party	9.1	2.6	2.7	5.9	11.2	8.5	7.5
5 Labour Party	46.1	48.8	46.4	43.8	44.1	48.0	43.1
7 Irish Republicans	0.3	0.3	0.6	0.2	0.4	0.5	0.7
10 Communist Party	0.3	0.1	0.1	0.1	0.2	0.2	0.1
11 Scottish National Party	0.0	0.0	0.0	0.1	0.2	0.5	1.1
12 Welsh Nationalists	0.1	0.0	0.2	0.3	0.3	0.2	0.6
Others	0.6	0.2	0.3	0.2	0.2	0.2	0.6

399

Table 22.17   UNITED KINGDOM   Number of Seats Won in the House of Commons 1950—1970

	1950	1951	1955	1959	1964	1966	1970
1 Conservative Party	298	321	345	365	304	253	330
2 Liberal Party	9	6	6	6	9	12	6
5 Labour Party	315	295	277	258	317	364	288
7 Irish Republicans	2	2	2	0	0	1	3
10 Communist Party	0	0	0	0	0	0	0
11 Scottish National Party	0	0	0	0	0	0	1
12 Welsh Nationalists	0	0	0	0	0	0	0
Others	1	1	0	1	0	0	2
Total Seats	625[1]	625[2]	630	630	630	630	630

[1] Including two unopposed returns.
[2] Including four unopposed returns.

Source: Craig, *British Parliamentary Election Statistics 1918—1970*, 1971 : 14-20.

Table 22.18   UNITED KINGDOM   Percentage of Seats Won in the House of Commons 1950—1970

	1950	1951	1955	1959	1964	1966	1970
1 Conservative Party	47.7	51.4	54.8	57.9	48.3	40.2	52.4
2 Liberal Party	1.4	1.0	1.0	1.0	1.4	1.9	1.0
5 Labour Party	50.4	47.2	44.0	41.0	50.3	57.8	45.7
7 Irish Republicans	0.3	0.3	0.3	0.0	0.0	0.2	0.5
10 Communist Party	0.0	0.0	0.0	0.0	0.0	0.0	0.0
11 Scottish National Party	0.0	0.0	0.0	0.0	0.0	0.0	0.2
12 Welsh Nationalists	0.0	0.0	0.0	0.0	0.0	0.0	0.0
Others	0.2	0.2	0.0	0.2	0.0	0.0	0.3

Table 22.19   UNITED KINGDOM   Number of Candidates 1950—1970

		1950	1951	1955	1959	1964	1966	1970
1	Conservative Party	619	617	624	625	630	629	628
2	Liberal Party	475	109	110	216	365	311	332
5	Labour Party	617	617	620	621	628	622	625
7	Irish Republicans	4	3	12	12	13	8	11
10	Communist Party	100	10	17	18	36	57	58
11	Scottish National Party	3	2	2	5	15	23	65
12	Welsh Nationalists	7	4	11	20	23	20	36
	Others	43	14	13	19	47	37	82
	Total	1,868	1,376	1,409	1,536	1,757	1,707	1,837

Source: Craig, *British Parliamentary Election Statistics 1918—1970*, 1971 : 14-20.

Table 22.20 UNITED KINGDOM Percentage of Seats Contested 1950—1970

	1950	1951	1955	1959	1964	1966	1970
1 Conservative Party	99.0	98.7	99.0	99.2	100.0	99.8	99.7
2 Liberal Party	76.0	17.4	17.5	34.3	57.9	49.4	52.7
5 Labour Party	98.7	98.7	98.4	98.6	99.7	98.7	99.2
7 Irish Republicans	0.6	0.5	1.9	1.9	2.1	1.3	1.7
10 Communist Party	16.0	1.6	2.7	2.9	5.7	9.0	9.2
11 Scottish National Party	0.5	0.3	0.3	0.8	2.4	3.7	10.3
12 Welsh Nationalists	1.1	0.6	1.7	3.2	3.7	3.2	5.7

403

Chapter 23

UNITED STATES OF AMERICA

The American Constitution of 1787 provides for the election of the President by an electoral college. Each state is entitled to as many electors as it has Congressmen. If no candidate receives a majority the election falls to the House of Representatives, where each state delegation has a single vote. The Constitution allows each state to decide how its electors are chosen. Initially in a majority of the states this was done by the state legislature. In a few states there was a popular election. Electors were chosen by plurality, either in districts or by the state as a whole. In the latter case, the list of electors which won a plurality obtained all the state's electoral college votes. The system is known as the 'unit rule'. By 1828 all the states except Delaware and South Carolina had decided to choose their electors by popular vote. Delaware followed suit in 1832, but the South Carolina legislature continued to choose the state's electors until 1860. Since 1828 the states have, with very rare exceptions, followed the 'unit rule'.

Franchise laws varied enormously from state to state. By 1860 income and property qualifications had mostly been abolished so that manhood suffrage was the rule. (Williamson, 1960:278) Negroes were excluded from the vote in the vast majority of the free states. Federal regulation of the franchise began with the passage of the Fifteenth Amendment of the Constitution in 1870, which sought to guarantee the vote on equal terms for whites and blacks. However, this provision was widely evaded. Women were given the vote in Wyoming in 1869; by 1917 they had the vote in 12 states (Seymour and Frary, 1918: 238). In 1920 a constitutional amendment forbade the denial of the right to vote on grounds of sex. The Civil Rights Acts of 1957, 1960, 1964 and 1965 included provisions designed to protect and extend the voting rights of blacks. Constitutional amendments in 1961 and 1965 gave the District of Columbia the right to vote in presidential elections and abolished the use of poll taxes as a qualification for voting in federal elections. The 1970 Civil Rights Act abolished the use of literacy tests as a voting qualification, and reduced the voting age to 18. At the time the minimum voting age in most states was 21. Voting provisions have varied considerably. The traditional English system of oral voting had been abandoned by most states by 1800. But because of the use of easily identified ballot papers provided by the contestants and because voting was in public, the vote was not effectively secret. In 1888 Massachusetts introduced secret voting and an official ballot paper. By 1896, 90 per cent of the states had followed suit. (Rusk 1970: 1,221 and Seymour and Frary, 1918: 246-251).

Sources:

Burnham, W.D., "The United States: the politics of heterogeneity" in R. Rose (ed.) *Electoral Behavior: a Comparative Handbook* (New York: Free Press, 1973).

Ferguson, E.E., *They Voted for Roosevelt: the Presidential Vote, 1932–1944.* (Stanford: University Press, 1947).

Rusk, J.G., "The effect of the Australian ballot on split ticket voting: 1876–1908" *American Political Science Review* 64: 1,200–1,238 (1970).

Scammon, R.M. *American Votes* (8) (Washington, D.C.: Governmental Affairs Institute, 1970).

Seymour, C. and Frary, C.P., *How the World Votes* (Springfield, Mass: Nichols, 1918).

U.S. Bureau of the Census, *Historical Abstract of the United States, Colonial Times to 1957* (Washington, D.C., 1960).

Ibid., Statistical Abstract of the United States, 1972 (Washington, D.C., 1972).

Williamson, C., *American Suffrage from Property to Democracy, 1760–1860* (Princeton: Princeton University Press, 1960).

Table 23.1
POLITICAL PARTIES IN THE UNITED STATES SINCE 1828

	Party Names	Elections contested	Number contested
1	Democrats	1828ff	37
2	National Republicans	1828-1832	2
3	Whigs	1836-1852	5
4	Liberty	1844	1
5	Free Soil	1848-1852	2
6	American	1856	1
7	Republicans	1856ff	30
8	Constitutional Union	1860	1
9	Democrat (Breckenridge)[1]	1860	1
10	Greenback-Labor	1880	1
11	Prohibition	1880ff	24
12	Union Labor	1888	1
13	Peoples Party	1892; 1900-1908	4
14	Socialist Labor Party	1892ff	21
15	Socialist Party	1900-1920; 1928-1956	14
16	Progressive (T. Roosevelt)	1912	1
17	Progressive (LaFollette)	1924	1
18	Communist Party[2]	1924-1940; 1968ff	7
19	Union	1936	1
20	Progressive (H. Wallace)	1948-1952	2
21	States Rights	1948	1
22	American Independent Party	1968ff	2

[1] Breckenridge was the candidate of the southern wing of the Democratic Party.
[2] In 1924 and 1928, the Workers Party.

Table 23.2
DATES OF PRESIDENTIAL ELECTIONS 1848–1972[1]

1.	7 November 1848	17.	5 November 1912
2.	2 November 1852	18.	7 November 1916
3.	4 November 1856	19.	2 November 1920
4.	6 November 1860	20.	4 November 1924
5.	8 November 1864	21.	6 November 1928
6.	3 November 1868	22.	8 November 1932
7.	5 November 1872	23.	3 November 1936
8.	7 November 1876	24.	5 November 1940
9.	2 November 1880	25.	7 November 1944
10.	4 November 1884	26.	2 November 1948
11.	6 November 1888	27.	4 November 1952
12.	8 November 1892	28.	6 November 1956
13.	3 November 1896	29.	8 November 1960
14.	6 November 1900	30.	3 November 1964
15.	8 November 1904	31.	5 November 1968
16.	3 November 1908	32.	7 November 1972

[1] The dates refer to the election of presidential electors. Before 1848 elections were held over a long time period, generally from early October to mid-November. Since 1848 the election has been held on the Tuesday following the first Monday in November.

Table 23.3 UNITED STATES   Total Votes 1828–1864[1]

	1828	1832	1836	1840	1844	1848	1852	1856	1860	1864
Valid Votes	1,155,350	1,217,691	1,505,278	2,402,405	2,700,861	2,874,572	3,142,395	4,043,918	4,689,568	4,010,725[2]
PARTY VOTES										
1 Democrats	647,286	687,502	765,483	1,127,781	1,338,464	1,222,342	1,601,117	1,832,955	1,382,713	1,803,787
2 National Republicans	508,064	530,189	–	–	–	–	–	–	–	–
3 Whigs	–	–	739,795	1,274,624	1,300,087	1,360,967	1,385,453	–	–	–
4 Liberty	–	–	–	–	62,300	–	–	–	–	–
5 Free Soil	–	–	–	–	–	291,263	155,825	–	–	–
6 American	–	–	–	–	–	–	–	871,731	–	–
7 Republicans	–	–	–	–	–	–	–	1,339,232	1,865,593	2,206,938
8 Constitutional Union.	–	–	–	–	–	–	–	–	592,906	–
9 Democrat (Breckenridge)	–	–	–	–	–	–	–	–	848,356	–

[1] Excludes unpledged tickets and candidates winning less than 10,000 votes.
[2] The Confederate states did not participate in the election.

Source: Bureau of the Census, 1960 : 682-683.

410

Table 23.4   UNITED STATES   Percentage of Votes 1828–1864

	1828	1832	1836	1840	1844	1848	1852	1856	1860	1864
PARTY VOTES										
1 Democrats	56.0	56.5	50.9	46.9	49.6	42.5	51.0	45.3	29.5	45.0
2 National Republicans	44.0	43.5	–	–	–	–	–	–	–	–
3 Whigs	–	–	49.1	53.1	48.1	47.3	44.1	–	–	–
4 Liberty	–	–	–	–	2.3	–	–	–	–	–
5 Free Soil	–	–	–	–	–	10.1	5.0	–	–	–
6 American	–	–	–	–	–	–	–	21.6	–	–
7 Republicans	–	–	–	–	–	–	–	33.1	39.8	55.0
8 Constitutional Union	–	–	–	–	–	–	–	–	12.6	–
9 Democrat (Breckenridge)	–	–	–	–	–	–	–	–	18.1	–

Table 23.5 UNITED STATES Number of Electoral College Votes 1828–1864

	1828	1832	1836	1840	1844	1848	1852	1856	1860	1864
1 Democrats	178	219	170	60	170	127	254	174	12	21
2 National Republicans	83	49	–	–	–	–	–	–	–	–
3 Whigs	–	–	113	234	105	163	42	–	–	–
4 Liberty	–	–	–	–	0	–	–	–	–	–
5 Free Soil	–	–	–	–	–	0	0	–	–	–
6 American	–	–	–	–	–	–	–	8	–	–
7 Republicans	–	–	–	–	–	–	–	114	180	212
8 Constitutional Union	–	–	–	–	–	–	–	–	39	–
9 Democrat (Breckenridge)	–	–	–	–	–	–	–	–	72	–
Others	–	20	11	–	–	–	–	–	–	–
Total	261	288	294	294	275	290	296	296	303	233

Table 23.6   UNITED STATES   Percentage of Electoral College Votes 1828—1864

	1828	1832	1836	1840	1844	1848	1852	1856	1860	1864
1 Democrats	68.2	76.0	57.8	20.4	61.8	43.8	85.8	58.8	4.0	9.0
2 National Republicans	31.8	17.0	–	–	–	–	–	–	–	–
3 Whigs	–	–	38.4	79.6	38.2	56.2	14.2	–	–	–
4 Liberty	–	–	–	–	0.0	–	–	–	–	–
5 Free Soil	–	–	–	–	–	0.0	0.0	–	–	–
6 American	–	–	–	–	–	–	–	2.7	–	–
7 Republicans	–	–	–	–	–	–	–	38.5	59.4	91.0
8 Constitutional Union	–	–	–	–	–	–	–	–	12.9	–
9 Democrat (Breckenridge)	–	–	–	–	–	–	–	–	23.8	–
Others	–	6.9	3.7	–	–	–	–	–	–	–

413

Table 23.7 UNITED STATES Total Votes 1868–1896[1]

	1868	1872	1876	1880	1884	1888	1892	1896
Valid Votes	5,720,250[2]	6,469,680[3]	8,402,329	9,186,260	10,055,539	11,381,427	12,053,259	13,777,055
PARTY VOTES								
1 Democrats	2,706,829	2,843,446	4,284,020	4,414,082	4,879,507	5,537,857	5,555,426	6,492,559[4]
7 Republicans	3,013,421	3,596,745	4,036,572	4,453,295	4,850,293	5,447,129	5,182,690	7,102,246
10 Greenback-Labor	–	–	–	308,578	175,370	–	–	–
11 Prohibition	–	–	–	10,305	150,369	249,506	264,133	132,007
12 Union Labor	–	–	–	–	–	146,935	–	–
13 Peoples Party	–	–	–	–	–	–	1,029,846	–
14 Socialist Labor Party	–	–	–	–	–	–	21,164	36,274
Others	–	29,489	81,737	–	–	–	–	13,969

[1] Excludes unpledged tickets and candidates winning less than 10,000 votes.
[2] Mississippi, Texas and Virginia did not participate in the election.
[3] Excluding Arkansas and Louisiana whose votes were disallowed.
[4] Includes votes cast for Peoples Party electors pledged to William Jennings Bryan who was also the Democratic Party candidate.

Source: Bureau of the Census, 1960 : 682.

Table 23.8 UNITED STATES Percentage of Votes 1868—1896

PARTY VOTES	1868	1872	1876	1880	1884	1888	1892	1896
1 Democrats	47.3	44.0	51.0	48.1	48.5	48.7	46.1	47.1
7 Republicans	52.7	55.6	48.0	48.5	48.2	47.9	43.0	51.6
10 Greenback-Labor	–	–	–	3.4	1.7	–	–	–
11 Prohibition	–	–	–	0.1	1.5	2.2	2.2	1.0
12 Union Labor	–	–	–	–	–	1.3	–	–
13 Peoples Party	–	–	–	–	–	–	8.5	–
14 Socialist Labor Party	–	–	–	–	–	–	0.2	0.3
Others	–	0.5	1.0	–	–	–	–	0.1

Table 23.9   UNITED STATES   Number of Electoral College Votes 1868—1896

		1868	1872	1876	1880	1884	1888	1892	1896
1	Democrats	80	63	184	155	219	168	277	176
7	Republicans	214	286	185	214	182	233	145	271
10	Greenback-Labor	–	–	–	0	0	–	–	–
11	Prohibition	–	–	–	0	0	0	0	0
12	Union Labor	–	–	–	–	–	0	–	–
13	Peoples Party	–	–	–	–	–	–	22	–
14	Socialist Labor Party	–	–	–	–	–	–	0	0
	Others	–	0	0	–	–	–	–	0
	Total	**294**	**349**	**369**	**369**	**401**	**401**	**444**	**447**

Table 23.10   UNITED STATES   Percentage of Electoral College Votes 1868—1896

	1868	1872	1876	1880	1884	1888	1892	1896
1 Democrats	27.2	18.1	49.9	42.0	54.6	41.9	62.4	39.4
7 Republicans	72.8	81.9	50.1	58.0	45.4	58.1	32.7	60.6
10 Greenback-Labor	–	–	–	0.0	0.0	–	–	–
11 Prohibition	–	–	–	0.0	0.0	0.0	0.0	0.0
12 Union Labor	–	–	–	–	–	0.0	–	–
13 Peoples Party	–	–	–	–	–	–	5.0	–
14 Socialist Labor Party	–	–	–	–	–	–	0.0	0.0
Others	–	0.0	0.0	–	–	–	–	0.0

Table 23.11   UNITED STATES   Total Votes 1900–1924[1]

	1900	1904	1908	1912	1916	1920	1924
Electorate[2]	n.a.	n.a.	n.a.	n.a.	n.a.	61,639,000	66,229,000
Valid Votes	13,962,065	13,521,935	14,888,240	15,037,535	18,480,224	26,776,068	29,089,084
PARTY VOTES							
1 Democrats	6,356,734[3]	5,084,223	6,412,294	6,296,547	9,127,695	9,130,328	8,385,283
7 Republicans	7,218,491	7,628,461	7,675,320	3,486,720	8,533,507	16,143,407	15,718,211
11 Prohibition	208,914	258,536	253,840	206,275	220,506	189,408	57,520
13 Peoples Party	50,373	117,183	29,100	–	–	–	–
14 Socialist Labor Party	39,739	31,249	14,021	28,750	13,403	31,715	36,428
15 Socialist Party	87,814	402,283	420,793	900,672	585,113	919,799	–
16 Progressive (T. Roosevelt)	–	–	–	4,118,571	–	–	–
18 Communist Party	–	–	–	–	–	–	36,386
17 Progressive (LaFollette)	–	–	–	–	–	–	4,831,289
Others	–	–	82,872	–	–	48,000	23,967

[1] Excludes unpledged tickets and candidates winning less than 10,000 votes.
[2] Estimates of the total voting-age population (U.S. Bureau of the Census, 1972 : 373 and 377).
[3] Includes votes cast for Peoples Party electors pledged to William Jennings Bryan, who was also the Democratic Party's candidate.

Sources: Bureau of the Census, 1960 : 682; *Ibid*, 1972 : 373, 377.

Table 23.12   UNITED STATES   Percentage of Votes 1900–1924

	1900	1904	1908	1912	1916	1920	1924
Valid Votes	n.a.	n.a.	n.a.	n.a.	n.a.	43.4	43.9
PARTY VOTES							
1 Democrats	45.5	37.6	43.1	41.9	49.4	34.1	28.8
7 Republicans	51.7	56.4	51.6	23.2	46.2	60.3	54.0
11 Prohibition	1.5	1.9	1.7	1.4	1.2	0.7	0.2
13 Peoples Party	0.4	0.9	0.2	–	–	–	–
14 Socialist Labor Party	0.3	0.2	0.1	0.2	0.1	0.1	0.1
15 Socialist Party	0.6	3.0	2.8	6.0	3.2	3.4	–
16 Progressive (T. Roosevelt)	–	–	–	27.4	–	–	–
18 Communist Party	–	–	–	–	–	–	0.1
17 Progressive (LaFollette)	–	–	–	–	–	–	16.6
Others	–	–	0.6	–	–	0.2	0.1

Table 23.13   UNITED STATES   Number of Electoral College Votes 1900—1924

	1900	1904	1908	1912	1916	1920	1924
1 Democrats	155	140	162	435	277	127	136
7 Republicans	292	336	321	8	254	404	382
11 Prohibition	0	0	0	0	0	0	0
13 Peoples Party	0	0	0	–	–	–	–
14 Socialist Labor Party	0	0	0	0	0	0	0
15 Socialist Party	0	0	0	0	0	0	–
16 Progressive (T. Roosevelt)	–	–	–	88	–	–	–
18 Communist Party	–	–	–	–	–	–	0
17 Progressive (LaFollette)	–	–	0	–	–	–	13
Others	–	–	0	–	–	0	0
Total	447	476	483	531	531	531	531

Table 23.14   UNITED STATES

Percentage of Electoral College Votes 1900—1924

	1900	1904	1908	1912	1916	1920	1924
1 Democrats	34.7	29.4	33.5	81.9	52.2	23.9	25.6
7 Republicans	65.3	70.6	66.5	1.5	47.8	76.1	71.9
11 Prohibition	0.0	0.0	0.0	0.0	0.0	0.0	0.0
13 Peoples Party	0.0	0.0	0.0	–	–	–	–
14 Socialist Labor Party	0.0	0.0	0.0	0.0	0.0	0.0	0.0
15 Socialist Party	0.0	0.0	0.0	0.0	0.0	0.0	–
16 Progressive (T. Roosevelt)	–	–	–	16.6	–	–	–
18 Communist Party	–	–	–	–	–	–	0.0
17 Progressive (LaFollette)	–	–	–	–	–	–	2.4
Others	–	–	0.0	–	–	0.0	0.0

Table 23.15   UNITED STATES   Total Votes 1928—1948[1]

	1928	1932	1936	1940	1944	1948
Electorate	71,000,000	75,768,000	80,174,000	84,728,000	85,654,000	95,573,000
Valid Votes	36,738,887	39,721,845	45,628,516	49,847,349	47,821,942	48,793,826
PARTY VOTES						
1 Democrats	15,016,169	22,809,638	27,752,869[2]	27,307,819[2]	25,606,585[3]	24,179,345[4]
7 Republicans	21,391,993	15,758,901	16,674,665	22,321,018	22,014,745	21,991,291
11 Prohibition	20,106	81,869	37,847	57,812	74,758	103,900
14 Socialist Labor Party	21,603	33,276	12,777	14,892	45,336	29,241
15 Socialist Party	267,835	881,951	187,720	99,557	80,518	139,572
18 Communist Party	21,181	102,785	80,159	46,251	–	–
19 Union	–	–	882,479	–	–	–
20 Progressive (H. Wallace)	–	–	–	–	–	1,157,326
21 States Rights	–	–	–	–	–	1,176,125
Others	–	53,425	–	–	–	17,026

[1] Until the 1948 election votes for unpledged tickets and candidates winning less than 10,000 votes are excluded.

[2] Includes votes cast for American Labor Party electors in New York State pledged to Franklin D. Roosevelt, the Democratic Party's candidate (Ferguson, 1947 : 199).

[3] Includes votes cast for American Labor Party and Liberal Party electors in New York State pledged to Franklin D. Roosevelt, the Democratic Party's candidate.

[4] Includes votes cast for Liberal Party electors in New York State pledged to support the Democratic Party's presidential candidate.

Sources: Bureau of the Census, 1960 : 682; *Ibid*, 1972 : 373, 377; Scammon, 1972 : 1.

Table 23.16   UNITED STATES   Percentage of Votes 1928–1948

	1928	1932	1936	1940	1944	1948
Valid Votes	51.7	52.4	56.9	58.8	55.8	51.1
PARTY VOTES						
1 Democrats	40.9	57.4	60.8	54.8	53.5	49.6
7 Republicans	58.2	39.7	36.5	44.8	46.0	45.1
11 Prohibition	0.1	0.2	0.1	0.1	0.2	0.2
14 Socialist Labor Party	0.1	0.1	0.0	0.0	0.1	0.1
15 Socialist Party	0.7	2.2	0.4	0.2	0.2	0.3
18 Communist Party	0.1	0.3	0.2	0.1	–	–
19 Union	–	–	1.9	–	–	–
20 Progressive (H. Wallace)	–	–	–	–	–	2.4
21 State Rights	–	–	–	–	–	2.4
Others	–	0.1	–	–	–	0.0

Table 23.17　　UNITED STATES　　Number of Electoral College Votes 1928—1948

	1928	1932	1936	1940	1944	1948
1 Democrats	87	472	523	449	432	303
7 Republicans	444	59	8	82	99	189
11 Prohibition	0	0	0	0	0	0
14 Socialist Labor Party	0	0	0	0	0	0
15 Socialist Party	0	0	0	0	0	0
18 Communist Party	0	0	0	0	–	–
19 Union	–	–	0	–	–	–
20 Progressive (H. Wallace)	–	–	–	–	–	0
21 States Rights	–	–	–	–	–	39
Others	–	0	–	–	–	0
Total	531	531	531	531	531	531

Table 23.18   UNITED STATES   Percentage of Electoral College Votes 1928—1948

	1928	1932	1936	1940	1944	1948
1 Democrats	16.4	88.9	98.5	84.6	81.4	57.1
7 Republicans	83.6	11.1	1.5	15.4	18.6	35.6
11 Prohibition	0.0	0.0	0.0	0.0	0.0	0.0
14 Socialist Labor Party	0.0	0.0	0.0	0.0	0.0	0.0
15 Socialist Party	0.0	0.0	0.0	0.0	0.0	0.0
18 Communist Party	0.0	0.0	0.0	0.0	–	–
19 Union	–	–	0.0	–	–	–
20 Progressive (H. Wallace)	–	–	–	–	–	0.0
21 States Rights	–	–	–	–	–	7.3
Others	–	0.0	–	–	–	0.0

Table 23.19   UNITED STATES   Total Votes 1952—1972

	1952	1956	1960	1964	1968	1972
Electorate	99,929,000	104,515,000	109,674,000	114,085,000	120,285,000	139,642,000
Valid Votes	61,550,918	62,026,908	68,838,219	70,644,592	73,211,875	77,718,554
PARTY VOTES						
1 Democrats[1]	27,314,992	26,022,752	34,226,731	43,129,566	31,275,166	29,195,978
7 Republicans	33,936,234	35,590,472	34,108,157	27,178,188	31,785,480	47,169,911
11 Prohibition	72,949	41,937	46,203	23,267	15,123	13,505
14 Socialist Labor Party	30,267	44,450	47,522	45,219	52,588	53,814
15 Socialist Party	20,203	2,126	–	–	–	–
18 Communist Party	–	–	–	–	1,075	25,595
20 Progressive (H. Wallace)	140,023	–	–	–	–	–
22 American Independent Party	–	–	–	–	9,906,473	1,099,482
Others	36,250	325,171[2]	409,606[3]	268,352[4]	175,970	185,864

[1] Includes votes cast for Liberal Party electors in New York State pledged to support the Democratic Party's presidential candidate.

[2] Includes 196,318 votes cast for Independent or unpledged States Rights tickets in several southern states.

[3] Includes 169,572 votes cast for Independent electors in Louisiana and 116,248 votes for an unpledged Democratic ticket in Mississippi.

[4] Includes 210,732 votes for an unpledged Democratic ticket in Alabama.

Sources: Scammon, 1972 : 1-11; Bureau of the Census, 1972 : 373, 377 and figures provided by the Elections Research Center, Washington, D.C.

Table 23.20   UNITED STATES   Percentage of Votes 1952–1972

	1952	1956	1960	1964	1968	1972
Valid Votes	61.6	59.3	62.8	61.9	60.9	55.7
PARTY VOTES						
1 Democrats	44.4	42.0	49.7	61.1	42.7	37.5
7 Republicans	55.1	57.4	49.5	38.5	43.4	60.7
11 Prohibition	0.1	0.1	0.1	0.0	0.0	0.0
14 Socialist Labor Party	0.0	0.1	0.1	0.1	0.1	0.1
15 Socialist Party	0.0	0.0	–	–	0.0	–
18 Communist Party	–	–	–	–	0.0	0.0
20 Progressive (H. Wallace)	0.2	–	–	–	–	–
22 American Independent Party	–	–	–	–	13.5	1.4
Others	0.1	0.5	0.6	0.4	0.2	0.2

Table 23.21   UNITED STATES   Number of Electoral College Votes 1952–1972

		1952	1956	1960	1964	1968	1972
1	Democrats	89	73	303	486	191	17
7	Republicans	442	457	219	52	301	520
11	Prohibition	0	0	0	0	0	0
14	Socialist Labor Party	0	0	0	0	0	0
15	Socialist Party	0	0	–	–	–	–
18	Communist Party	–	–	–	–	0	0
20	Progressive (H. Wallace)	0	–	–	–	–	–
22	American Independent Party	–	–	–	–	46	0
	Others	0	1[1]	15[2]	0	0	1[3]
	Total	**531**	**531**	**537**	**538**	**538**	**538**

[1] One of the Democratic electors from Alabama voted for Walter B. Jones and Herman Talmadge rather than the national Democratic candidates.

[2] Six Democratic electors from Alabama, 8 unpledged Democratic electors from Mississippi and one Republican elector from Oklahoma voted for Senator Harry F. Byrd rather than the national Democratic candidate.

[3] One Republican elector voted for John Hospers, the Libertarian Party candidate.

Table 23.22   UNITED STATES   Percentage of Electoral College Votes 1952—1972

		1952	1956	1960	1964	1968	1972
1	Democrats	16.8	13.7	56.4	90.3	35.5	3.2
7	Republicans	83.2	86.1	40.8	9.7	55.9	96.7
11	Prohibition	0.0	0.0	0.0	0.0	0.0	0.0
14	Socialist Labor Party	0.0	0.0	0.0	0.0	0.0	0.0
15	Socialist Party	0.0	0.0	–	–	–	–
18	Communist Party	–	–	–	–	0.0	0.0
20	Progressive (H. Wallace)	0.0	–	–	–	–	–
22	American Independent Party	–	–	–	–	8.6	0.0
	Others	0.0	0.2	2.8	0.0	0.0	0.2

APPENDIX

THE MECHANICS OF ELECTORAL SYSTEMS*

Electoral systems have been usefully described as laws which 'govern the process by which electoral preferences are articulated as votes and by which these votes are translated into distributions of governmental authority (typically parliamentary seats) among the competing political parties' (Rae, 1971:14). As the polemical and scholarly literature indicates, electoral systems are important. Not only do they effect the relationship between votes and parliamentary seats, but also, through franchise requirements, the initial distribution of party votes.

There are four principal types of electoral systems: plurality, majority, list systems of proportional representation and the single transferable vote. There are very considerable national variations in the application of these basic patterns; they are mentioned in the appropriate chapters. Most Anglo-American countries have usually employed the plurality system. During the nineteenth century, versions of the majority system were used in most continental European countries. From the end of the nineteenth century these countries increasingly adopted one of the many versions of proportional representation. (Rokkan, 1970:155–158).

A) *The plurality system*

In plurality systems (often known as 'relative majority' or 'first past the post') the party that takes the largest number of votes in a single-member constituency wins, even if this figure is less than half the total vote. The plurality system tends to favour larger parties. The single non-transferable vote used in Japan is designed to obviate this difficulty. Each elector has only one vote although more than one representative is to be chosen. The winning candidates are chosen in order of their share of the total vote until all the seats in the electoral district have been filled.

B) *Majority systems*

In majority systems, a seat is won by the party which wins an absolute majority of votes, that is, more votes than all the other parties combined. In the event of no party winning a majority on the first ballot, a majority can be guaranteed in one of two ways: the second ballot or the alternative vote. In the second ballot a plurality of votes may suffice or a majority may be created by the elimination of all but the two leading contenders before the second round. Instead of a second contest, each voter can have a transferable or alternative vote. In this system the voter lists the candidates in order of his

---

* Thanks are due to Professor W.J.M. Mackenzie of the University of Glasgow and D.W. Urwin of the University of Bergen for their helpful comments on an earlier draft of this Appendix.

preference. A candidate is only elected at the first count if he gains an absolute majority. In the example in Table A.1 the first count did not produce a majority.

TABLE A.1 *The alternative vote system*

Party	Initial Vote	Second Count	Third Count	Fourth Count
A	7,000	7,250 (+250)	8,250 (+1,000)	9,250 (+1,000)
C	5,500	6,000 (+500)	6,900 (+900)	10,750 (+3,850)
E	4,000	4,150 (+150)	4,850 (+700)	—
B	2,500	2,600 (+100)	—	—
D	1,000	—	—	—
Total	20,000	20,000 (+1,000)	20,000 (+2,600)	20,000 (+4,850)

Source: adapted from Mackenzie (1958:56)

At the second count D, the candidate winning fewest votes is eliminated and his second preferences redistributed among the remaining candidates. As no candidate has yet gained a majority, B is eliminated and the second preferences of his supporters are redistributed among the three remaining candidates. Since a majority has still not been obtained, candidate E is eliminated, and the redistribution of his second preferences among the two remaining candidates gives a majority to C.

C) *List systems of proportional representation*

Proportional representation systems (PR) are designed to ensure a high degree of correspondence between the proportion of a party's vote and its seats in the legislature. While plurality and majority systems may be operated with either single or multiple-member constituencies, P.R. must employ multiple-member constituencies so that seats in a constituency can be apportioned amongst the most popular parties; in a single-member constituency the candidate with the most votes must win all, that is, the sole seat. The number of seats in a constituency varies widely. In extreme cases (Israel and the Netherlands) the entire country is treated as a single constituency. Usually the apportioning of seats is done on a constituency basis. In order to introduce greater proportionality additional seats may be allocated at the regional or national level to parties relatively disadvantaged by constituency-level distributions. To prevent very small parties from sharing in the distribution of parliamentary seats a barrier clause is often employed; parties which fail to meet minimum vote requirements are excluded.

The voter is presented with a number of party lists. In some cases the voter can only choose between the lists. In other cases he may also express a preference for one or more of the individual candidates included in the list. In systems where the voter has more than one vote he may be allowed to divide his votes between different party lists (*panachage*). The three principal versions of P.R. are:

1) *Largest Remainder System*

A quota is computed for each electoral district by dividing the total number of votes cast by the total number of seats to be distributed. This quota is in turn divided into the vote of each party, and the party receives a seat for each resulting whole number. Frequently this procedure leaves seats